Correct Writing SIXTH EDITION

Sixth Edition

Correct Writing

Eugenia Butler
University of Georgia

Mary Ann Hickman
University System of Georgia

Patricia J. McAlexander
University of Georgia

Lalla Overby
Gainesville College

D. C. Heath and Company
Lexington, Massachusetts· ■ Toronto

Address editorial correspondence to:

D. C. Heath and Company
125 Spring Street
Lexington, MA 02173

Acquisitions Editor: Paul A. Smith
Developmental Editor: Linda M. Bieze
Production Editor: Renée M. Mary
Production Coordinator: Richard Tonachel
Text Permissions Editor: Margaret Roll

To the Instructor

College instructors who wish to give students a strong foundation in the basics of Standard English grammar will find *Correct Writing*, Sixth Edition, a versatile and comprehensive aid in teaching grammar, punctuation, mechanics, and diction.

Correct Writing is a distinctive combination of the best features of a grammar and composition text, a workbook of exercises, and a convenient reference handbook. The body of grammatical information meets the needs of instructors whose courses emphasize sentence-level writing skills. Brief but lucid definitions of all terms are provided, along with careful explanation of the principles involved in sentence structure. These definitions and explanations come at the earliest mention of a term, so that students can begin to apply what they learn in completing the exercises. Another especially convenient feature of *Correct Writing* is its cross-reference system, through which a brief definition refers the reader to more detailed discussions of the topic in other chapters.

Several exercises follow each chapter of text, with sentences designed to illustrate the specific point of the chapter, thus giving students the immediate opportunity to apply their knowledge of the material just studied. As in previous editions, all exercises in this book are new. Whenever possible, the sentences in these exercises are somewhat simplified to make them obviously illustrative of the grammatical principles involved. Explanation of these principles is presented to students in straightforward terms, yet is far more extensive than those in other workbooks. Though discussion of many aspects of grammar is not intended to be exhaustive, it is always sufficiently thorough for students to grasp and learn without the instructor's having to spend classroom time in prolonged explanation.

Correct Writing, Sixth Edition, contains enlarged lists and explanations of sentence elements that are especially challenging for students. These include expanded lists of pronouns and their cases; discussion of the problems of tense, voice, and mood of verbs; modifiers of all kinds; and comprehensive dicussions of punctuation and mechanics. Also enlarged are the lists of difficult spelling words and irregular verbs. In the chapter on spelling, for instance, special attention is given to homonyms. Along with the discussion there is a list of homonyms commonly confused by student writers. These lists are another handy reference source.

A strong aspect of *Correct Writing* is that rules of punctuation are given in individual chapters and relate to the particular elements of sentence structure under discussion. For example, in the chapters on clauses, specific examples are presented for the punctuation of both independent and dependent clauses.

When students reach Chapters 19 and 20, which are devoted exclusively to punctuation and mechanics, they will already have learned most of the rules laid out in these chapters. Instead of an arbitrary listing of rules to be memorized, these chapters then serve as reinforcement and review. They are also quick references to any questions on punctuation and mechanics.

An unusually helpful section of *Correct Writing* is the Glossary of Faulty Diction, which appears in Chapter 22. Students are constantly exposed, through television and other media, to trite, slangy, and ungrammatical usage. Recognizing this fact, the authors make careful distinction between informal, stale, and incorrect written expressions and those that are acceptable as Standard English. The Glossary has been updated for this edition, with new entries added and outdated terms withdrawn. Arranged in alphabetical order, it is another readily available reference.

Popular features of past editions of *Correct Writing* have been retained in this edition. "Paragraph Tests" offer practical application because they are whole, integrated paragraphs in the same format that students encounter in their everyday reading and writing. Within the paragraphs are grammatical, punctuation, diction, and spelling errors of all the kinds studied in this book. The Paragraph Tests provide a realistic method of determining whether students have learned to be alert to unexpected errors in their everyday reading and writing. The Glossary of Grammatical Terms, which appears at the back of the book, incorporates easily understood definitions that are accompanied by simple examples that clarify and enhance the definitions.

The section of Sentence-Combining Exercises, introduced in the Fifth Edition, has proved a valuable teaching tool. Most college instructors find that students can usually increase their ability to use subordination and to reduce wordiness as a means of achieving texture and variety, thus developing a perspective on the relative importance of several ideas within a single sentence. These exercises provide strong additional practice in these areas.

One central point that should emerge through a student's careful use of this text is that the study of grammar and sentence elements is the necessary first step in improving communication and understanding. *Correct Writing*, Sixth Edition, will be valuable in furthering the teacher's goal of providing that improvement.

The following individuals helped us with their suggestions for revisions: Paul Beran, North Harris College; Carol Eiten, Carl Sandburg College; Sally Hanson, University of South Dakota; Kaye W. Jefferey, Utah Valley Community College; R. K. Kalia, Mesa Community College; Thomas A. Mozola, Macomb Community College; Karen K. Reid, Midwestern State University; Marcia Rogers, Utah Valley Community College; Cecilia M. Russo, Saint John's University; Sid Silvester, Bob Jones University; and Darla Tice, Midwestern State University.

Eugenia Butler
Mary Ann Hickman
Patricia J. McAlexander
Lalla Overby

To the Student

This book is a combination textbook, workbook, and reference handbook. It contains a great deal of information in the various chapters that precede the exercises. It is a workbook in which you will be able to write your answers concerning grammatical principles that you have just studied. When you have worked all the exercises as well as the Review and Achievement Tests, you will still have a convenient reference handbook in which you can check points of grammar, usage, punctuation, and mechanics whenever you need to. The Glossary of Faulty Diction and the Glossary of Grammatical Terms will be of special help to you in questions of usage and in providing familiarity with grammatical terminology that you are likely to encounter.

Working conscientiously through the chapters and exercises of *Correct Writing* will put you well on your way to a mastery of grammar and usage, which in turn will help you to write and speak accurately and effectively.

Contents

x   Contents

Diagnostic Test

In the following sentences identify the part of speech of each *italicized* word by writing one of the following numbers in the space at the right:

1 if it is a *noun,*   5 if it is an *adverb,*
2 if it is a *pronoun,* 6 if it is a *preposition,*
3 if it is a *verb,*   7 if it is a *conjunction,*
4 if it is an *adjective,* 8 if it is an *interjection.*

1. We will arrive in *London* early tomorrow morning. _____

2. *Where* is your car? _____

3. *Neither* Tricia *nor* her brother came to the party. _____

4. All History 202 classes were filled *at* registration. _____

5. Most atmospheric scientists accept the *existence* of the "greenhouse effect." _____

6. No *one* knows exactly where or when April Fools' Day began. _____

7. The band played too *loud.* _____

8. The Grand Canyon offers many *spectacular* sights. _____

9. Donna *and* Renée studied together for their physics final. _____

10. Winston *has received* numerous awards for service and leadership. _____

11. I could *not* afford this expensive hardcover edition. _____

12. Ansel Adams's *photographs* demonstrate his exceptional ability. _____

13. In 1914 Omicron Delta Kappa *was founded* at Washington and Lee University. _____

14. Aimee dreams about *exotic* places in distant lands. _____

15. Miriam, have *you* washed the dishes? _____

16. On the bank *behind* the house is my favorite rosebush. _____

17. *Yes,* I loved that movie. _____

18. Erika is a *senior* at Duquesne University. _____

19. That very tall, handsome *young* man is Curtis. _____

20. Uncle Tim will not eat *sweet-and-sour* pork. _____

21. They will be late, *but* they are coming. _____

22. *In* the yard are my rake, hoe, and clippers. _____

23. The *acronym* for the North Atlantic Treaty Organization is NATO. _____

24. Alaska is the only state *without* houseflies. _____

25. His research has focused on the *sociological* basis of personality. _____

Each of the following sentences either contains an error in grammar or is correct. Indicate the error or the correctness by writing one of the following numbers in the space at the right:

    1 if the case of the pronoun is incorrect,
    2 if the subject and verb do not agree,
    3 if a pronoun and its antecedent do not agree,
    4 if an adjective or an adverb is used incorrectly,
    5 if the sentence is correct.

26. My brother was always stronger than me. _____

27. Their neighbors are real nice people. _____

28. We appreciate you helping us with this research. _____

29. Are you going with Jeff and I? _____

30. Everyone patiently waited their turn. _____

31. There is several reasons why I enjoyed the festival. _____

32. At lunch I talked with the nurse who I met at the doctor's office. _____

33. Each of us are to submit suggestions for the spring concert to the choral director. _____

34. The soccer team elected Jason to represent them at the association's meeting. _____

35. Maria, you will be real happy with your recommendation from Dean Frederic. _____

36. Except for she and Morgan, the whole team was at the bonfire last night. _____

37. Are either of these rowing machines in good working order? _____

38. One of us sure needs to call home today or tomorrow. _____

39. In our town the media often lends support to worthy money-raising projects. _____

40. My guess is that a whole regiment of soldiers is in this convoy. _____

41. He can swing a golf club as smooth as anyone I know. _____

42. Just between you and I, bungee jumping is a sport for somebody else. _____

43. It seemed as if every man, woman, and child in town had lined up to have Michael autograph his book for them. _____

44. Twelve gallons is all that this gas tank will hold. _____

45. Jerry does appreciate you agreeing to give an interview to the campus newspaper. _____

46. The visiting lecturer views the international situation different than Dr. Conrad does. _____

47. Neither Martie nor Josephine have a record of her membership in the health club. _____

48. Please explain to whomever is on duty at the desk that I'll drop the room key in the mail. _____

49. The perfume that Nathan gave me for my birthday smells divinely. _____

50. Ernest is one of those rare friends who is always willing to listen. _____

Each of the following sentences either contains an error in sentence structure or is correct. Indicate the error or the correctness by writing one of the following numbers in the space at the right:

    1 if the sentence contains a *dangling modifier,*
    2 if the sentence contains a *misplaced modifier,*
    3 if the sentence contains a *faulty reference of a pronoun,*
    4 if the sentence contains *faulty parallelism,*
    5 if the sentence is correct.

51. Never having tasted one, the mango was delicious. _____

52. Either the Thompsons need less baggage or a larger automobile. _____

53. I wish that you had come earlier because I only talked to Mother a few minutes ago. _____

54. The slight young woman, having enjoyed gymnastics since childhood, was an accomplished one. _____

55. His grandparents are great rummy players, which occupies many of their evenings. _____

56. On clear afternoons the sun always has shone and always will through these kitchen windows. _____

57. To understand the philosopher's ideas, defining his terms was my first order of business. _____

58. Arnold left the city hall just after five o'clock, and this caused him to be late for dinner. _____

59. Before going to bed, the lamp on the hall table needs to be turned off. _____

60. This jean skirt is too long, too tight, and I have trouble climbing stairs in it. _____

61. Yesterday I learned about Marie Curie's research in our science lab. _____

62. One has less chance of catching a cold if you get enough sleep and eat well. _____

63. It was below freezing, but we were warm in our fleece-lined coats. _____

64. Damaged in the accident, there was nothing for him to do but take his car to a paint-and-body shop. _____

65. Diane told her sister that she needed to consider going on the grapefruit diet. _____

66. We had hardly walked any distance before we spotted a bus stop. _____

67. Before finishing the test, the fire alarm went off. _____

68. Many college students think that dormitories are comfortable, practical, and offer financial savings. _____

69. Gripping the bat tightly, Casey swung at the ball. _____

70. The motel rates were high, which made me decide not to go to the Georgia-Florida game. _____

71. Remember to park in the West Langdon Street lot only during the summer. _____

72. While traveling through the South, the fast-growing, broad-leafed vine called kudzu fascinated us. _____

73. The president of the club asked me briefly to speak. _____

74. I either want you to go with me or to stay at home. _____

75. When asleep, your incision won't hurt you. _____

Each of the following sentences contains an error in punctuation or mechanics or is correct. Indicate the error or the correctness by writing one of the following numbers in the space at the right:

1 if a comma has been omitted,
2 if a semicolon has been omitted,
3 if an apostrophe has been omitted,
4 if quotation marks have been omitted,
5 if the sentence is correct.

76. My parents enjoy coming to the college football games and my being a cheerleader gives them an extra reason to attend. _____

77. Every time I begin to study my friends come to visit. _____

78. Harry's was more than a restaurant, it was a gathering place for all types of people. _____

79. Lying beside the pool on a hot afternoon is a good way to relax. _____

80. Robert Frost, a famous New England poet, read his poem The Gift Outright at the inauguration of John Fitzgerald Kennedy. _____

81. Students who have an *A* average in this course are not required to take the exam. _____

82. The noisy rowdy football players piled into the waiting bus. _____

83. The trees were no longer covered with red and gold leaves, they had become bare, black skeletons. _____

84. Rushing to catch the bus Maurice fell and sprained his ankle. _____

85. Divorce is a major issue in todays society. _____

86. Mrs. Brown strolled about the classroom, then she went to the blackboard and began to write on it. _____

87. Its a shame that you had to miss my party. _____

88. Even athletes who are red-shirted are required to go to all the team's meetings and practices. _____

89. Everyone should travel abroad at least once, commented Dr. Roper. _____

90. The childrens toys were scattered all over the floor. _____

91. When I asked my student what was wriggling around in his bookbag he took out his pet snake. _____

92. He doesn't like being in the bookbag; he wants to wrap himself around my neck, the student said. _____

93. Snakes may make good pets, however, I prefer my cat. _____

94. My youngest son Ed can do a wonderful imitation of Hulk Hogan. _____

95. Have you read John Updike's story A & P? _____

96. That kitten never gets tired of chasing its tail! _____

97. My library books were due three months ago, I know I'll have to pay a big fine. _____

98. "The Gambler" by Kenny Rogers is Harry's favorite song. _____

99. My parents think that holding a job builds character, thus they have encouraged me to work during summer vacations. _____

100. On September 7, 1993 I left home to go to college. _____

The Parts of Speech

Our own language is one of the most fascinating subjects that we can investigate, and those of us who speak and write English can find pleasure in seeking to understand its various aspects. The concern of this book is Standard English and its use in contemporary writing. The study and description of Standard English, based on the thoughtful use of language by educated people, provide standards for correct writing. Although the English language is flexible and continually changing, it is possible to follow certain principles and to observe certain characteristics of usage which can make grammar a relatively exact study and one which can widen the scope of the individual in a satisfying way.

An understanding of the accurate and effective use of English is important not only as a means of communication but also as a vital element of creative thought. Because words are used to formulate conscious thought, precise grammatical usage promotes clear thinking and encourages logical and systematic transmission of ideas.

Knowledge of Standard English and its acceptable forms is basic to the education of all college students. Learning grammatical terms is an essential first step toward understanding what is correct and what is incorrect in the writing of English prose. The best place to begin this learning of terms is with the various elements that make up a sentence, elements called **parts of speech.** Many words may function as more than one part of speech, and any word's designation as a particular part of speech depends entirely upon its use within its sentence. (See Section 1i as well as the Glossary of Grammatical Terms at the end of this book.) The names of the eight parts of speech are as follows:

| noun | adjective | adverb | conjunction |
| pronoun | verb | preposition | interjection |

▪ 1a Noun

A **noun** (from Latin *nomen*, name) is the name of a person, place, thing, or idea. All nouns are either proper nouns or common nouns. A **proper noun** is the name of a particular person, place, or thing and is spelled with a capital letter:

John F. Kennedy	London, England
California	The Washington Monument
The Vatican	O'Keefe Junior High School

A **common noun** is the name of a class of persons, places, things, or ideas and is not capitalized:

girl	park	honesty
teacher	street	disgust
student	dog	friendship
home	automobile	poverty

Nouns may also be classified as **individual** or **collective. Collective nouns** name groups of persons, places, or things that sometimes function as units:

flock	team	the rich
jury	dozen	club

Finally, nouns may be classified as **concrete** or **abstract. The concrete noun** names a person, place, or thing that can be perceived by one of the five senses. It can be seen, felt, smelled, heard, or tasted. Here are some examples of concrete nouns:

door	woman	scream
dress	city	snow
tree	odor	museum

An **abstract noun** is the name of a quality, condition, action, or idea. The following are examples of abstract nouns:

beauty	truth	kindness
fear	loneliness	campaign
dismissal	hatred	courtesy

A noun is said to belong to the **nominative,** the **objective,** or the **possessive case,** depending upon its function within a sentence. Subjects are in the nominative case (The *truck* stopped), objects are in the objective case (He saw the *parade*), and nouns showing possession are in the possessive case (That car is *John's*).

As you can see, there is no difference in form between nouns in the nominative and the objective cases. The possessive case, however, changes a noun's form. (See Chapter 12 for a thorough discussion of case.)

A noun may be **singular** or **plural,** forming its plural generally by the addition of *-s* or *-es* to the end of the singular form (*girl, girls; potato, potatoes*).

Nouns, together with pronouns and other words or expressions that function as nouns, are sometimes called **substantives.**

■ 1b Pronoun

A **pronoun** (from Latin *pro*, for, and *nomen*, name) is a word used in place of a noun. A pronoun usually refers to a noun or other substantive already mentioned, which is called its **antecedent** (from Latin *ante*, before, and *cedere*, to go). Most pronouns have antecedents, but some do not.

Pronouns are divided into eight categories:

PERSONAL PRONOUNS: I, you, he, she, it, we, they, and their inflected forms (*See table below.*)

DEMONSTRATIVE PRONOUNS: this, that, these, those

INDEFINITE PRONOUNS: all, any, anyone, anything, each, everyone, everything, either, neither, one, several, some, someone, something

INTERROGATIVE PRONOUNS: what, which, who, whom, whose

RELATIVE PRONOUNS: which, who, whom, whose, that

REFLEXIVE PRONOUNS: myself, yourself, himself, herself, itself, ourselves, yourselves, themselves

INTENSIVE PRONOUNS: I *myself*, you *yourself*, he *himself*, she *herself*, (the dog, the book, the car) *itself*, we *ourselves*, you *yourselves*, they *themselves*

RECIPROCAL PRONOUNS: each other, one another

The personal pronouns have differing forms depending upon whether they are subjects (*I* will help Mr. Curtis) or objects (Gene told *him* the plan) or show possession (The red coat is *hers*). These differences in form, which are seen only in the possessive case of nouns, occur in all three cases (*nominative, objective,* and *possessive*) of these pronouns.

Personal pronouns, like nouns, are singular and plural, but their plurals are irregularly formed: I, *we*; he, *they*; she, *they*; it, *they*; etc. The following table shows the various forms of the personal pronouns:

Singular			
	Nominative	Objective	Possessive
1st person	I	me	my, mine
2nd person	you	you	your, yours
3rd person	he, she, it	him, her, it	his, her, hers, its
Plural			
	Nominative	Objective	Possessive
1st person	we	us	our, ours
2nd person	you	you	your, yours
3rd person	they	them	their, theirs

■ 1c Adjective

An **adjective** (from Latin *adjectivum,* something that is added) modifies, describes, limits, or adds to the meaning of a noun or pronoun (*strange, lovely, three, French,* *those*). In other words, adjectives modify substantives. The articles *the, a,* and *an* are adjectives. Nouns in the possessive case (*Martha's* book, the *cat's* whiskers) and some possessive forms of the personal pronouns are used as adjectives:

my	our
your	your
his, her, its	their

Many demonstrative, indefinite, and interrogative forms may be used as either pronouns or adjectives:

DEMONSTRATIVE: this, that, these, those

INDEFINITE: each, any, either, neither, some, all, both, every, many, most

INTERROGATIVE: which, what, whose

When one of these words appears before a noun or other substantive, describing it or adding to its meaning (*this* cake, *those* gloves, *any* person, *some* food, *which* dress), it is an adjective. When the word stands in the place of a noun (*Those* are pretty roses), it is, of course, a pronoun.

Adjectives are often formed from words that are essentially nouns, but because they modify or describe other words that are themselves substantives, they become adjectives (*service* station, *velvet* dress, *straw* hat, *flower* garden).

Adjectives formed from proper nouns are called **proper adjectives** and are spelled with capital letters (*German, Christian, Shakespearean*).

■ 1d Verb

A **verb** (from Latin *verbum*, word) is a word used to state or ask something and usually expresses an action (*spoke, tells, ran, argued, fights*) or a state of being (*is, seemed, existed, appears*). As its Latin origin indicates, the verb is *the* word in the sentence, for every sentence must have a verb, either expressed or understood.

Transitive and Intransitive Verbs

A verb is called **transitive** if its action is directed toward some receiver, which may be the object of the verb or even its subject. (*David flew the plane,* or *The plane was flown by David.* Whether *plane* is the subject or object of the verb, the fact remains that David flew the plane, making *plane* in both sentences the receiver of the verb's action.)

Note: The term *action* should not be misinterpreted as always involving physical activity. The so-called "action" of a verb may not refer to a physical action at all: Mr. Lee *considered* the plan, Amanda *believed* Frank's story, Louise *wants* a new car. The verbs *considered, believed,* and *wants* are transitive verbs; and their objects *plan, story,* and *car* are receivers of their "action," even though there is no physical action involved.

A verb is called **intransitive** if its action is not directed toward some receiver. (*Lightning strikes. Mother is ill.*) Most verbs may be either transitive or intransitive, simply depending on whether or not a receiver of the verb's action is present in the sentence: *Lightning strikes tall trees* (*strikes* is transitive because *trees* is its object). *Lightning strikes suddenly* (*strikes* is intransitive because no receiver of its action is present). The action is complete without an object.

Linking Verbs

There is a special group of intransitive verbs that make a statement not by expressing action but by indicating a state of being or a condition. These verbs are called **linking verbs** because their function is to link the subject of a sentence with a noun, pronoun, or other substantive that identifies it or with an adjective that describes it. A subject and a linking verb cannot function together as a complete sentence without the help of the substantive or adjective needed to complete the thought; for example, in the sentence *Dorothy is my sister* the word *sister* is necessary to complete the sentence, and it identifies *Dorothy*, the subject. In the sentence *Dorothy is vigorous* the word *vigorous* is necessary, and it describes the subject.

The most common linking verb is the verb *to be* in all its forms (see table on page 9), but any verb that expresses a state of being and is followed by a noun or an adjective identifying or describing the subject is a linking verb. Following is a list of some of the most commonly used linking verbs:

appear	look	smell
become	remain	sound
feel	seem	taste*
grow		

You will notice that those verbs referring to states of being perceived through the five senses are included in the list: *look, feel, smell, sound,* and *taste.* (Sally *looks* happy, I *feel* chilly, The coffee *smells* good, The ticking of the clock *sounded* loud, The plum pudding *tastes* spicy.)

Active and Passive Voice

Transitive verbs are said to be in the **active voice** or the **passive voice. Voice** is the form of a verb that indicates whether the subject of the sentence performs the action or is the receiver of the action of the verb. If the subject performs the action, the verb is in the *active voice* (*Andy ate soup for lunch today*). If the subject

---

* These verbs are not exclusively linking verbs; they may also be used in an active sense, possibly having objects, as in the following:

The dog cautiously *smelled* the food in its bowl.
We *looked* everywhere for the lost key.
Sharon *felt* the warmth of the log fire across the room.
Nick *tasted* the chowder and then added salt.
Dr. Ambrose *sounded* the bell for class to begin.

receives the action, the verb is in the *passive voice* (*Soup was eaten by Andy for lunch today*).

Tense

Tense is the form a verb takes in order to express the time of an action or a state of being, as in these examples: *Helen walks* (**present tense**); *Helen walked* (**past tense**). These two tenses, present and past, change the verb's simple form to show the time of the verb's action. The other four of the six principal tenses found in English verbs are formed through the use of **auxiliary** (helping) verb forms like the following:

am	was	have
are	were	has
is	will	had

The use of these auxiliary verbs creates **verb phrases** (groups of related words that function as single parts of speech). These verb phrases enable the writer to express time and time relationships far beyond those found in the simple present and past forms: She *has gone* to the office; Maggie *will ride* with me; He *had expected* to win the prize; I *am planning* a trip. Verb phrases are also created by the combination of verbs and words like *must, can,* and *do,* often called modal auxiliaries: I *can walk* to class in five minutes; You *must finish* your dinner; *Do* you *have* the time?

Conjugation of Verbs

Showing all forms of a verb in all its tenses is called **conjugation**. Any verb may be conjugated if its **principal parts** are known. These are (1) the first person singular, present tense, (2) the first person singular, past tense, (3) the past participle. (The **participle** is a verbal form that must always be accompanied by an auxiliary verb when it is used to create one of the verb tenses.)

The principal parts of the verb *to call* are (1) *call,* (2) *called,* (3) *called.* The first two of these provide the basic forms of the simple tenses; the third is used with the auxiliary verbs to form verb phrases for the other tenses. The conjugation in the **indicative mood** (that form used for declarative sentences, which make a statement, or interrogative sentences, which ask a question) of the verb *to call* is given below:

ACTIVE VOICE	
Present tense	
Singular	Plural
1. I call	We call
2. You call	You call
3. He, she, it calls	They call

ACTIVE VOICE	
Singular	Plural
Past tense	
1. I called	We called
2. You called	You called
3. He, she, it called	They called
Future tense	
1. I will (shall) call	We will (shall) call
2. You will call	You will call
3. He, she, it will call	They will call
Present perfect tense	
1. I have called	We have called
2. You have called	You have called
3. He, she, it has called	They have called
Past perfect tense	
1. I had called	We had called
2. You had called	You had called
3. He, she, it had called	They had called
Future perfect tense	
1. I will (shall) have called	We will (shall) have called
2. You will have called	You will have called
3. He, she, it will have called	They will have called
PASSIVE VOICE	
Present tense	
1. I am called	We are called
2. You are called	You are called
3. He, she, it is called	They are called
Past tense	
1. I was called	We were called
2. You were called	You were called
3. He, she, it was called	They were called
Future tense	
1. I will (shall) be called	We will (shall) be called
2. You will be called	You will be called
3. He, she, it will be called	They will be called
Present perfect tense	
1. I have been called	We have been called
2. You have been called	You have been called
3. He, she, it has been called	They have been called

PASSIVE VOICE	
Singular	Plural
Past perfect tense	
1. I had been called	We had been called
2. You had been called	You had been called
3. He, she, it had been called	They had been called
Future perfect tense	
1. I will (shall) have been called	We will (shall) have been called
2. You will have been called	You will have been called
3. He, she, it will have been called	They will have been called

Note: You have probably noticed that in the future and future perfect tenses the auxiliary verb *shall* is used as an alternate to *will* in the first persons singular and plural. Traditionally, written English has required *shall,* but contemporary grammarians now suggest that the distinction need be made only rarely and that *will* may be used throughout a conjugation. For emphasis, however, *shall* may occasionally be needed, especially to express strong determination or invitation:

We *shall* overcome!

Shall we dance?

Progressive Tenses

To express an action or state in progress either at the time of speaking or at the time spoken of, forms of the auxiliary verb *to be* are combined with the present participle (see Chapter 3, Section C) as follows:

Progressive present tense	
1. I am calling	We are calling
2. You are calling	You are calling
3. He, she, it is calling	They are calling
Progressive past tense	
1. I was calling	We were calling
2. You were calling	You were calling
3. He, she, it was calling	They were calling

This process may be continued through the various tenses of the active voice, as indicated below:

PROGRESSIVE FUTURE TENSE: I will (shall) be calling, etc.

PROGRESSIVE PRESENT PERFECT TENSE: I have been calling, etc.

PROGRESSIVE PAST PERFECT TENSE: I had been calling, etc.

PROGRESSIVE FUTURE PERFECT TENSE: I will (shall) have been calling, etc.

In the passive voice, the progressive is generally used only in the simple present and past tenses:

PROGRESSIVE PRESENT TENSE: I am being called, etc.

PROGRESSIVE PAST TENSE: I was being called, etc.

In the remaining tenses of the passive voice, the progressive forms — though feasible — become awkward (*I will be being called, I have been being called*, etc.).

Auxiliary Verbs *To Be* and *To Have*

As you have seen, the verbs *to be* and *to have* are used to form certain tenses of all verbs. Following are the conjugations of these two auxiliary verbs in the indicative mood, active voice.

The principal parts of *to be* are (1) *am*, (2) *was*, and (3) *been*.

Present tense	
Singular	Plural
1. I am	We are
2. You are	You are
3. He, she, it is	They are
Past tense	
1. I was	We were
2. You were	You were
3. He, she, it was	They were
Future tense	
1. I will (shall) be	We will (shall) be
2. You will be	You will be
3. He, she, it will be	They will be
Present perfect tense	
1. I have been	We have been
2. You have been	You have been
3. He, she, it has been	They have been
Past perfect tense	
1. I had been	We had been
2. You had been	You had been
3. He, she, it had been	They had been
Future perfect tense	
1. I will (shall) have been	We will (shall) have been
2. You will have been	You will have been
3. He, she, it will have been	They will have been

The principal parts of the verb *to have* are (1) *have*, (2) *had*, and (3) *had*.

Present tense	
Singular	Plural
1. I have	We have
2. You have	You have
3. He, she, it has	They have
Past tense	
1. I had	We had
2. You had	You had
3. He, she, it had	They had
Future tense	
1. I will (shall) have	We will (shall) have
2. You will have	You will have
3. He, she, it will have	They will have
Present perfect tense	
1. I have had	We have had
2. You have had	You have had
3. He, she, it has had	They have had
Past perfect tense	
1. I had had	We had had
2. You had had	You had had
3. He, she, it had had	They had had
Future perfect tense	
1. I will (shall) have had	We will (shall) have had
2. You will have had	You will have had
3. He, she, it will have had	They will have had

Mood

Mood is the form a verb may take to indicate whether it is intended to make a statement, to give a command, or to express a condition contrary to fact. Besides the **indicative** mood shown in the conjugations above, there are the **imperative** and the **subjunctive** moods.

The **imperative** mood is used in giving commands or making requests, as in *TAKE me out to the ball game*. Here *TAKE* is in the imperative mood. The subject of an imperative sentence is *you*, usually understood, but sometimes expressed for the sake of emphasis, as in *You get out of here!*

The **subjunctive** mood is most often used today to express a wish or a condition contrary to fact. In the sentences *I wish I WERE going* and *If I WERE you, I would not go*, the verbs in capitals are in the subjunctive mood.

■ 1e Adverb

An *adverb* (from Latin *ad*, to or toward, and *verbum*, word) usually modifies or adds to the meaning of a verb, an adjective, or another adverb. Sometimes, however, it may be used to modify or qualify a whole phrase or clause, adding to the meaning of an idea that the sentence expresses. The following sentences illustrate the variety of uses of the adverb:

He ran *fast*. [*Fast* modifies the verb *ran*.]

The judges considered the contestants *unusually* brilliant. [*Unusually* modifies the adjective *brilliant*.]

She sang *very* loudly. [*Very* modifies the adverb *loudly*.]

The doves were flying *just* outside gun range. [*Just* modifies either the preposition *outside* or the whole prepositional phrase *outside gun range*.]

He had driven carefully *ever* since he was injured. [*Ever* modifies either the conjunction *since* or the whole clause *since he was injured*.]

Unfortunately, she has encountered rejection everywhere. [*Unfortunately* modifies the whole idea expressed in the sentence and cannot logically be attached to a single word.]

■ 1f Preposition

A **preposition** (from Latin *prae*, before, and *positum*, placed) is a word placed usually before a substantive, called the *object of the preposition*, to show relationship between that object and some other word in the sentence. The combination of a preposition, its object, and any modifiers of the object is called a **prepositional phrase** (*in the mood, on the porch, of human events, toward the beautiful green lake*). You will see how necessary prepositions are to our language when you realize how often you use most of the ones in the group below, which includes some of the most commonly used prepositions:

about	below	except	through
above	beneath	for	throughout
across	beside	from	to
after	besides	in	toward
against	between	into	under
along	beyond	like	underneath
amid	but (meaning	of	until
among	*except*)	off	up
around	by	on	upon
at	concerning	over	with
before	down	past	within
behind	during	since	without

Ordinarily a preposition precedes its object, as its name indicates. Although a sentence ending with a preposition is frequently unemphatic or clumsy, it is in no way contrary to English usage. *She asked what they were cooked in* is better English than *She asked in what they were cooked.*

■ 1g Conjunction

A **conjunction** (from Latin *conjungere,* to join) is a word used to join words or groups of words. There are two kinds of conjunctions: **coordinating conjunctions** and **subordinating conjunctions.**

Coordinating Conjunctions

Coordinating conjunctions join sentence elements of equal rank. In the sentence *She was poor but honest* the conjunction *but* joins the two adjectives *poor* and *honest.* In *She was poor, but she was honest* the conjunction *but* joins the two independent statements *She was poor* and *she was honest.* The common coordinating conjunctions are the following:

and	or	for
but	nor	

Yet in the sense of *but,* and *so* in the sense of *therefore* are also coordinating conjunctions. **Correlative conjunctions,** used in pairs (*either . . . or . . . , neither . . . nor . . . , not only . . . but also . . .*), are coordinating conjunctions too.

Subordinating Conjunctions

Subordinating conjunctions introduce certain subordinate or dependent elements and join them to the main or independent part of the sentence. In *Jack has gone home because he was tired* the subordinating conjunction *because* subordinates the clause that it is part of and joins it to the main part of the sentence, *Jack has gone home.* There are many subordinating conjunctions. Some common ones are the following:

after	because	since	unless	whenever	whether
although	before	so that	until	where	while
as	if	than	when	wherever	why
as if	in order that	that			

Note: Words like *however, therefore, nevertheless, moreover, in fact, consequently, hence,* and *accordingly* are essentially adverbs, not conjunctions; they are sometimes called **conjunctive adverbs.**

■ 1h Interjection

An **interjection** (from Latin *inter,* among or between, and *jectum,* thrown) is an exclamatory word like *oh, ouch, please, why, hey* thrown into a sentence or sometimes used alone. An interjection is always grammatically independent of the rest of the sentence. Adjectives, adverbs, and occasionally other parts of speech become interjections when used as independent exclamations (*good! horrible! fine! what! wait!*).

■ 1i Varying Sentence Functions of Words

The introductory paragraphs in this chapter pointed out that there are many words in the English language that may function as more than one part of speech and that the designation of a word as a particular part of speech is dependent upon its function within its own sentence. It will be helpful for you to see a few examples of this assertion. The word *cause*, for instance, may be a noun, as in the sentence *What was the cause of her distress?* or a transitive verb, as in the sentence *Will the rain cause a delay in the baseball game?* The word *fire* may be a noun, a verb, or an adjective, as shown in the following sentences: *The fire at the warehouse was set by an arsonist; John fired the pistol;* and *We had a fire drill at school yesterday.* The word *near* may be an adverb, an adjective, or a preposition, as in the following sentences: *The end of the year is drawing near; I will make my decision in the near future; Our house is near the campus.*

Exercise 1 Nouns and Pronouns

Write in the first blank at the right any *italicized* word that is a noun and in the second any that is a pronoun.

	Noun	Pronoun
Example: My *father bought me* a new Porsche.	*father*	*me*

1. *She* lives *in* the next *apartment*.   _____   _____

2. *We* spent the *entire day* at SciTrek.   _____   _____

3. *This* is *an* incomplete *address*.   _____   _____

4. The Durdens have invited *us* to *dinner on* Sunday.   _____   _____

5. Professor Gibson read *some* of Walt Whitman's *poetry to* the class.   _____   _____

6. The *stray* dog followed *us* into the *building*.   _____   _____

7. *Someone* had *already* re-served the conference *room*.   _____   _____

8. *Both* of us *left* our *umbrellas* in the dormitory.   _____   _____

9. Marvin looked *everywhere* for his *keys* but didn't find *them*.   _____   _____

10. I will meet *you* in the *morn-ing* at the snack bar.   _____   _____

11. The birds were *fearful* of the *cat* in the *yard*.   _____   _____

12. After *work* on Fridays Bob and Sue usually go to the mountains *for* the weekend.   _____   _____

	Noun	Pronoun

13. My aunt and uncle invited *us over* for *leftovers*.

14. *Each* of us has a *special* place in *society*.

15. Did you paint that *picture yourself*?

16. Peanuts are *one* of the largest cash *crops* in Georgia.

17. The *U.S. Census* is *conducted* every ten *years*.

18. *They* are installing a *Jacuzzi in* their new home.

19. They did *not* understand the *attorney's question*; did *you*?

20. Mary Kay envisions *herself president* of a large Manhattan bank.

21. Phil promised *them* a *surprise*.

22. *Every* night *he* refuses to go to *bed without* his teddy bear.

23. *We* all need *time* for work, study, *and* recreation.

24. *Whom* will your *parents* take with them to Germany?

25. After graduation *they* are *gathering* on the *beach* for an all-night party.

Exercise 2 Pronouns

In the sentences below identify the *italicized* pronouns as personal, demonstrative, indefinite, relative, interrogative, intensive, or reflexive by writing **P, D, Indef, Rel, Inter, Inten,** or **Ref** in the space at the right.

Example: *This* is not the right address.   *D*

1. My brother, *who* is two years older than I, teaches at the University of Texas.   _____

2. *What* did you do after the party?   _____

3. Gail sent *me* a present from Venice.   _____

4. Will you bring me the book *yourself*?   _____

5. During our Australian tour *we* saw kangaroos and koala bears.   _____

6. James bought Rose Hill, *which* was his father's birthplace.   _____

7. The manager called *us* all together for a brief meeting.   _____

8. Randy will enjoy *these*.   _____

9. Alex will fly to Portland by *himself*.   _____

10. He did not recognize *either* of them.   _____

11. The book *that* I had misplaced was in my car.   _____

12. *This* was his choice, not mine.   _____

13. *Several* of our Drama Club members are in the spring play.   _____

14. *What* is your favorite restaurant in Phoenix?   _____

15. Professor Baxter gave *us* extra time on our final examination.   _____

16. I discussed these changes with the director *himself*.   _____

17. I ordered that software package for *myself*.   _____

18. Nearly *everyone* will attend this week's rock concert.   _____

19. When do you want *these* delivered?   _____

20. Angie, *who* is quite prompt, will be here on time.   _____

21. *Anyone* who needs a ride to the game should sign up.   _____

22. He *himself* said that the job was too demanding.   _____

23. The woman *whom* you met in the store is my attorney.   _____

24. *He* said the temperature will be below freezing tonight.   —————

25. She cut *herself* on the broken window pane.   —————

Exercise 3 Adjectives and Adverbs

In the following sentences underline once all the adjectives and words used as adjectives except the articles *a, an,* and *the.* Underline all adverbs twice.

Example: Jeff speaks Russian <u>fluently</u>.

1. My cousin is extremely shy.
2. The team played well.
3. During the hot summer the house is unusually cool.
4. The university awarded him a full academic scholarship.
5. Maria told us many funny stories about her childhood.
6. The dark, damp cave was very unpleasant.
7. Everyone left the party early.
8. Our company recycles tons of office paper daily.
9. The first day of spring brought one of the year's heaviest snowfalls.
10. Chris remembered that he saw Jess at the campus library late in the afternoon.
11. Did you read *The Diary of a Young Girl* for your English class?
12. Captain James Cook was killed by the same native Hawaiians who had earlier welcomed him.
13. Suddenly the cat raced across the room and leaped onto the new couch.
14. The defense witness contradicted himself several times.
15. By the time the tour director stopped for lunch, we were very hungry.
16. The tone of the letter reveals a person who is extremely angry.
17. I recently read a very informative article about trap-door spiders.
18. Art currently lives in an apartment on the twenty-fifth floor.
19. Everyone agrees that she is lovely.
20. Josh lives near the Okefenokee Swamp and has acquired the great gift of observation.

Exercise 4 | Verbs

In the following sentences underline all verbs and then write them in the first column at the right. In the second column write **T-A** for each transitive verb in the active voice, **T-P** for each transitive verb in the passive voice, or **I** for each intransitive verb.

	Verb	T-A, T-P, or I
Example: Chris <u>seemed</u> sleepy during class yesterday.	*seemed*	*I*
1. I bought a new dress for the dance.		
2. The dance will be held on the day after Christmas.		
3. Jane and Wanda donated holly and magnolia boughs for the decorations.		
4. Lilacs smell sweet.		
5. The wind howled around the house.		
6. The big billboard on Main Street was damaged by the storm.		
7. Guinea pigs are good pets.		
8. Do you want a drink of water?		
9. I left Denver at 10:00 A.M.		
10. I arrived in Houston at noon.		
11. Snow had fallen throughout the night.		
12. My favorite movie is *Gone with the Wind*.		
13. For some reason I felt very secure and content.		

	Verb	T-A, T-P, or I

14. She felt the raindrops on her face. _____ _____

15. That portrait was painted by an unknown artist. _____ _____

16. My chocolate bar melted in the sun. _____ _____

17. Columbus sailed the ocean blue in 1492. _____ _____

18. In the middle of the night an owl hooted mournfully. _____ _____

19. The Grand Canyon is over one mile deep. _____ _____

20. Lech Walesa has been the president of Poland since 1990. _____ _____

21. Herschel Walker was awarded the Heisman Trophy in 1982. _____ _____

22. The car engine whined and sputtered all the way up the hill. _____ _____

23. Like the legendary gods of old, today's fictional superheroes have magical powers. _____ _____

24. My nephew collects baseball cards. _____ _____

25. Our beagle was named George. _____ _____

Exercise 5   Prepositions

Write the prepositions in the following sentences in the spaces of the first column at the right. Write the objects of the prepositions in the second column. If a sentence contains no preposition, leave the spaces blank.

	Prep.	Object
Example: The Johnsons have two daughters in Seattle.	*in*	*Seattle*
1. I have scheduled all my classes except physics.		
2. In Betsy I have a dear friend.		
3. The crackling of the cozy fire made me sleepy.		
4. Native Americans are divided into many different tribes.		
5. I did not find Sonny's baseball cards among the others.		
6. Catalina Island is off the California coast.		
7. During the night I heard a lonesome train whistle.		
8. They will meet you outside the bookstore.		
9. Jessica has done everything well throughout her career.		
10. We were all there but Joseph.		
11. By the time we arrived, all the food had been eaten.		
12. The Colorado River runs behind our house.		
13. Between you and me, I think his plan is more cost-effective than ours.		
14. William's plane should arrive within the hour.		

	Prep.	Object

15. We simply cannot go without the twins.

16. Uncle Joe found his tennis shoes under his bed.

17. After the morning speech we will leave.

18. Does Sally want a pickle with her salami sandwich?

19. He will leave *Time* magazine on the hall table.

20. Is that Jake walking toward us?

21. The community action group appeared before the zoning board and requested an exemption.

22. Bruce is planning a trip to Iowa this summer.

23. He was regional sales manager for his company.

24. Gordon has left Tim a message on the computer.

25. We cooked enough fried chicken for everyone.

Exercise 6   Conjunctions

In the following sentences there are both coordinating and subordinating conjunctions. Write the conjunction(s) in the space at the right, and after it write **C** if it joins sentence elements of equal rank or **S** if it joins unequal elements.

Example: Jim and Mark will oversee the renovation of the gym.   *and, C*

1. Laureen will be here, but she will be late.   _____

2. We spent several hours visiting galleries and antique shops in Soho.   _____

3. When we left New York, we were exhausted.   _____

4. Will, help me move this desk before you go.   _____

5. Aunt Norinne will call you if she can come on Sunday.   _____

6. We can meet you for dinner and the theater Friday evening.   _____

7. Either Shannon or her sister will meet you at the airport.   _____

8. Since I saw him last, many wonderful things have happened to him.   _____

9. Rodney is my best friend and confidant.   _____

10. Although they are planning an extended trip this summer, they will be back in time for Heather's wedding.   _____

11. Mother took a well-deserved nap while everyone was watching the tennis match.   _____

12. My cousin has lived in New Zealand most of his life and only recently moved to St. Louis.   _____

13. Professor Salier's seminars are not only interesting but also informative.   _____

14. I hope David cleaned out the refrigerator before he left.   _____

15. After work I will pick up some Chinese or Italian food for supper.   _____

16. I first met my husband in the sixties while I was attending the University of Alaska.   _____

17. Jill and Greg have spent the last several weeks cleaning out their attic.   _____

18. As the world gets smaller, our marketplace gets larger.   _____

19. I will always remember Dr. Fincher because he was kind to me personally and helpful to me professionally.   _____

20. Even though he has finished all his work, he cannot leave until Amy gets here.   _____

Exercise 7   Review of Parts of Speech

In the following sentences identify the part of speech of each *italicized* word by writing one of the following abbreviations in the space at the right:

N for noun,	**Adv** for adverb,
V for verb,	**Prep** for preposition,
P for pronoun,	**C** for conjunction,
Adj for adjective,	**I** for interjection.

Example: Will *you* bring me the paper?   *P*

1. Are Becky and Robyn going to the *beach*?   *N*

2. Let's sit in the kitchen *and* talk.   *C*

3. My physical therapist *has done* wonders for me.   *V*

4. Cameron spent her *junior* year at the University of Edinburgh.   *Adj*

5. The little boy squatted *on* his heels and watched the kittens play.   *prep*

6. *All* of the tables and chairs had been removed for the dance.   ~~prep~~ *adv*

7. I can't go tonight *because* I have a science report due tomorrow.   *C*

8. It's *too* late for lunch.   *adv*

9. There are still a few gaslights in *downtown* Atlanta.   *adj*

10. *Each* of the students must bring a sandwich for lunch.   *adj*

11. The massive Stonehenge monoliths remain a *mystery*.   *N*

12. *During* the summers his family has visited many of the national parks.   *prep*

13. Tony has had Professor Hayes *before*.   *prep*

14. Our cabin overlooks a peaceful *mountain* lake.   *adj*

15. *No!* We can't afford a new car now.   *I*

16. Ralph is packing his snorkeling gear *for* the trip.   *prep*

17. Marge *never* has any extra money.   *adv*

18. Almost all of my friends had joined a fitness center *before* I did.   *prep*

19. The entire class is *somewhat* anxious about final grades.   *adv*

20. *They* are leaving early in the morning.   P

Exercise 8 Review of Parts of Speech

In the following sentences identify the part of speech of all *italicized* words by writing one of the following abbreviations in the space at the right:

N for noun,	**Adv** for adverb,
V for verb,	**Prep** for preposition,
P for pronoun,	**C** for conjunction,
Adj for adjective,	**I** for interjection.

Example: Maurice is *quite* unpredictable.   *Adv*

1. They will come *if* they can bring the children.   _____

2. A bibliophile is a person *who* loves and collects books.   _____

3. The bicycle is the prevailing mode *of* transportation in China.   _____

4. Nashville, Tennessee, is the home of *country* music.   _____

5. *Not only* women *but also* men are having cosmetic surgery.   _____

6. The addition of fluoride to toothpaste has *drastically* reduced tooth decay.   _____

7. A mango is a delicious yellow-red tropical fruit *with* a thick rind and a hard stone.   _____

8. *Oh, no!* I locked my keys in the car.   _____

9. "Sesame Street" is a *worthwhile* program for little children.   _____

10. Yogurt is an excellent low-fat *substitute* for ice cream.   _____

11. Jennifer traded her motorized wheelchair for a new lighter-weight *one*.   _____

12. Windsor Castle *has been* a residence of the English monarchy since the time of William the Conqueror.   _____

13. We registered for the conference *before* we received the program.   _____

14. *Underneath* his stern expression lies a sympathetic heart.   _____

15. College and high school students flock to the *beaches* during spring break.   _____

16. Athletes hurt *themselves* when they lift too many weights.   _____

17. Cape Cod is *among* my favorite vacation spots.   _____

18. Our building *was evacuated* yesterday because of a gas leak.   _____

19. *Yes,* I do like that dress very much.   _____

20. There are *various* colors of African violets   _____

Recognizing Subjects, Verbs, and Complements

2a The Sentence

A **sentence** is made up of single parts of speech combined into a pattern that expresses a complete thought. In other words, a sentence is a group of words that expresses a complete thought. When written, it begins with a capital letter and ends with a period, a question mark, or an exclamation mark. In its simplest form this complete statement is an independent clause or a **simple sentence.**

2b Subject and Predicate

Every simple sentence must have two basic elements: (1) the thing we are talking about, and (2) what we say about it. The thing we are talking about is called the **subject,** and what we say about it is called the **predicate.** The subject is a noun, a pronoun, or some other word or group of words used as a noun. The essential part of the predicate is a verb — a word that tells something about the subject. It tells that the subject *does* something or that something *is true* of the subject. A subject and a verb are, therefore, the fundamental parts of every sentence. In fact, it is possible to express meaning with just these two elements:

Pilots fly.

Flowers bloom.

She sings.

Note that in each example the verb says that the subject does something.

■ 2c Finding the Verb

Finding verbs and subjects of verbs in a sentence is the first step in determining whether or not a group of words expresses a complete thought. Look first for the verb, the most important word in the sentence, and then for its subject.

The verb may sometimes be difficult to find. It may come anywhere in the sentence; for instance, it may precede the subject, as in some interrogative sentences (*Where is my pencil?*). It may consist of a single word or a group of two or more words; it may have other words inserted within the verb phrase; it may be combined with the negative *not* or with a contraction of *not*. To find the verb, look for the word or group of words that expresses an action or a state of being. In the following sentences the verbs are in italics:

> His friend *stood* at his side. [The verb *stood* follows the subject *friend*.]
>
> At his side *stood* his friend. [The verb *stood* precedes the subject *friend*.]
>
> His friend *was standing* at his side. [The verb *was standing* consists of two words.]
>
> His friend *cannot stand* at his side. [The verb *can* is combined with the negative adverb *not*, which is not part of the verb.]
>
> *Did* his friend *stand* at his side? [The two parts of the verb *did stand* are separated by the subject.]

■ 2d Finding the Subject

Sometimes finding the subject may also be difficult, for, as we have just seen, the subject does not always come immediately before the verb. Often it comes after the verb; often it is separated from the verb by a modifying element. Always look for the noun or pronoun about which the verb asserts something and disregard intervening elements:

> *Many* of the children *come* to the clinic. [A prepositional phrase comes between the subject and the verb. The object of a preposition is never a subject.]
>
> There *are flowers* on the table. [The subject comes after the verb. The word *there* is never a subject; in this sentence it is an **expletive,** an idiomatic introductory word.]
>
> In the room *were* a *cot* and a *chair*. [The subjects come after the verb.]

In an **imperative sentence,** a sentence expressing a command or a request, the subject *you* is usually implied rather than expressed. Occasionally, however, the subject *you* is expressed:

> Come in out of the rain.
>
> Shut the door!
>
> *You* play goalie.

Either the verb or the subject or both may be **compound;** that is, there may be more than one subject and more than one verb:

The *boy* and the *girl* played. [Two subjects.]

The boy *worked* and *played*. [Two verbs.]

The *boy* and the *girl* *worked* and *played*. [Two subjects and two verbs.]

In the first sentence the compound subject is *boy* and *girl*. In the second sentence there is a compound verb, *worked* and *played*. In the third sentence both the subject and the verb are compound.

■ 2e Complements

Thus far we have discussed two functions of words: that of nouns and pronouns as subjects and that of verbs as predicates.

A third function of words that we must consider is that of completing the verb. Nouns, pronouns, and adjectives are used to complete verbs and are called **complements**. A complement may be a **direct object**, an **indirect object**, a **predicate noun** or **pronoun**, a **predicate adjective**, an **objective complement**.

A **direct object** is a noun or noun equivalent that completes the verb and receives the action expressed in the verb:

> The pilot flew the *plane*. [*Plane* is the direct object of *flew*. Just as the subject answers the question *"who?"* or *"what?"* before the verb (Who flew?), so the direct object answers the question *"whom?"* or *"what?"* after the verb (Flew what?).]

An **indirect object** is a word (or words) denoting the person or thing indirectly affected by the action of a transitive verb. It is the person or thing to which something is given or for which something is done. A sentence cannot contain an indirect object without also containing a direct object. Such words as *give, offer, grant, lend, teach* represent the idea of something done for the indirect object:

> We gave *her* the book. [*Her* is the indirect object of *gave*. The indirect object answers the question *"to (for) whom or what?"* after the verb *gave* (Gave to whom?).]

Certain verbs that represent the idea of taking away or withholding something can also have indirect objects:

> The judge *denied him* the opportunity to speak in his own defense.

> Father *refused Frances* the use of the car.

A **predicate noun** (also called **predicate nominative**) is a noun or its equivalent that renames or identifies the subject and completes such verbs as *be, seem, become,* and *appear* (called linking verbs):

> The woman is a *doctor*. [The predicate noun *doctor* completes the intransitive verb *is* and renames the subject *woman*.]

> My best friends are *she* and her *sister*. [The predicate pronoun *she* and the predicate noun *sister* complete the intransitive verb *are* and rename the subject *friends*.]

Mary has become a *surgeon*. [The predicate noun *surgeon* completes the intransitive verb *has become* and renames the subject *Mary*.]

A **predicate adjective** is an adjective that completes a linking verb and describes the subject:

The man seems *angry*. [The predicate adjective *angry* completes the intransitive verb *seems* and describes the subject *man*.]

An **objective complement** is a noun or an adjective that completes the action expressed in the verb and refers to the direct object. If it is a noun, the objective complement is in a sense identical with the direct object; if it is an adjective, it describes or limits the direct object. It occurs commonly after such verbs as *think, call, find, make, consider, choose,* and *believe*:

Jealousy made Othello a *murderer*. [The objective complement *murderer* completes the transitive verb *made* and renames the direct object *Othello*.]

She thought the day *disagreeable*. [The objective complement *disagreeable* is an adjective that describes the direct object *day*.]

Exercise 9   Subjects and Verbs

In each of the following sentences underline the subject once and the verb twice. Then write the subject in the first column and the verb in the second column at the right.

	Subject	**Verb**
Example: How many <u>students</u> <u><u>are coming</u></u> to tonight's concert?	*students*	*are coming*

1. One hundred years after his death Walt Whitman remains one of America's most important poets.   _____   _____

2. Dan flew to Anchorage last Monday.   _____   _____

3. They spent last weekend in Dallas.   _____   _____

4. During the afternoon we browsed through the Furniture Mart.   _____   _____

5. The brick house around the corner was built by Tom's uncle.   _____   _____

6. Russ didn't reach Annapolis until after midnight.   _____   _____

7. Jody has already planned her schedule for next semester.   _____   _____

8. With each player's shot the emotions at the basketball game intensified.   _____   _____

9. I cannot finish this lab experiment this afternoon.   _____   _____

	Subject	Verb
10. Sam has offered his help.	_____	_____
11. Dr. Brown's article will be published in the spring.	_____	_____
12. Summer vacation passes too quickly.	_____	_____
13. Chandra enjoys daydreaming.	_____	_____
14. The Grand Old Opry popularized country music.	_____	_____
15. Bighorn sheep have huge horns and inhabit the Rocky Mountains.	_____	_____
16. They are anticipating renovations to their apartment building.	_____	_____
17. Cheryl's wedding dress was beautifully made.	_____	_____
18. Did you understand that poem?	_____	_____
19. There were several different models of antique cars for sale at the auction.	_____	_____
20. The mother cat with her new kittens was on the porch.	_____	_____

Exercise 10 Subjects and Verbs

In each of the following sentences underline the subject(s) once and the verb(s) twice. Then copy the subject(s) in the first column and the verb(s) in the second column at the right.

	Subject	Verb
Example: Have <u>you</u> ordered our tickets for the game Saturday?	*you*	*Have ordered*
1. The company has assumed the responsibility of health care for its employees.		
2. We enjoyed the concert from start to finish.		
3. Is Wayne looking forward to his retirement?		
4. The dog as well as her puppies was excited by the knock on the door.		
5. During the tournament we could hardly hear the referee.		
6. They followed his instructions carefully but did not find the restaurant.		
7. The houses in the next block were built in the early 1920's.		
8. The five-minute video was used for recruitment purposes.		
9. There was a renaissance of Native American graphic art in the 1930's.		
10. Several members of our law firm are attending the San Francisco conference.		
11. Has Laura read Madeleine L'Engle's *A Circle of Quiet*?		

	Subject	Verb

12. Rhonda is taking a two-year
degree in sign language.

13. In spite of himself he usually
sticks his foot in his mouth.

14. Will you meet me in the cafeteria
for lunch?

15. All government managers will take
a course in ethics.

16. In 1803 the United States
purchased the Louisiana Territory
from France.

17. At the first of this year, Joe sent
his résumé to twenty-five companies.

18. Many employees in our company
work and attend evening school.

19. During recent years college tuition
costs have increased greatly.

20. The senior concert will be held on
Monday evening.

21. Jane, approximately how many
telephone calls do you receive
daily?

22. After lengthy debate the framers
of the Constitution adopted a
strong executive branch.

23. Both of us are planning the party
for Vernon and Helen.

24. In the cabinet on the top shelf is
Zoe's recipe for jambalaya.

25. All of the exhibits are displayed in
the lobby of the museum.

Exercise 11   Direct Objects and Predicate Nouns

In each of the following sentences underline the complement. Then identify the complement by writing in the space at the right one of the following abbreviations:

DO if it is a direct object,
PN if it is a predicate noun.

Example: The office staff gave Tammy and Shawn a double
rocking <u>chair</u> as a wedding gift.   _DO_

1. Dr. Rose is a pediatrician in Baltimore.   _____

2. No one in the room understood a word that he said.   _____

3. After dinner we visited Martha and her new baby.   _____

4. Dr. Voight is a French professor at the University of South
   Dakota.   _____

5. In 1783 the signing of the Treaty of Paris ended the American
   Revolution.   _____

6. The treasurer of the college requested our presence at the
   alumni dinner.   _____

7. The president-elect of the board has always been the
   presiding officer.   _____

8. At the class reunion I renewed old friendships.   _____

9. Has Crystal given you the invitation list?   _____

10. She has really become a wizard with computers.   _____

11. Robert Shaw is Music Director emeritus and Conductor
    Laureate of the Atlanta Symphony Orchestra.   _____

12. Will the organist perform two different programs?   _____

13. The station welcomes your comments and suggestions.   _____

14. His cousin became the first woman on the company's board
    of directors.   _____

15. I forgot the most important thing on my grocery list.   _____

16. Daniel Boone made his first expedition west of the
    Appalachians in 1767.   _____

17. I really do not like answering machines.   _____

18. Uncle Jesse was the first member of our family to graduate from college.   _____

19. Nevada is definitely my choice for our family reunion.   _____

20. In 1974 Hank Aaron became the all-time leading home-run hitter.   _____

Exercise 12 Indirect Objects and Objective Complements

In each of the following sentences identify the *italicized* complement by writing in the space at the right one of the following abbreviations:

IO if it is an indirect object,
OC if it is an objective complement.

Example: The librarian gave *me* Stephen King's most recent novel. _*IO*_

1. From the market Grandmother brought *us* several pieces of candy. _____

2. Professor Owen wrote *Sue* a complimentary note on her essay. _____

3. The committee found her attitude *offensive*. _____

4. Dave Justice gave *José* his autograph. _____

5. Until now James has considered Don his best *friend*. _____

6. While at the old gem mine, Uncle Rush found *each* of the children several beautiful but worthless gems. _____

7. From the catalog we ordered *Wesley* a new tent. _____

8. The road crew made the highway *broader* north of the bridge. _____

9. Professor Nouwen considered Vincent the brightest *student* in the class. _____

10. Carlos is teaching *me* ballet. _____

11. They elected Gwen *captain* of the tennis team. _____

12. Ross dyes his hair *auburn*. _____

13. My grandfather told *me* my first ghost story. _____

14. The coach threw *her* a fast pitch. _____

15. The realtor had the entire house painted a light *gray*. _____

16. Will the doorman call *us* a cab? _____

17. The poet read the *class* some of his poetry. _____

18. I will prepare *them* supper before leaving. _____

19. Before finals, Josh, keep your mind *clear*. _____

20. Write *him* a letter when you get home. _____

Exercise 13   Complements

A. In each of the following sentences identify the *italicized* word by writing one of the following abbreviations in the space at the right:

      PN if it is a predicate noun,   **IO** if it is an indirect object,
      PA if it is a predicate adjective,   **OC** if it is an objective complement.
      DO if it is a direct object,

Example: I repeated my *story* to Rita.   *DO*

1. The speaker appeared unusually *nervous*.   _____

2. Trees are a special *gift* from nature.   _____

3. In 1777 Congress approved a *design* for the American flag.   _____

4. In spite of what I know, I consider all snakes *dangerous*.   _____

5. Dolores is extremely *creative*.   _____

6. The mimes provided the *audience* a hilarious evening.   _____

7. My favorite variety of summer corn is *Silver Queen*.   _____

8. Samuel Pepys was a famous English *diarist*.   _____

9. Can you bring *me* a quart of milk from the store?   _____

10. The teacher gave *us* a pop test today.   _____

11. I found him very *sensitive*.   _____

12. In 1903 the Wright brothers made the first successful *flight* in a motorized airplane.   _____

13. Bryan thought Twain's novel *splendid*.   _____

14. This painting is an unusual *example* of the Hudson River School of art.   _____

15. Fame made him unbearably *egotistical*.   _____

B. Write sixteen sentences, four of which contain direct objects; four, indirect objects; four, predicate nouns; four, predicate adjectives. In the space at the right, write **DO** (direct object), **IO** (indirect object), **PN** (predicate noun), or **PA** (predicate adjective) as the case may be.

1. _____ _____

2. _____ _____

3. _____ _____

4. _____ _____

5. _____ _____

6. _____ _____

7. _____ _____

8. _____ _____

9. _____ _____

10. _____ _____

11. _____ _____

12. _____ _____

13. _____ _____

14. _____ _____

15. _____ _____

16. _____ _____

Verbals

You may sometimes have trouble in recognizing sentence verbs because you may confuse them with certain verb forms that function partly as verbs and partly as other parts of speech. (The *sentence verb* is the verb that states something about the subject, one capable of completing a statement.) These other verb forms are made from verbs but also perform the function of nouns, adjectives, or adverbs. In other words, they constitute a sort of half-verb. They are called **verbals.** The three verbal forms are the **gerund,** the **participle,** and the **infinitive.**

■ 3a Verbals and Sentence Verbs

It is important that you distinguish between the use of a particular verb form as a verbal and its use as a main verb in a sentence. An illustration of the different uses of the verb form *running* will help you to make this distinction:

> *Running* every day is good exercise. [*Running* is a **gerund** and is the subject of the verb *is.*]
>
> *Running* swiftly, he caught the bandit. [*Running* is a **participle** and modifies the pronoun *he.*]
>
> The boy *is running* down the street. [*Is running* is the **sentence verb.** It is formed by using the present participle with the auxiliary verb *is.*]

It must be emphasized that *a verbal cannot take the place of a sentence verb* and that *any group of words containing a verbal but no sentence verb is a sentence fragment:*

> The boy *running* [A sentence fragment.]
>
> *To face* an audience [A sentence fragment.]

The boy *running* up the steps is Charles. [A complete sentence.]

To face an audience was a great effort for me. [A complete sentence.]

The following table shows the tenses and voices in which verbals appear:

Gerunds and participles		
Tense	Active voice	Passive voice
Present	doing	being done
Past		done (This form applies only to participles.)
Present perfect	having done	having been done
Progressive present perfect	having been doing	
Infinitives		
Tense	Active voice	Passive voice
Present	to do	to be done
Present perfect	to have done	to have been done
Progressive present	to be doing	
Progressive present perfect	to have been doing	

■ 3b The Gerund

A **gerund** is a verbal used as a noun and in its present tense always ends in -*ing*. Like a noun, a gerund is used as a subject, a complement, an object of a preposition. It can also be used as an appositive (see Chapter 4, Section f). Do not confuse the gerund with the present participle, which has the same form but is used as an adjective:

> *Planning* the work carefully required a great deal of time. [*Planning* is a gerund used as subject of the sentence.]

> She was not to blame for *breaking* the vase. [*Breaking* is a gerund used as object of the preposition *for*.]

> I appreciated your *taking* time to help me. [*Taking* is a gerund used as direct object of *appreciated*.]

> His unselfish act, *giving* Marty his coat, plainly showed Ed's generosity. [*Giving* is a gerund used as the appositive of *act*.]

In the sentences above, you will note examples of gerunds functioning as nouns but also taking objects as verbs do. In the first sentence the gerund *planning* is used as the subject of the verb *required*. *Planning* itself, however, is completed by the object *work* and is modified by the adverb *carefully*. This dual functioning of the gerund is apparent in the other three sentences as well.

It is important to remember a rule concerning the modification of gerunds: always use the possessive form of a noun or pronoun before a gerund. Because gerunds are nouns, their modifiers, other than the adverbial ones just mentioned, must be adjectival; therefore, the possessive form, which has adjectival function, is the correct modifier:

Mr. Bridges was surprised at *Doug's* offering him the motorboat.

NOT

Mr. Bridges was surprised at Doug offering the motorboat.

■ 3c The Participle

A **participle** is a verbal used as an adjective. The present participle is formed by adding *-ing* to the verb: *do — doing*. Again, remember not to confuse the gerund and the present participle, which have the same form but do not function similarly. The past participle is formed in various ways. It may end in *-ed, -d, -t,* or *-n: talk — talked, hear — heard, feel — felt, know — known*. It may also be formed by a change of vowel: *sing — sung*.

The baby, *wailing* pitifully, refused to be comforted. [*Wailing* is a present participle. It modifies *baby*.]

The *broken* doll can be mended. [*Broken* is a past participle, passive voice. It modifies *doll*.]

An old coat, *faded* and *torn,* was her only possession. [*Faded* and *torn* are past participles, passive voice, modifying *coat*.]

Having been warned, the man was sent on his way. [*Having been warned* is the present perfect participle, passive voice. It modifies *man*.]

Like the gerund, the participle may have a complement and adverbial modifiers. In the sentence *Wildly waving a red flag, he ran down the track,* the participle *waving* has the object *flag* and the adverbial modifier *wildly*.

■ 3d The Infinitive

An **infinitive** is a verbal consisting usually of the simple form of the verb preceded by *to* and used as a noun, an adjective, or an adverb:

To err is human. [*To err* is used as a noun, the subject of *is*.]

He wanted *to go* tomorrow. [*To go* is used as a noun, the object of the verb *wanted*.]

He had few books *to read*. [*To read* is used as an adjective to modify the noun *books*.]

Frank seemed eager *to go*. [*To go* is used as an adverb to modify the adjective *eager*.]

She rode fast *to escape* her pursuers. [*To escape* is used as an adverb to modify the verb *rode*.]

Sometimes the word *to* is omitted:

> Susan helped carry the packages. [*To* is understood before the verb *carry*. *(To) carry* is used as a noun and is the object of *helped*.]

Note: An adverbial infinitive can frequently be identified if the phrase "in order" can be placed before it, as in *Katy paid ten dollars* (in order) *to get good seats for the play*.

Like the gerund and the participle, the infinitive may have a complement and adverbial modifiers:

> He did not want *to cut the grass yesterday*. [The infinitive *to cut* has the object *grass* and the adverbial modifier *yesterday*.]

Exercise 14   Verbs and Verbals

In the following sentences identify each *italicized* expression by writing on the line at the right

> **V** if it is a verb,   **Part** if it is a participle,
> **Ger** if it is a gerund,   **Inf** if it is an infinitive.

Example: Our company has hired a *consulting* firm.   *Part*

1. He bores me with his constant *complaining*. _____

2. Samuel is competing in the national *spelling* contest. _____

3. Are you planning *to invite* everyone in the office? _____

4. *Riding* a horse down the trail into the Grand Canyon is a memorable experience. _____

5. Interstate highways make *driving* long distances less stressful than two-lane roads that go through every small town. _____

6. In 1925 Noel Coward had three plays *running* simultaneously in London. _____

7. Disposable contact lenses are now available *to replace* the hard lenses. _____

8. Two of my friends love *walking* in the warm spring rain. _____

9. The audience was delighted by Betty Ann Wylie's *storytelling*. _____

10. The children enjoyed her *dancing* puppets. _____

11. Professor Pankey's *acting* class is full. _____

12. *To complete* the financial report will take several hours. _____

13. Sumac, a poisonous plant, *belongs* to the same family as the cashew. _____

14. They came home early *to change* their clothes. _____

15. *Lifting* weights increases muscle strength. _____

16. The hiking club delights in *finding* new paths. _____

17. In an effort *to improve* public education, businesses are adopting schools. _____

18. Many of her colleagues are eager *to read* her recently published novel. _____

19. Santa Fe is an *enchanting* place.   ———

20. Ballet is a way *to demonstrate* emotions with movements.   ———

21. The first-period class *was given* another book list.   ———

22. Our children have always enjoyed *making* cookies.   ———

23. Lightning caused the television picture tube *to explode*.   ———

24. Have you found my *lost* keys?   ———

25. His parents *bought* him a computer.   ———

Exercise 15 Gerunds

In the following sentences underline each gerund. Copy the gerund in the first column at the right. In the second column write **S** if the gerund is the subject of the verb, **PN** if the gerund is the predicate nominative, **DO** if the gerund is the direct object, **OP** if the gerund is the object of the preposition.

	Gerund	Use
Example: Recovering from a long illness requires patience and determination.	*Recovering*	S

1. By adding storm windows, she saved on her heating bill.

    adding   OP

2. One of Annie's favorite pastimes is telling African folktales.

    telling   PN ~~DO~~

3. We enjoyed his singing and dancing.

    Singing/Dancing   DO

4. Last night my roommate's coughing disturbed my sleep.

    Coughing ~~Singing~~   DO

5. Landing a jet plane on an aircraft carrier requires precision flying.

    landing/flying   S/DO

6. The executive committee of the board of directors will consider implementing the strategic plan.

    implementing   DO ~~~~

7. Grooming Fifi for the county fair took both of us several hours.

8. The ringing of church bells reminds us of our spiritual needs.

9. Strong ankles are needed for ballet dancing.

10. Good bidding is essential for an exciting game of bridge.

11. Tim will find practicing yoga a rewarding exercise.

12. There is something to be said for taking the less traveled roads.

	Gerund	Use

13. Remote control makes watching television too easy for "couch potatoes." _____ _____

14. Portraying violence on television may be psychologically damaging to small children. _____ _____

15. In many colleges and universities a course in critical thinking is being offered. _____ _____

16. Jenny loves watching "Sesame Street," particularly when Big Bird is on. _____ _____

17. Shortly after reading Eugenia Price's novel *Savannah*, we visited the coastal city. _____ _____

18. Painting his house took longer than he had thought it would. _____ _____

19. After working in an office all day, Mike spends his evenings at work in his yard. _____ _____

20. Before returning home, stop by the store for some milk and bread. _____ _____

21. The only thing that his friends disliked was his loud talking. _____ _____

22. Filing her income tax on time each year was almost impossible. _____ _____

23. Trading baseball cards has become a full-time job for John. _____ _____

24. This weekend I will need extra money for lessons in skiing. _____ _____

25. The official grand opening of the new building will take place on June 10 during a special ceremony. _____ _____

Exercise 16 Participles

Underline the participle in each of the following sentences, and then write in the space at the right the word that the participle modifies.

Example: Surely you won't wear that <u>faded</u> dress to the
party.   _____*dress*_____

1. Using his money wisely, Dan buys secondhand text-
books.   _____

2. Having arrived late, her application will not be
handled in the same manner as all the others.   _____

3. The old man was wearing a tattered and faded coat.   _____

4. Having expressed her hope that the entire family
would be home for Christmas, my mother began to
plan her menu.   _____

5. How many of the returning students have received
their room assignments?   _____

6. The broken glass was scattered everywhere.   _____

7. The little girl shivered each time she walked by the
tall, locked door.   _____

8. The creaking stairs also frightened her.   _____

9. Having locked his keys in the car, Tom called home
for help.   _____

10. They had baked lobster for supper last night.   _____

11. His scheduled departure time is about six o'clock
tomorrow evening.   _____

12. Do you have a guaranteed reservation for Saturday
night?   _____

13. Chasing the puppy around the yard, Danny tripped
and fell.   _____

14. He ordered two chicken sandwiches, fried green
tomatoes, and a large root beer.   _____

15. They found his missing papers in a trash can.   _____

16. Aristotle is one of the world's best-known philosophers.   _____

17. Realizing her mistake, she quickly apologized.   _____

18. We are driving to Madison County Sunday to see an old covered bridge.   _____

19. The electrician installed recessed lighting in the kitchen.   _____

20. Chief Inspector Morse always uncovers the well-kept secrets.   _____

21. The old man, having slowly walked across the street, seemed to be looking for someone.   _____

22. After the storm we returned to a house lighted only by candles.   _____

23. Rain was predicted for Friday; therefore, we canceled our scheduled visit to Lewis-Clark State College.   _____

24. The children were sitting on the sofa watching television.   _____

25. The young woman sitting next to the piano has been invited to join the medical school honor society.   _____

26. Having chosen his major, Vincent felt good.   _____

27. He went into the kitchen for a snack, tiptoeing each step of the way.   _____

28. Serving consistently delicious food at her restaurant, she never lacks customers.   _____

29. Because of Aunt Ellie's great sense of humor, I always enjoy reading her cleverly written letters.   _____

30. Having spent most of his childhood in Germany, Todd spoke excellent German.   _____

Exercise 17 Infinitives

Underline the infinitive in each of the following sentences, and in the space at the right indicate its use in the sentence by writing **N** for noun, **Adj** for adjective, and **Adv** for adverb.

Example: To act professionally takes much dedication and work.   _N_

1. I wanted to take German 101 at nine o'clock.   _____

2. I had five chapters of the novel to read before Wednesday.   _____

3. Gary liked his job as a short-order cook once he learned
   to prepare ten different orders at the same time.   _____

4. She worked in her air-conditioned office to escape the heat.   _____

5. Mary's parents approved of her decision to attend summer
   school.   _____

6. I hope to finish mowing the lawn before it rains.   _____

7. Tom learned to write the kind of articles his editor wanted.   _____

8. My sister was acting so strangely that I began to suspect something was wrong.   _____

9. I was sorry that I had to turn down the invitation to the party.   _____

10. I had promised to baby-sit with my history professor's children
    that night.   _____

11. My mother told me to come home right away.   _____

12. My sister plans to marry her boyfriend this spring.   _____

13. Many people chew gum during an airplane's takeoff and landing
    to relieve the pressure in their ears.   _____

14. How would you like to go to the dairy store for ice cream cones?   _____

15. Gloria was too tired to finish her dinner.   _____

16. I love to hear the ocean breakers pounding against the shore.   _____

17. His ability to become a professional football player was
    unquestioned.   _____

18. If everyone cooperates, we will be able to finish this project by
    Monday.   _____

19. Rebecca planned to run three miles every morning before breakfast. _____

20. My first impulse was to telephone my parents. _____

21. I wish you had had a chance to meet my mother. _____

22. After working as a teacher's aide, Phyllis decided to get her degree in early childhood education. _____

23. To have loved and lost is sad. _____

24. However, it is sadder never to have loved at all. _____

25. My roommate told me to study longer. _____

26. Jane wanted to visit Venice while she was in Italy. _____

27. Do you prefer to eat here or at the beach? _____

28. John did not have enough time to consider all the options. _____

29. Brad will have to make both free throws to win the game. _____

30. I do not like to disappoint my friends. _____

Exercise 18 Verbals

In the following sentences underline each verbal. In the first column at the right identify the type of verbal by writing

      Ger for gerund,
      Part for participle,
      Inf for infinitive.

In the second column at the right indicate the *use* of the verbal by writing

      Adj for adjective,   **PN** for predicate nominative,
      Adv for adverb,   **DO** for direct object,
      S for subject,   **OP** for object of a preposition.

	Type	Use
Example: A favorite Southern dish is <u>fried</u> chicken.	*Part*	*Adj*

1. Whenever a cat comes into the room, Bill begins to sneeze. _____ _____

2. Diving from a great height can be dangerous. _____ _____

3. Purring loudly, the kitten jumped into my lap. _____ _____

4. I want to visit my friend who lives on St. Simons Island. _____ _____

5. Tired after a long day of work, Jim fell asleep. _____ _____

6. Our first goal is to raise a million dollars. _____ _____

7. She earns extra money by typing students' papers. _____ _____

8. The sky looked threatening. _____ _____

9. To keep up on current events, I watch CNN daily. _____ _____

10. She gave him ten dollars for changing her flat tire. _____ _____

11. My sister seemed refreshed by her bath and nap. _____ _____

12. The most challenging course I ever took was calculus. _____ _____

13. Raising a child is not easy. _____ _____

14. Aunt Maude gave her nephew many educational videos to watch. _____ _____

15. One of the best forms of exercise is swimming. _____ _____

	Type	Use

16. The plum pudding, steaming and fragrant, was served for dessert. _____ _____

17. I expect to inherit a great deal of money someday. _____ _____

18. The barbecued chicken was delicious. _____ _____

19. We tried to find the house where my father was born. _____ _____

20. By comparing prices carefully, Allan found the car he wanted for a reasonable price. _____ _____

21. Patsy occupied herself with reading an Agatha Christie mystery. _____ _____

22. My brother drove all the way from Memphis to celebrate our father's birthday. _____ _____

23. The car, dented on the driver's side, was found two miles outside of town. _____ _____

24. Helen is too young to travel to Europe alone. _____ _____

25. One should usually be suspicious of sweeping generalizations. _____ _____

4

Recognizing Phrases

A **phrase** is a group of related words, generally having neither subject nor predicate and used as though it were a single word. It cannot make a statement and is therefore not a clause.

A knowledge of the phrase and how it is used will suggest to you ways of diversifying and enlivening your sentences. Variety in using sentences will remedy the monotonous "subject first" habit. The use of the participial phrase, for instance, will add life and movement to your style because the participle is an action word, having the strength of its verbal nature in addition to its function as a modifier.

We classify phrases as **gerund, participial, infinitive, absolute, prepositional,** and **appositive.** The following sentences will show how the same idea may be expressed differently by the use of different kinds of phrases:

Sue swam daily. She hoped to improve her backstroke. ["Subject first" sentences.]

By *swimming daily,* Sue hoped to improve her backstroke. [Gerund phrase.]

Swimming daily, Sue hoped to improve her backstroke. [Participial phrase.]

Sue's only hope of improving her backstroke was *to swim daily.* [Infinitive phrase.]

With a daily swim Sue hoped to improve her backstroke. [Prepositional phrase.]

Sue knew of one way to improve her backstroke: *swimming daily.* [Appositive phrase.]

■ 4a The Gerund Phrase

A **gerund phrase** consists of a gerund and any complement or modifiers it may have. The function of the gerund phrase is always that of a noun:

Being late for breakfast is Joe's worst fault. [The gerund phrase is used as the subject of the verb *is*.]

She finally succeeded in *opening the camera*. [The gerund phrase is the object of the preposition *in*.]

Bill hated *driving his golf balls into the lake*. [The gerund phrase is the object of the verb *hated*.]

His hobby, *making furniture*, is enjoyable and useful. [The gerund phrase is an appositive.]

■ 4b The Participial Phrase

A **participial phrase** consists of a participle and any complement or modifiers it may have. It functions as an adjective:

Disappointed by his best friend, Roger refused to speak to him. [The participial phrase modifies the proper noun *Roger*.]

Having written the letter, Julie set out for the post office. [The participial phrase modifies the proper noun *Julie*.]

The boy *standing in the doorway* is the one who asked to borrow our rake. [The participial phrase modifies the noun *boy*.]

Punctuation: *Introductory participial phrases are set off by commas. Other participial phrases are also set off by commas unless they are essential to the meaning of the sentence. (See Chapter 19, Section b.)*

■ 4c The Infinitive Phrase

An **infinitive phrase** consists of an infinitive and any complement or modifiers it may have. Infinitives function as adjectives, adverbs, or nouns:

She had a plane *to catch at eight o'clock*. [The infinitive phrase modifies the noun *plane*.]

To be in Mr. Foster's class was *to learn the meaning of discipline*. [The first infinitive phrase is the subject of the verb *was*. The second infinitive phrase is the predicate nominative after the linking verb *was*.]

Millie left early *to avoid the heavy traffic*. [The infinitive phrase modifies the verb *left*.]

After the night outdoors we were happy *to be warm and dry again*. [The infinitive phrase modifies the adjective *happy*.]

Ted has no plans except *to watch television*. [The infinitive phrase is the object of the preposition *except*.]

We decided *to go for a long walk*. [The infinitive phrase is the direct object of the verb *decided*.]

Her fiancé seems *to be very pleasant*. [The infinitive phrase is the predicate adjective after the linking verb *seems*.]

Punctuation: *Introductory infinitive phrases used as modifiers are set off by commas.* (See Chapter 19, Section b.)

■ 4d The Absolute Phrase

A noun followed by a participle may form a construction grammatically independent of the rest of the sentence. This construction is called an **absolute phrase.** It is never a subject, nor does it modify any word in the sentence, but it is used *absolutely* or independently:

> *The bus having stopped,* the tourists filed out.
>
> *The theater being nearby,* I decided to walk.
>
> I shall do as I please, *all things considered.*

Punctuation: *An absolute phrase is always separated from the rest of the sentence by a comma.* (See Chapter 19, Section b.)

■ 4e The Prepositional Phrase

A **prepositional phrase** consists of a preposition followed by a noun or pronoun used as its object, together with any modifiers the noun or pronoun may have. The prepositional phrase functions usually as an adjective or an adverb:

> The plan *of the house* is very simple. [The prepositional phrase modifies the noun *plan.*]
>
> The river runs *through rich farmland.* [The prepositional phrase modifies the verb *runs.*]
>
> *Throughout the house* there was an aroma of corned beef and cabbage. [The introductory prepositional phrase modifies the verb *was.*]

Punctuation: *An introductory prepositional phrase, unless unusually long, is not set off by a comma.* (See Chapter 19, Section b.)

■ 4f The Appositive Phrase

An **appositive** is a word or phrase that explains, identifies, or renames the word it follows. An appositive may be a noun phrase (that is, a noun and its modifiers), a gerund phrase, an infinitive phrase, or a prepositional phrase:

> This book, *a long novel about politics,* will never be a best-seller. [Noun phrase used as an appositive.]
>
> Jean knew a way out of her difficulty: *telling the truth.* [Gerund phrase used as an appositive.]

His greatest ambition, *to make a million dollars,* was doomed from the start. [Infinitive phrase used as an appositive.]

The rustler's hideout, *in the old cave by the river,* was discovered by the posse. [Prepositional phrase used as an appositive.]

An appositive may be **essential** (sometimes called **fused**) or **nonessential;** it is essential if it positively identifies that which it renames, frequently by use of a proper noun. Examples of both essential and nonessential appositives occur in the sentences below:

The Victorian poets *Tennyson and Browning* were outstanding literary spokesmen of their day. [The appositive, *Tennyson and Browning,* identifies *poets* and thus is essential.]

Tennyson and Browning, *two Victorian poets,* were outstanding literary spokesmen of their day. [The appositive, *two Victorian poets,* is nonessential because the poets are already identified by their names.]

Punctuation: *An appositive phrase is enclosed with commas unless it is essential.* (See Chapter 19, Section b.)

Exercise 19   Phrases

In each of the following sentences identify the *italicized* phrase by writing in the space at the right

       Prep if it is a prepositional phrase,   **Inf** if it is an infinitive phrase,

       Part if it is a participial phrase,   **App** if it is an appositive phrase,

       Ger if it is a gerund phrase,   **Abs** if it is an absolute phrase.

Example: I have never known anyone else *with his stage presence.*   *__Prep__*

1. Will they be here *for lunch*?   _____

2. *Adjusting the draperies* took longer than he had expected.   _____

3. *The lights having come on,* the band began to play again.   _____

4. Do you think that they have registered *to vote in this election*?   _____

5. Several students say they are interested in *studying the Japanese language.*   _____

6. When the baseball sailed *through the window,* it nearly hit Art.   _____

7. Reynolds Price, *a Rhodes scholar,* published his first novel in 1962.   _____

8. Midshipmen at the U.S. Naval Academy are encouraged *to read newspapers and news magazines.*   _____

9. Information technology will lead to the creation *of new business.*   _____

10. John Atlitude, *a local attorney,* has donated his time and expertise to our business club this year.   _____

11. *During our stay* in New York we plan to visit the Whitney Museum of American Art.   _____

12. *Business having been slow,* the computer store offered generous discounts on personal computers.   _____

13. *Moving quietly and carefully,* the cat surprised the mouse.   _____

14. *Taking tests* has always been a challenge to him.   _____

15. Jonathan, *known for his computer expertise,* will assume the responsibility for the computer lab.   _____

16. *Giving children responsibility* helps them develop a good self-image.   _____

17. *To eat heartily* will please the cook.   ———

18. After he had mowed the yard, he took a long shower *followed by a nap.*   ———

19. Jana received her doctorate *from Rutgers University.*   ———

20. *Living in America* offers many opportunities.   ———

Exercise 20 Phrases

The sentences in the following exercise contain prepositional, verbal, and appositive phrases. Underline each phrase, and in the first space at the right, identify its type; in the second space show how each phrase is used by writing **Adj** for adjective, **Adv** for adverb, or **N** for noun.

Example: The handball courts <u>at the gym</u> are being
              repaired.   *Prep*   *Adj*

1. Reading Shakespeare's love sonnets is a romantic
   experience.   _____   _____

2. Olivia, my niece, has read all of Stephen King's
   books.   _____   _____

3. I seldom want to sleep late.   _____   _____

4. Austin thinks that he saw his aunt shopping at
   the mall.   _____   _____

5. The team will meet the coach at the auditorium.   _____   _____

6. Among the staff we can raise five hundred
   dollars.   _____   _____

7. The game proved challenging to all the players.   _____   _____
8. Both were ready to leave the mall.   _____   _____
9. Did you remember to feed the dog?   _____   _____

10. We will leave the jeep here and walk the rest
    of the way.   _____   _____

11. To find real happiness is everyone's dream.   _____   _____

12. Even when she was a child, she liked helping
    others.   _____   _____

13. Having wrapped the presents, Amy went to bed.   _____   _____

14. Henri Nouwen, author and educator, wrote
    Genesee Diary.   _____   _____

15. Ed looked everywhere for a newspaper to read.   _____   _____

16. Eugene O'Neill, a twentieth-century dramatist,
    used his plays to explain his life.   _____   _____

17. Limiting dietary fat is an important lifestyle
    modification.   _____   _____

18. Erich Maria Remarque's *All Quiet on the Western
    Front* changed the world's perception of war.   _____   _____

19. Cheri was present at the game, cheering Cameron
    every minute.   _____   _____

20. For summer vacation he suggested her reading
    Josephine Humphrey's *Dreams of Sleep*.   _____   _____

21. Having worked all day and attended evening
    school three nights a week, Edie had very little
    energy left.   _____   _____

22. Dr. Ellis's research was funded by the institute's
    research foundation.   _____   _____

23. Women athletes enjoy playing field hockey as
    much as men athletes do.   _____   _____

24. The salesman, an unusually patient individual,
    finally sold his customer a new coat.   _____   _____

25. We missed seeing Nadine last week.   _____   _____

Exercise 21 Phrases

In each of the following sentences underline the phrase(s). In the first column at the right identify the *type* of phrase by writing

Prep for prepositional phrase,   **Inf** for infinitive phrase,
Part for participial phrase,   **App** for appositive phrase.
Ger for gerund phrase,

Then in the second column indicate its *use* by writing **Adj, Adv,** or **N.**

	Type	Use
Example: Exploring our national parks has provided my family many fond memories.	*Ger*	*N*

1. Archaeologists spend their lives seeking answers to the world's mysteries. _____ _____

2. We had already assembled the tools to use the next day. _____ _____

3. Many companies interviewing seniors say they will be hiring more graduates this year than last year. _____ _____

4. The stadium was quiet after the game. _____ _____

5. Having spent a year abroad, he reluctantly returned home. _____ _____

6. Planting trees will reduce her heating and cooling bills. _____ _____

7. The committee selected the film to be shown spring quarter. _____ _____

8. The business manager, an extremely abrupt person, almost always says no. _____ _____

9. Losing weight gradually gives the body time to adjust. _____ _____

10. Robert Russ, a professor of applied mathematics, teaches in the Fuqua School of Business. _____ _____

11. Why does she want to spend her summer here? _____ _____

	Type	Use

12. In last night's play every aspect of the lead character was exaggerated.   ———   ———

13. Yesterday he locked his keys in the car again.   ———   ———

14. Anne Rivers Siddons, an Atlanta author, will sign her latest novel at the Oxford Bookstore.   ———   ———

15. During his investigation the attorney uncovered important evidence critical to his case.   ———   ———

16. To swim alone is never wise.   ———   ———

17. Solving problems quickens one's wit.   ———   ———

18. Some biologists believe that amphibians are more sensitive to environmental changes than other animals.   ———   ———

19. Her truck, an old and rusted jalopy, was the only transportation she had.   ———   ———

20. Herman Melville completed a work called "The Isle of the Cross," a manuscript that was only recently found.   ———   ———

Exercise 22   Phrases

A. Combine the following pairs of sentences, making one sentence a participial phrase. Punctuate each sentence correctly.

Example: Karen has decided to take an improvisation class this summer. She wants to improve her storytelling skills.

Wanting to improve her storytelling skills, Karen has decided to take an improvisation class this summer.

1. Grandmother had stirred her tea thoughtfully. She began telling a story.

2. Yellowstone National Park was established in 1872. It represented the first major effort of the government to legislate recreational use of land.

3. Dave hit a home run with the bases loaded. He won the game for the University.

4. Venus was noted for her beauty. She was married to Vulcan, the god of fire and the ugliest of the Greek gods.

5. *The Seven Storey Mountain* was written by Thomas Merton. The book describes his journey from his student days to the time of his decision to become a Trappist monk.

6. In 1964 Robert C. Weaver was appointed Secretary of Housing and Urban Development. He was the first black member of a presidential cabinet.

7. President Hoff arrived only minutes before the graduation procession began. He had little time to collect his thoughts for his address.

8. The Georgia Institute of Technology is located in Atlanta, Georgia. It is a part of the state's university system.

9. Christina had worked with the same company for twenty-five years. She requested that she be allowed to retire early.

—

10. Our oldest dog, Spot, bit the postman. Spot had to spend ten days at the veterinarian's.

B. Combine the following pairs of sentences, making one of the sentences an *appositive* phrase.

Example: We visited her home during the holidays. She lives in a resort town near Banff National Park.

During the holidays we visited her home town, a resort near Banff National Park.

1. Betsy and Gail spent the weekend with me in the mountains. They were my college roommates.

2. The children had an Alaskan malamute. They would not go anywhere without it.

3. Dr. Williams is a professor of meteorology. He believes that some forecasts of global warming are fraught with misconceptions.

4. My uncle graduated from Weber State College. He is now a professor of physics at his alma mater.

5. Denise is one of the actors in the community theater. She is a volunteer.

6. Professor Worts is our soccer coach. She also teaches English literature.

7. He had one goal in life. He wanted to make a million dollars by the time he was thirty.

8. When Sally was angry, everyone knew what she would do. She would go to her tree house.

9. Our assignment was to read "The Raven." It is a poem of contrasting images.

10. Voltaire was a nineteenth-century philosopher and writer. He was not a democrat.

Exercise 23   Punctuation of Phrases

In the following sentences insert all commas required by the rules stated in Chapter 4. In the blanks write the commas with the words that precede them. When the sentence requires no comma, write **C** in the space.

Example: Taking the advice of his physician Andy quit smoking.

Taking the advice of his physician, Andy quit smoking.   *physician,*

1. To tell the truth I think that I have already read *Women Who Run with the Wolves.* _____

2. Everyone having left we took off our shoes, relaxed, and had coffee. _____

3. Her brother an international computer consultant has invited her to visit him while he is in Rome. _____

4. To get the best possible results he carefully measured the ingredients before combining them. _____

5. I cannot believe that we are finally going to Alaska all things considered. _____

6. Encouraged by her success she tried even harder than before. _____

7. His hobby collecting first-edition books was expensive. _____

8. The travel agent a friend of the family planned an interesting itinerary for us. _____

9. Darwin's greatest work *Origin of Species* was completed in 1859. _____

10. The old man leaning on the mantel is Pam's great-uncle. _____

11. To reach the airport on time the French ambassador had to secure a police escort. _____

12. Senator Smith an incumbent will be difficult to defeat. _____

13. After meeting for three hours the board adjourned without resolving the problem. _____

14. The American poets Robert Frost and Maya Angelou have very different writing styles. _____

15. Machiavelli a fifteenth-century political theorist advocated expediency and duplicity in all dealings. _____

16. To support their communities many people give their time to volunteer activities. _____

17. Mt. Everest the highest peak in the world is located in the Himalayan Mountains. _____

18. The child learning to walk held a blanket for security. _____

19. The grandmother sat on the porch rocking her new grandson. _____

20. *Vogue* a fashion magazine for women is more than one hundred years old. _____

Independent Clauses

■ 5a Independent Clauses

A group of words containing a subject and a verb and expressing a complete thought is called a sentence or an **independent clause.** Some groups of words that contain a subject and a verb, however, do not express a complete thought and therefore cannot stand alone as a sentence. Such word groups are dependent on other sentence elements and are called **dependent clauses.**

Sometimes an independent clause stands alone as a sentence. Sometimes two or more independent clauses are combined into one sentence without a connecting word. Then a semicolon is used to connect the independent clauses:

> The day is cold.
>
> The day is cold; the wind is howling.

Sometimes independent clauses are connected by one of the coordinating conjunctions, *and, but, for, or, nor, so,* and *yet.* Independent clauses joined by a coordinating conjunction are separated by commas. Therefore, to punctuate correctly, you must distinguish between independent clauses and other kinds of sentence elements joined by coordinating conjunctions. In the following examples note that only independent clauses joined by coordinating conjunctions are separated by commas:

> The day was *dark* and *dreary.* [The conjunction *and* joins two adjectives, *dark* and *dreary.* No comma permitted.]
>
> The fallen tree *blocked* the highway and *delayed* travel. [The conjunction *and* joins the two verbs. No comma permitted.]
>
> She ran *up the steps* and *into the house.* [The conjunction *and* joins two phrases. No comma permitted.]

Mrs. Brown caught the fish, and *her husband cooked them.* [The conjunction *and* connects two independent clauses, and these are separated by a comma.]

Sometimes two independent clauses are connected by a **conjunctive,** or **transitional, adverb** such as one of the following:

however	moreover	nevertheless	therefore
then	accordingly	otherwise	thus
hence	besides	consequently	

A semicolon is necessary before any of these words beginning a second clause. After the longer conjunctive adverbs a comma is generally used:

We drove all day; *then* at sundown we began to look for a place to camp.

It rained during the afternoon; *consequently,* our trip to the mountains had to be postponed.

Note: Conjunctive adverbs can be distinguished from subordinating conjunctions by the fact that the *adverbs* can be shifted to a later position in the sentence, whereas the *conjunctions* cannot:

It rained during the afternoon; our trip to the mountains, *consequently,* had to be postponed.

Summary of punctuation: From the foregoing discussion and examples we can establish the following rules for the punctuation of independent clauses:

1. *Two independent clauses connected by a coordinating conjunction are separated by a comma:*

   Our goat chewed up the morning paper, *and* Father is angry.

   You should call Hank tonight, *for* he is all alone.

2. *Two independent clauses not connected by a coordinating conjunction are separated by a semicolon.* Remember that this rule also holds true when the second clause begins with a conjunctive adverb:

   Philip is quite strong; he is much stronger than I.

   We both wanted to go to the toboggan race; *however,* Mother had asked us to be home by six.

3. *A semicolon is used to separate independent clauses that are joined by a coordinating conjunction but are heavily punctuated with commas internally:*

   Being somewhat excited and, incidentally, terribly tired, Ellen's two children, Mary and Fred, became unruly; but they went quickly to sleep on the trip home.

4. *Short independent clauses, when used in a series with a coordinating conjunction preceding the final clause, may be separated by commas:*

   The audience was seated, the lights were dimmed, and the curtain was raised.

Note: A series consists of at least three elements.

■ 5b The Comma Splice

Use of a comma between two independent clauses not joined by a coordinating conjunction (Rule 2) is a major error called the **comma splice** (this term comes from the idea of splicing or "patching" together two clauses that should be more strongly separated):

COMMA SPLICE: I enjoyed his company, I do not know that he enjoyed mine.

CORRECTION: I enjoyed his company, but I do not know that he enjoyed mine. (Rule 1)

I enjoyed his company; I do not know that he enjoyed mine. (Rule 2)

OR

I enjoyed his company; however, I do not know that he enjoyed mine. (Rule 2)

■ 5c The Run-together Sentence

The **run-together sentence** results from omitting punctuation between two independent clauses not joined by a conjunction. Basically the error is the same as that of the comma splice; it shows ignorance of sentence structure:

Twilight had fallen it was dark under the old oak tree near the house.

When you read the sentence just given, you have difficulty in getting the meaning at first because the ideas are run together. Now consider the following sentence:

Twilight had fallen, it was dark under the old oak tree near the house.

The insertion of the comma is not a satisfactory remedy, for the sentence now contains a comma splice. There are, however, four reliable devices for correcting the run-together sentence and the comma splice:

1. Connect two independent clauses by a comma and a coordinating conjunction if the two clauses are logically of equal importance:

   Twilight had fallen, and it was dark under the old oak tree near the house.

2. Connect two independent clauses by a semicolon if they are close enough in thought to make one sentence and you want to omit the conjunction:

   Twilight had fallen; it was dark under the old oak tree near the house.

3. Write the two independent clauses as separate sentences if you wish to give them separate emphasis:

   Twilight had fallen. It was dark under the old oak tree near the house.

4. Subordinate one of the independent clauses:

   When twilight had fallen, it was dark under the old oak tree near the house.

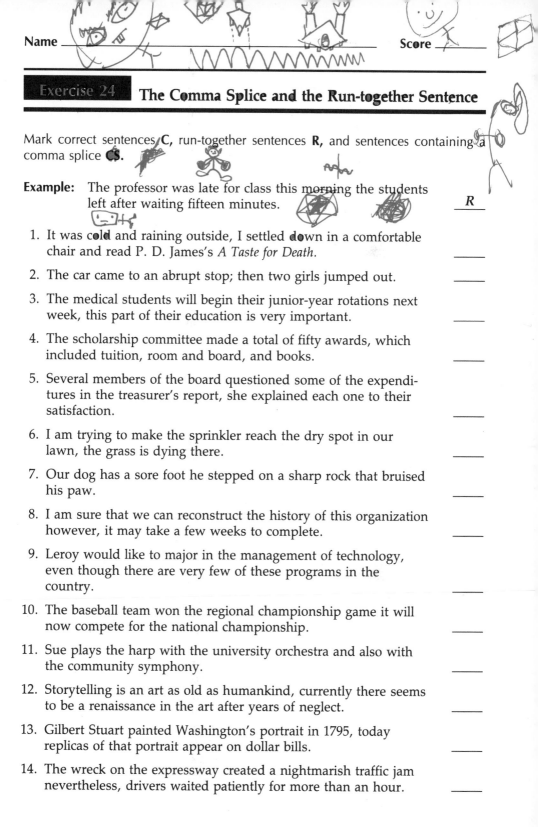

Name _____   Score _____

Exercise 24 The Comma Splice and the Run-together Sentence

Mark correct sentences **C**, run-together sentences **R**, and sentences containing a comma splice **CS**.

Example: The professor was late for class this morning the students left after waiting fifteen minutes.   _R_

1. It was cold and raining outside, I settled down in a comfortable chair and read P. D. James's *A Taste for Death*.   _____

2. The car came to an abrupt stop; then two girls jumped out.   _____

3. The medical students will begin their junior-year rotations next week, this part of their education is very important.   _____

4. The scholarship committee made a total of fifty awards, which included tuition, room and board, and books.   _____

5. Several members of the board questioned some of the expenditures in the treasurer's report, she explained each one to their satisfaction.   _____

6. I am trying to make the sprinkler reach the dry spot in our lawn, the grass is dying there.   _____

7. Our dog has a sore foot he stepped on a sharp rock that bruised his paw.   _____

8. I am sure that we can reconstruct the history of this organization however, it may take a few weeks to complete.   _____

9. Leroy would like to major in the management of technology, even though there are very few of these programs in the country.   _____

10. The baseball team won the regional championship game it will now compete for the national championship.   _____

11. Sue plays the harp with the university orchestra and also with the community symphony.   _____

12. Storytelling is an art as old as humankind, currently there seems to be a renaissance in the art after years of neglect.   _____

13. Gilbert Stuart painted Washington's portrait in 1795, today replicas of that portrait appear on dollar bills.   _____

14. The wreck on the expressway created a nightmarish traffic jam nevertheless, drivers waited patiently for more than an hour.   _____

15. Her new sports car is really handsome, but I would not want her sixty installment payments. _____

16. We have experienced a gradual increase in our sales during the previous twelve months, therefore, we are considering expanding our marketing. _____

17. Although as a boy Derek enjoyed reading Twain's *Huckleberry Finn,* he recently reread the book and found that he enjoyed the second reading even more. _____

18. The kitten played with a ball of yarn for nearly an hour, then it became bored and went to sleep. _____

19. Is there a possibility that former President Carter will be our graduation speaker? _____

20. College graduates in increasing numbers are returning home after graduation they seem to delay leaving the nest. _____

Exercise 25 — The Comma Splice and the Run-together Sentence

Mark correct sentences **C,** run-together sentences **R,** and sentences containing a comma splice **CS.**

Example: The bride-to-be chose a designer dress for her wedding,
she also wanted a special hairdresser to do her hair.   *CS*

1. Living plant cells produce amino acids these are the chief
components of proteins.   _____

2. Because transport trucks frequently fail to observe the speed
limit, they are dangerous to others on the highway.   _____

3. Sabrina and her husband recently bought a hammock for their
yard, however, because both of them work, they have very little
time to enjoy it.   _____

4. After last night's freeze, the sidewalks were icy Tyler slipped
and fell while walking to the bus stop.   _____

5. The East Germans built the Berlin Wall in 1961, it was torn
down in 1989.   _____

6. For over fifty years Lassie was the all-time favorite movie and
television animal at one time Lassie was probably more popular
than Mickey Mouse.   _____

7. They had only recently completed landscaping the back yard
when the heavy rains came and destroyed the retaining wall,
washing away a flower garden.   _____

8. The University of Oregon has acquired the papers of one of its
most famous alumni, the papers will be housed in the main
library in a special collection.   _____

9. The ability to discern the character and motives of an individual
is extremely important it is particularly important to a personnel
manager.   _____

10. Vegetarian meals have few calories, they are also economical.   _____

11. Economists and producers agree that the red-meat market in this
country has changed drastically in the last decade, Americans
are eating more chicken and fish and less beef than in the past. _____

12. Robby finally gave me her mother's recipe for clam chowder she
had promised to give it to me several weeks ago.   _____

13. During our vacation we visited an old gold mine and panned for gold, however, we did not find any.   _____

14. While I waited in the dentist's office, I thumbed through several magazines.   _____

15. Travis left the party early his car was making strange sounds that he could not identify.   _____

16. The team had traveled to New Mexico to compete in the playoffs because of one error the game was lost.   _____

17. Over the weekend Nathan read the mystery novel *The Cat Who Knew a Cardinal*, although the ending did not surprise him, the death of the cardinal did.   _____

18. Each morning before it gets hot, Jim takes a walk in the park, but if it is raining, he walks at the mall.   _____

19. Erica is always complaining that she is bored, if she would read more, she would not be bored.   _____

20. This summer Kendra has a job with an advertising firm since she is interested in the advertising program of the university, this opportunity is important to her.   _____

21. Kelly is one of five children and therefore is very independent.   _____

22. One way to deal with unwanted calls is not to answer the telephone an answering machine is another way.   _____

23. I ran after that crazy dog for two blocks, then I just let him go.   _____

24. My speech will be on a subject with which I am familiar, as I did not have time to research a new subject.   _____

25. The minister preached longer than usual however, the congregation remained attentive.   _____

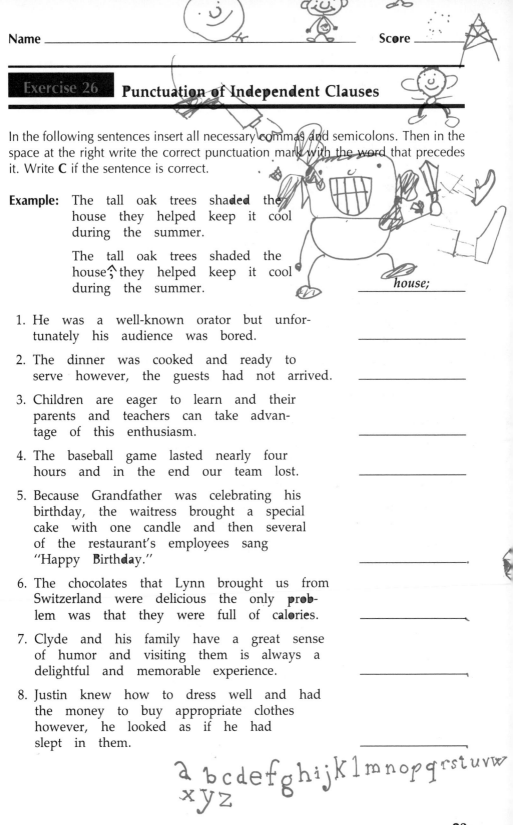

Name _____   Score _____

In the following sentences insert all necessary commas and semicolons. Then in the space at the right write the correct punctuation mark with the word that precedes it. Write **C** if the sentence is correct.

Example: The tall oak trees shaded the house they helped keep it cool during the summer.

The tall oak trees shaded the house they helped keep it cool during the summer.   *house;* _____

1. He was a well-known orator but unfortunately his audience was bored.   _____

2. The dinner was cooked and ready to serve however, the guests had not arrived.   _____

3. Children are eager to learn and their parents and teachers can take advantage of this enthusiasm.   _____

4. The baseball game lasted nearly four hours and in the end our team lost.   _____

5. Because Grandfather was celebrating his birthday, the waitress brought a special cake with one candle and then several of the restaurant's employees sang "Happy Birthday."   _____

6. The chocolates that Lynn brought us from Switzerland were delicious the only problem was that they were full of calories.   _____

7. Clyde and his family have a great sense of humor and visiting them is always a delightful and memorable experience.   _____

8. Justin knew how to dress well and had the money to buy appropriate clothes however, he looked as if he had slept in them.   _____

9. They bought an old farmhouse to restore but they had no idea of the time or the money that the restoration would require.   _____

10. Even though she was getting old, Aunt Lucy planned her life as though she would live forever her family and friends said that attitude was what kept her young.   _____

11. Her hobbies have become a full-time job thus, if she is unable to hire an assistant, she will be forced to give up her job at the bank.   _____

12. Sue Grafton, a mystery writer, will autograph her latest book Saturday at the bookstore and I hope I can be there.   _____

13. An *oxymoron* is two contradictory words or concepts that are combined the term *jumbo shrimp* is an example.   _____

14. Our political science class was assigned Arthur Schlesinger's *The Disunity of America* for outside reading the discussions based on the book were enlightening.   _____

15. The Romans played a game known as *paganica,* which was the forerunner of golf the player used a bent stick and a leather ball stuffed with feathers.   _____

16. Although the *Titanic* sank on April 15, 1912, interest in the tragedy is still strong and rumors continue to swirl around the questions of how and why the ship sank.   _____

17. *Spartina* is the story of a man's struggle to survive changes in a fishing village the title of the book comes from the name of the protagonist's fishing boat and of the marsh grass native to the area.   _____

18. As a self-denying man, Gandhi became India's ideal, accessible to the poor and privileged alike later he became a symbol of selflessness to the world. _____

19. Some students require more study time than others knowing which type of student one is may mean the difference between success and failure in college. _____

20. *The Old Curiosity Shop* by Charles Dickens is one of my favorite novels but my cousin complains that it is too long and descriptive. _____

Dependent Clauses

As you remember, a dependent clause is one that cannot stand alone as a sentence: although it has both a subject and a verb, it does not express a complete thought. Any clause beginning with a subordinating word like *what, that, who, which, when, since, before, after,* or *if* is a **dependent clause.** Dependent clauses, like phrases, function as grammatical units in a sentence — that is, as nouns, adjectives, and adverbs:

I went to school.

Too much time had elapsed.

[Both clauses are independent.]

When I went to school, I studied my lessons. [The first clause is dependent.]

Since too much time had elapsed, she remained at home. [The first clause is dependent.]

In the last two sentences *I studied my lessons* and *she remained at home* are complete statements. But the clauses *When I went to school* and *Since too much time had elapsed* do not express complete thoughts. They depend upon the independent statements to complete their meanings. Both of these dependent clauses function as adverbs.

■ 6a Noun Clauses

A **noun clause** is a dependent clause used as a noun, that is, as a subject, complement, object of a preposition, or appositive. Noun clauses are usually introduced by *that, what, why, whether, who, which,* or *how.* Some of these introductory words can introduce both noun and adjective clauses, since the function of the whole clause in the sentence, and not its introductory word, determines its classification. Most sentences containing noun clauses differ from those containing adjective and adverbial clauses in that, with the clause removed, they are no longer complete sentences.

> Your *plan* is interesting. [This is a simple sentence, containing no dependent clause. The subject is the noun *plan*. The following example sentences show that dependent noun clauses may be substituted for the word *plan*, and vice versa.]
>
> *What you intend to do* [your plan] is interesting. [The italicized noun clause is the subject of the verb *is*. Notice that the noun *plan* can be substituted for the clause.]
>
> Tell me *what you intend to do* [your plan]. [The italicized noun clause is the direct object of the verb *tell*.]
>
> That is *what you intend to do* [your plan]. [The italicized noun clause is a predicate nominative.]
>
> I am interested in *what you intend to do* [your plan]. [The italicized noun clause is the object of the preposition *in*.]
>
> The fact *that he had not told the truth* soon became apparent. [The italicized noun clause is in apposition with the noun *fact*.]
>
> Bob's problem, *how he could open the locked door*, seemed insoluble. [The italicized noun clause is in apposition with the noun *problem*.]

Punctuation: *Noun clauses used as nonessential appositives are set off by commas.*

■ 6b Adjective Clauses

An **adjective clause** is a dependent clause that modifies a noun or pronoun. The common connective words used to introduce adjective clauses are the relative pronouns *who* (and its inflected forms *whom* and *whose*), *which*, *that*, and relative adverbs like *where*, *when*, and *why*. (*Where* and *when* can introduce all three kinds of clauses.)

The italicized clauses in the following sentences are all adjective clauses:

> She is a woman *who is respected by everyone.*
>
> Mr. Johnson, *whose son attends the University of Oklahoma*, is our minister.
>
> He saw the place *where he was born.*
>
> It was a time *when money did not count.*
>
> I know the reason *why I failed the course.*

Adjective clauses are classified as **essential** (restrictive) and **nonessential** (nonrestrictive).

An *essential* clause, as its name indicates, is necessary in a sentence, for it identifies or points out a particular person or thing; a *nonessential* clause adds information about the word it modifies, but it is not essential in pointing out or identifying a person or thing:

Thomas Jefferson, *who was born on the frontier*, became President of the United States. [The name *Thomas Jefferson* has identified the person, and the italicized clause is not essential.]

A person *who loves to read* will never be lonely. [The italicized adjective clause is essential in identifying a particular kind of person.]

My father, *who was a country boy*, has lived in the city for years. [Since a person has only one father, an identifying clause is not essential.]

The girl *by whom I sat in class* is an honor student. [The italicized adjective clause is essential to the identification of *girl*.]

To determine whether an adjective clause is essential, you may apply this test: read the sentence leaving out the adjective clause and see whether the removal omits necessary identification. Try this test on the following sentence:

Jet pilots, *who work under a great deal of stress*, must stay in excellent physical condition.

You will see that the removal of the adjective clause does not change the basic meaning of the sentence. The italicized adjective clause is, therefore, nonessential.

Now read the following sentence, leaving out the italicized adjective clause:

Jet pilots *who are not in excellent physical condition* should not be allowed to fly.

If the adjective clause of this sentence is removed, the statement is not at all what the writer meant to say. The adjective clause is, therefore, essential.

Punctuation: *Nonessential adjective clauses are set off from the rest of the sentence by commas.* (See Chapter 19, Section b.)

■ 6c Adverbial Clauses

An **adverbial clause** is a dependent clause that functions exactly as if it were an adverb. Like an adverb it modifies a verb, an adjective, an adverb, or the whole idea expressed in the sentence's independent clause; for example, *As luck would have it*, we missed his telephone call.

An adverbial clause is used to show *time, place, cause, purpose, result, condition, concession, manner,* or *comparison*. Its first word is a subordinating conjunction. Common subordinating conjunctions and their uses are listed below:

1. Time (*when, before, since, as, while, until, after, whenever*)

   I will stay *until you come.*

   When the whistle blew, the laborer stopped.

2. Place (*where, wherever, whence, whither*)

   He went *where no one had ever set foot before.*

   Wherever you go, I will go also.

3. Cause (*because, since, as*)

   Since I had no classes on Saturday, I went home.

   Because he was afraid of being late, Bob ran all the way.

4. Purpose (*in order that, so that, that*)

   My family made many sacrifices *so that I could have an education.*

   Men and women work *that they may eat.*

5. Result (*so . . . that, such . . . that*)

   The weather was *so* cold *that I decided not to walk to school.*

6. Condition (*if, unless*)

   You will hurt your hand *if you are not careful.*

   Unless you apply at once, your name will not be considered.

7. Concession (*though, although*)

   Although she had no money, she was determined to go to college.

8. Manner (*as, as if, as though*)

   She looked *as though she wanted to laugh.*

   Do *as you like,* but take the consequences.

9. Comparison (*as, than*)

   He is older *than his brother.*

   He is as tall *as his brother.*

Note: The last two sentences contain examples of ellipsis, which is a grammatically incomplete expression whose meaning is nevertheless clear. It is frequently a dependent clause from which subject and/or verb is omitted. Thus, the sentence *He is older than his brother* omits *is* following *brother,* but the meaning of the clause is understood.

Punctuation: *Introductory adverbial clauses are always set off by commas:*

   Although he had tests to take and a term paper to write, he went home for the weekend.

   While I was eating lunch, I had a phone call from my brother.

■ 6d Kinds of Sentences

For the purpose of varying style and avoiding monotony, you may need to be able to distinguish the four basic types of sentences. According to the number and kind of clauses (phrases do not affect sentence type), sentences may be grouped into four types: **simple, compound, complex,** and **compound-complex.**

1. A **simple** sentence is a single independent clause with one subject and one predicate. The one subject, however, may consist of more than one noun or pronoun, and the one predicate may consist of more than one verb.

Robert has a new car. [Single subject and single predicate.]

Robert and his *brother* have a new car. [There is one verb, *have*, but the subject consists of two nouns.]

Robert *washed* and *polished* his new car on Sunday. [There is one subject, *Robert*, but two verbs.]

Robert and his *brother washed* and *polished* their new car. [The subject consists of two nouns, *Robert* and *brother*; and the predicate consists of two verbs, *washed* and *polished*.]

2. A **compound** sentence contains at least two independent clauses and no dependent clause:

Mary likes the mountains, but Jackie prefers the seashore.

A lamp was lighted in the house, the happy family was talking together, and supper was waiting.

3. A **complex** sentence contains only one independent clause and one or more dependent clauses (the dependent clauses are in italics):

The toy truck *that you gave Molly for her birthday* is broken.

Why he refused to contribute to the fund we do not know.

4. A **compound-complex** sentence has at least two independent clauses and one or more dependent clauses (the independent clauses are in italics):

My friend was offended by my attitude, and *I was sorry* that she was hurt.

We spent the morning looking for the home of the woman who paints landscapes, but *we were unable to find it.*

Exercise 27 Clauses

In the following sentences underline each dependent clause. In the space at the right, write **Adj** if the clause is an adjective clause, **Adv** if it is an adverbial clause, and **N** if it is a noun clause. If the sentence contains no dependent clause, leave the space blank.

Example: He was sitting <u>where he could see each guest arrive.</u>   *Adv*

1. Although many factors contributed to the market crash of 1929, a main cause was the lack of procedures to control and regulate the sale of securities.   _____

2. Anne told us that she is of Scottish ancestry.   _____

3. He is a reporter who spends most of his time in London.   _____

4. Jason will not be going with us because he is spending the weekend with his grandfather.   _____

5. His belief that all people are created equal caused Gandhi to reject the caste system in his country.   _____

6. For those who want to see spring wild flowers there will be a guided hike after lunch.   _____

7. Storytellers, if they are good, have generally been held in high esteem.   _____

8. That Melissa became an English professor surprised no one.   _____

9. Professor Davis took a position at the University of Montana, where he taught for three years.   _____

10. Realizing that they had seen very little of America, the couple planned a year-long tour.   _____

11. The investigator will call campus security before he comes.   _____

12. Do you know who has been invited to the dinner?   _____

13. One of the most vivid memories that I have from my childhood is my first day in school.   _____

14. The tour, which includes five countries, is very expensive.   _____

15. A reception for the organist will be held after the concert is over.   _____

16. Did you understand the speaker? _____

17. The rodeo, which was one of the major events at the carnival, was well attended. _____

18. Treasured possessions can be ruined if a leaky roof is not repaired. _____

19. I read the morning paper while I waited for the post office to open. _____

20. Because it has rained very little this spring, the crops have been hurt. _____

21. Who lives in the house that has the green shutters and the red door? _____

22. Procedures that become effective next year will determine the company's vacation policy. _____

23. The decision that we should all ride in one van was an economical one. _____

24. The van waited until noon before it left. _____

25. Deciduous trees, which block the hot summer sun and cold winter winds, should be planted on the south and west sides of a house. _____

26. As far as the box office knows, the concert will begin at the scheduled time. _____

27. What he requested was reasonable. _____

28. That Eugenia Price has so many devoted readers does not surprise me. _____

29. My grandfather, who lived in El Paso, Texas, was a trail boss and horse trader in his youth. _____

30. It is I who am at a disadvantage in this debate, not Russ. _____

Exercise 28   Clauses

Give the function of each of the *italicized* clauses by writing one of the following abbreviations in the space at the right:

S for subject,   **OP** for object of a preposition,
DO for direct object,   **Adj** for adjective modifier,
PN for predicate nominative,   **Adv** for adverbial modifier.

Example: *After we eat lunch,* we need to study.   *Adv*

1. Dr. White, *who is acknowledged as the best lecturer on campus* and *who has written numerous books,* is leaving the university.   _____

2. In the not-so-distant future/the university will have a new fine arts center, *which a wealthy alumna has offered to finance.*   _____

3. She wishes *that she could remember all of her grandmother's recipes.*   _____

4. *When Cara was a child,* she sat with her grandparents and listened to stories of their childhood.   _____

5. Many students *who are attending college* pay for a major portion of their tuition and other expenses.   _____

6. *Why he had arrived late* was the question.   _____

7. Jane Yolen, *who is winner of the 1992 Regina Medal,* has written 120 books for children.   _____

8. Bangladesh, *which ranks ninth in population among the countries of the world,* covers an area no larger than Wisconsin.   _____

9. *That we will miss the first act* does not concern him.   _____

10. Do you remember *where you put the car keys?*   _____

11. Carlos said *that he did not agree with the critic's interpretation.*   _____

12. The reason that Marge ran so well was *that she had trained longer than the other runners had.*   _____

13. The political science faculty realized *that remaining up-to-date is difficult in a rapidly changing world.*   _____

14. Their grandmother read Greek myths to them *before they started school.*   _____

15. At last month's meeting in Kansas City, the committee reviewed the objectives *that had been reached* and those *that had not.*   _____

16. *What Professor Banks expects of his students* is sometimes unreasonable.   _____

17. Everyone was waiting for *what the board would decide about moving the company.*   _____

18. We decided to eat *while the others shopped.*   _____

19. During the spring break we visited the Folger Shakespeare Library, *which is in Washington, D.C.*   _____

20. From *what was said at today's meeting,* we believe that the conference will be held in Portland.   _____

21. *After the poet's papers have been catalogued,* they will be made available to faculty and students.   _____

22. Jeff gave directions to the church to *whoever needed them.*   _____

23. *That the bank closed at noon on Wednesday* surprised me.   _____

24. The winner of "Jeopardy" will be *whoever has won the most money at the end of the game.*   _____

25. *How one responds to the reporter's questions* depends on careful listening.   _____

Name _____   Score _____

Exercise 29 Review of Clauses

In the following sentences enclose the dependent clauses in parentheses. In the spaces at the right indicate the number of independent and dependent clauses in each sentence. Be sure that you understand the function of each of the dependent clauses. (Note that some sentences may not contain a dependent clause.)

	Ind.	Dep.
Example: Her basket was filled with the vegetables (that she was carrying to a friend.)	1	1

1. Three children, who lived next door, were playing basketball.

2. The pumpkin bread that her friend had baked was delicious.

3. June is a month when many couples marry.

4. While the other girls played bridge, Jan studied chemistry.

5. Roger, until you try, you will never know what you can do.

6. Although it was not the rush hour, traffic was heavy, driving was difficult, and we were late for the meeting.

7. Ginny, do you think that good things happen to people who deserve them or that good things just happen whether they are deserved or not?

8. Many career-oriented people, when they are young, begin planning for retirement, but many others make few plans for retirement until they are middle-aged.

9. Math was a difficult course for Walter, but he excelled in English.

10. Gardening is therapeutic for those who enjoy working in the yard and who have time for a hobby.

	Ind.	Dep.

11. While Doug read, the baby was happily playing with a string of spools; however, it was not long before the child became bored.   ____   ____

12. Having a job that one enjoys is a great asset.   ____   ____

13. As he and his father walked down the dusty road, they discussed the crops and the future of their farm.   ____   ____

14. For the first time in four months, she balanced her checkbook, a task that was difficult because she had not recorded each check written.   ____   ____

15. The boy shared his duplicate baseball cards with his cousin, who had only recently started a collection.   ____   ____

16. Until I tried to collect a set of baseball cards, I had no idea that collecting them was big business; for many collectors baseball cards are a financial investment.   ____   ____

17. The fans were cheering for their team to win, and during the last ten seconds, the player who was the poorest shooter on the court sank a three-point basket.   ____   ____

18. A friend of ours, who is somewhat unconventional, suggested that we crash a political fund-raising event that was a black-tie affair.   ____   ____

19. During World War I, air power played a limited role, but its potential was recognized by General Billy Mitchell, who developed a reputation for aggressively promoting the idea of air power.   ____   ____

20. The Nineteenth Amendment to the Constitution, which gave women the right to vote, was not ratified until 1920.   ____   ____

21. Dr. Woodruff, who is internationally known as an advocate for liberal arts education, will be a visiting professor on our campus this year.   ____   ____

Ind.   Dep.

22. That her father was a philanthropist was well known; however, no one knew how much money he had given to the community.   ____   ____

23. E. M. Forster wrote *Howards End,* which is a novel that portrays a person's emotional attachment to the place where she was born and on which her identity depends.   ____   ____

24. Irene has decided that she will stop by an exclusive boutique and buy herself something new because today is her birthday.   ____   ____

25. When she was a little girl, she sold lemonade so that she could make money to go to the Saturday-afternoon movie.   ____   ____

Exercise 30   Clauses

Complete each of the sentences below by writing in the spaces an *adjective clause,* an *adverbial clause,* or a *noun clause* as indicated above each space.

(adverbial clause)

Example: *When I was young,* I went to Camp Illahee in North Carolina.

(adjective clause)

1. Plants _____ are generally very
   healthy.

(adverbial clause)

2. We were all relieved _____

(adjective clause)

3. Last year, her little sister grew two inches, _____

   _____

(adverbial clause)

4. _____ the grocery store was almost
   empty.

(noun clause)

5. _____ was important to the
   Student Advisory Council.

(noun clause)

6. She tried to remember _____

(adjective clause)

7. Do you recognize the person _____

(adverbial clause)

8. We sent Derek a jigsaw puzzle _____

(noun clause)

9. Everyone knew _____

(adjective clause)

10. An old proverb _____ says, "Waste not, want not."

Exercise 31 Punctuation of Clauses

In the following sentences supply commas and semicolons where they are needed. In the spaces at the right, write the marks of punctuation with the words that precede them. Write **C** if the sentence is correct.

Example: On that cold morning when the car finally started, Henry was greatly relieved.

                                                   started,

1. Margaret Farber who has always had unusual interests is deep into Chinese calligraphy. _____

2. What will intrigue her next is anybody's guess. _____

3. Meet me at Park Square we'll have lunch and then look for those boots that you want. _____

4. After Dad has scanned everything else in the newspaper he studies the sports section. _____

5. I got up early to study for my geology test but spent much of the time looking for my notes. _____

6. The financial analyst who addressed the seminar discussed the interrelationship of the two economies. _____

7. The day that Jerry received his notice for jury duty he was terribly annoyed he knew he would be in the midst of writing the annual report. _____

8. Once he had actually served on a jury he decided that the experience was one that nobody should miss. _____

9. We turned left immediately after we had passed the town square then we drove somewhat less than a mile. _____

10. There on the left stood the craft shop that we had read about in *Yankee*. _____

11. What we were interested in seeing was the work of Anna Dickens who teaches at the nearby college.   _____

12. I wasn't sure how we were going to get all our belongings into the car but Harry proved to be an expert packer.   _____

13. Although the economy remained sluggish the utility company posted a fourth-quarter profit.   _____

14. The showroom was filled with so many sofas and chairs and tables that we had difficulty reaching any sort of agreement.   _____

15. While I parked the car Smithson picked up our tickets at the box office nevertheless we almost missed the opening curtain.   _____

16. Whenever the telephone rings in the middle of the night of course I think that the worst has happened.   _____

17. Last night the insistent ring of the telephone woke me up "the worst" was that my roommate had run out of gas over on Mitchell Boulevard.   _____

18. The first hurricane of the season was a threat to the shipping lanes but not to the coastline.   _____

19. Because the weather is usually rather cool in May I didn't think that it was a good idea to plan to go camping with the children.   _____

20. This May was as warm as any June and we struck out for the mountains the first chance that we had.   _____

21. When you have a minute or two read the lead editorial in the Sunday paper.   _____

22. The writer opposes the idea of building a causeway to the island until we have exhausted all other possibilities.   _____

23. She does not support the notion of building a bridge nor is she enthusiastic about a ferry.   _____

24. Paddling one's own canoe appears to be the only acceptable alternative thus the island may well continue to enjoy its splendid isolation. _____

25. We wanted to see the software exhibit before we went to the general meeting however, in the lobby we ran into Marge whom neither of us had talked with for months. _____

Exercise 32   Kinds of Sentences

Identify the type of sentence by writing one of the following abbreviations in the space at the right:

S if the sentence is simple,   **Cx** if the sentence is complex,
Cp if the sentence is compound,   **Cp-Cx** if the sentence is compound-
                                                              complex.

Example: Once the days grew longer, we often saw picnickers in
               the park.   _Cx_

1. That Madge is interested in backpacking comes as no surprise
   to me.   _____

2. Fred told us about the large crowds at the new seafood restaurant, so we decided to be there at six o'clock.   _____

3. He was exactly right, and though we had to stand in line, the
   crab cakes were well worth the wait.   _____

4. My neighbor has never had more beautiful irises than those
   that are blooming on the north side of her house.   _____

5. I don't know which I prefer: the bright yellow ones or those
   that are a gorgeous shade of purple.   _____

6. Their being planted in front of the split-rail fence makes them
   all the more attractive.   _____

7. In Friday's paper there was a feature story about consignment
   shops, and I read it with great interest.   _____

8. I immediately decided to gather together all those odds and
   ends that I no longer used but that were taking up valuable
   space in kitchen cabinets.   _____

9. My collection included four vases, two unusual pitchers,
   several teacups of an unknown pattern, and one ceramic
   calico cat.   _____

10. After careful consideration I decided that these items were
    more suitable for a yard sale than for a consignment shop.   _____

11. Tina had not finished the essay that was due at nine o'clock
    Monday morning; moreover, she was very tired.   _____

12. To finish the paper by midnight, she had counted on a wonderful spurt of energy as well as a brilliant flash of imagination. _____

13. Neither was forthcoming, nor did the chocolate bar and mug of coffee seem to help matters. _____

14. As a last resort she climbed into bed and set the alarm for four o'clock. _____

15. Surely a bit of sleep would recharge those "little grey cells" made famous by Agatha Christie's Hercule Poirot. _____

16. Although I have usually associated freelancing with writers and photographers, persons with other skills and talents enjoy its advantages. _____

17. For instance, I recently read of a city planner who freelances; a computer has enabled her to exchange her office at city hall for one at home. _____

18. Freelancing has a lengthy history, however, beginning at least as long ago as when independent knights sold their services to beleaguered overlords. _____

19. Nathan remembered going as a child to a secondhand bookstore with his father. _____

20. The shop was dark and musty, with shelves everywhere: under the windows, above the doors, and when space allowed, from floor to ceiling. _____

21. The large woman sitting at my right had close-cropped blond hair and a bright square face. _____

22. Once we began talking, I became increasingly aware of her eyes; no one in the dining room escaped their notice. _____

23. Clearly my new acquaintance was evaluating one of the guests and then another. _____

24. John, if you are interested in finding out what people are buying and selling, just read the want ads in Sunday's paper. _____

25. Advertised for sale under "Collectibles" is everything from postcards to jukeboxes to antique maps, and under "Antiques" is mentioned a log cabin, which the owner says was built in 1865. _____

The Sentence Fragment

■ 7a Grammatical Fragments

If you are not careful to have both a subject and a predicate in your sentences and to express a complete thought, you will write sentence fragments instead of complete sentences. Observe, for example, the following:

> A tall, distinguished-looking gentleman standing on the corner in a pouring rain.
>
> Standing on the corner in a pouring rain and shielding himself from the deluge with a large umbrella.

The first of these groups of words is no more than the subject of a sentence or the object of a verb or preposition. It may be part of such a sentence, for example, as *We noticed a tall, distinguished-looking gentleman standing on the corner in a pouring rain*. The second group is probably a modifier of some kind, the modifier of a subject, for instance: *Standing on the corner in a pouring rain and shielding himself from the deluge with a large umbrella, a tall, distinguished-looking gentleman was waiting for a cab.*

Another type of fragment is seen in the following illustrations:

> Because I had heard all that I wanted to hear and did not intend to be bored any longer.
>
> Who was the outstanding athlete of her class and also the best scholar.
>
> Although he had been well recommended by his former employers.

Each of these groups of words actually has a subject and a predicate, but each is still a fragment because the first word of each is a subordinating element and clearly indicates that the thought is incomplete, that the thought expressed

109

depends upon some other thought. Such fragments are subordinate parts of longer sentences like the following:

> I left the hall because I had heard all that I wanted to hear and did not intend to be bored any longer.

> The valedictorian was Alice Snodgrass, who was the outstanding athlete of her class and also the best scholar.

> He did not get the job although he had been well recommended by his former employers.

■ 7b Permissible Fragments

A sentence fragment is often the result of ignorance or carelessness and is the sign of an immature writer. On the other hand, much correctly spoken and written English contains perfectly proper fragments of sentences. The adverbs *yes* and *no* may stand alone, as may other words and phrases in dialogue (though our chief concern remains written prose). There is nothing wrong, for example, in such fragments as the following:

> The sooner, the better

> Anything but that.

> Same as before.

Interjections and exclamatory phrases may also stand alone as independent elements. The following fragments are correct:

> Ouch!

> Tickets, please!

> Not so!

■ 7c Stylistic Fragments

There is another kind of fragment of rather common occurrence in the writing of some of the best authors. It is the phrase used for realistic or impressionistic effect, the piling up of words or phrases without any effort to organize them into sentences: "The blue haze of evening was upon the field. Lines of forest with long purple shadows. One cloud along the western sky partly smothering the red." This kind of writing, if it is to be good, is very difficult. Like free verse it may best be left to the experienced writer. You should learn to recognize a sentence fragment when you see one. You should use this form sparingly in your own writing. And you should remember two things: first, that the legitimacy of the sentence fragment depends upon whether it is used intentionally or not, and second, that *in an elementary course in composition most instructors assume that a sentence fragment is unintended.*

Study carefully the following sentence fragments and the accompanying comments:

A large woman of rather determined attitude who says that she wishes to see you to discuss a matter of great importance. [This is a typical fragment unintended by the writer, who seems to have felt that it is a complete sentence because there are a subject and a predicate in each subordinate clause.]

He finally decided to leave school. Because he was utterly bored with his work and was failing all his courses. [Here the second group of words is an unjustifiable fragment. It is a subordinate clause and should be attached to the main clause without a break of any kind.]

There were books everywhere. Books in the living room, books in the bedroom, books even in the kitchen. [The second group of words is a fragment, but it may be defended on grounds of emphasis. Many writers, however, would have used a colon after *everywhere* and made a single sentence.]

Exercise 33   The Sentence Fragment

Indicate in the space at the right by writing **C** or **F** whether the following groups of words are complete sentences or fragments. Rewrite any fragment, making it a complete sentence.

Example: Butterfly bushes, with their colorful, fragrant flowers, attracting butterflies.

Butterfly bushes, with their colorful, fragrant flowers, attract butterflies.   _____*F*_____

1. Ever since the third grade when I watched a tadpole develop into a frog.   _____

2. To conquer our fears and face the unknown.   _____

3. The Amazons of Greek legend were female warriors.   _____

4. Unable to study because of the noise in the dormitory and the heat of the room.   _____

5. Wait to see the movie until it comes out on video.   _____

6. My sister, who has a horse, a dog, a bird, and three cats. _____

7. My friend, an animal rights enthusiast, believes that all species have equal rights. _____

8. Although a blizzard was predicted for the following day. _____

9. The two squirrels that are doing gymnastic feats as they try to get at the birdseed in the squirrel-proof feeder. _____

10. Eating barbecue and corn on the cob and savoring every bite. _____

11. Many college athletes enjoy living in separate dormitories. _____

12. Americans' dreams of houses, cars, money, and security. _____

13. Mary, while arranging a bouquet of flowers. _____

14. Riding our bicycles for ten miles along the edge of the ocean.   _____

15. Have you ever taken the bus tour of New York City?   _____

16. Worrying about her persistent cough.   _____

17. As we left the island and saw the sign for Interstate 95.   _____

18. What I would really like to do on my next vacation.   _____

19. Because of the heavy traffic and the bad weather.   _____

20. If I could live in the North in the summer and the South in the winter.   _____

Exercise 34   The Sentence Fragment

Some of the following groups are fragments. Some are fragments and sentences. Some are complete sentences. Rewrite each group in such a way as to leave no fragment. If the group of words is already a complete sentence, leave it as it is and mark it **C.**

Example: Even though his parents wanted John to attend college near home. John decided to go to Stanford, a continent away.

Even though his parents wanted John to attend college near home, John decided to go to Stanford, a continent away.   _____F_____

1. Working on a construction crew was not difficult. Except when the temperature went over ninety degrees.   _____

2. Aunt Dot gave Edward a subscription to *Sports Illustrated.* A weekly magazine that deals exclusively with sports and sports issues.   _____

3. There are many challenges when one first goes to college. Learning to get along with a roommate. Managing money. Resisting the constant temptation to socialize rather than study.   _____

4. The 1996 Summer Olympics will be held in Atlanta, Georgia.   _____

5. After the game was over and everyone had gone home.   _____

6. For gardening Adele wore old, comfortable clothes. Blue jeans, a baggy sweatshirt, and dingy athletic shoes.   _____

7. Since no one has applied for the job. We will advertise it again in next week's newsletter.   _____

8. My roommate, Sandra, riding her bike across campus, her bookbag on her back.   _____

9. At the conference I heard a number of interesting speakers. Speakers who gave me ideas I'll remember all my life.   _____

10. I realized that if I had not done my science project on the environment. I would still not fully understand the importance of recycling.   _____

11. Janet went to the door of her teacher's office to see if the grades were posted. To see if she had kept her *A*.   _____

12. News reporters often print or broadcast stories about the personal lives of famous people. Sports figures, politicians, musicians.   _____

13. I did not go to Europe with my parents last summer. The reason being that I wanted to work at home.   _____

14. When new teachers first enter the classroom and face row upon row of students seated before them.   _____

15. Pikes Peak, a mountain in central Colorado, is 14,110 feet high.   _____

Exercise 35   The Sentence Fragment

Complete or revise the following sentence fragments in such a way as to make complete sentences.

Example: Even as I was speaking to the police officer about my missing roommate.

Even as I was speaking to the police officer about my missing roommate, she appeared in the doorway.

1. American movies of the 1930's and 1940's, following the Motion Picture Production Code of 1930.

2. This Code, which decreed that movies should not arouse the sympathy of the audience on the side of wrongdoing or show wrongdoing in any detail.

3. That if a product is good, it doesn't need to be advertised.

4. Although advertisements are usually necessary so that people will know about the existence of the product.

5. The ducks swimming close to the edge of the lake or waddling along the banks, looking for handouts from humans.

6. In New York City, where the towering skyscrapers make concrete canyons of the sidewalks.

7. After studying for two hours by myself and then reviewing for two more with a classmate.

8. The beautiful Mohawk River, winding its way across upstate New York.

9. Two of my best friends from college — Agnes and Meg.

10. The complex tangle of entrance and exit ramps off Interstate 85 near Atlanta known as "Spaghetti Junction."

Tense, Voice, Mood

In Chapter 1 you found that a single verb may be classified according to **tense**, **voice**, and **mood**; therefore, it is not surprising that choosing the appropriate verb form occasionally presents difficulty.

■ 8a Principal Parts of Verbs

There are three **principal parts** of a verb. These are (1) **the first person singular, present indicative;** (2) **the first person singular, past indicative;** (3) **the past participle.** The first two of these provide the basic forms of the present, past, and future tenses; the third is used as the basis for the three perfect tenses:

Principal parts: *begin, began, begun*		
Present:	I begin	
Past:	I began	
Future:	I will (shall) begin———————	(This form based on present tense *begin*)
Present Perfect:	I have begun	(These forms based on past participle *begun*)
Past Perfect:	I had begun	
Future Perfect:	I will (shall) have begun	

If you know the principal parts of a verb and the way to form the various tenses from them, you should never make a mistake such as the one contained in the following sentence: "The play had already began when I arrived." If the speaker had known that the principal parts of *begin* are *begin, began, begun* and that the past perfect tense is formed by using *had* with the past participle, he or she would have known that the correct form is *had begun*.

Regular verbs — that is, those verbs that form their past tense and past participle by adding *-d* or *-ed* to the present tense — rarely cause difficulty. It is the **irregular verbs** that are most frequently used incorrectly. When necessary, consult a dictionary for their principal parts. The following list contains the principal parts of certain troublesome irregular verbs. Study them:

Present	Past	Past participle	Present	Past	Past participle
ask	asked	asked	know	knew	known
bite	bit	bitten	lead	led	led
blow	blew	blown	ride	rode	ridden
break	broke	broken	ring	rang (rung)	rung
burst	burst	burst	run	ran	run
choose	chose	chosen	see	saw	seen
come	came	come	shake	shook	shaken
dive	dived (dove)	dived	sing	sang (sung)	sung
do	did	done	speak	spoke	spoken
drag	dragged	dragged	steal	stole	stolen
draw	drew	drawn	sting	stung	stung
drink	drank	drunk	suppose	supposed	supposed
drown	drowned	drowned	swim	swam	swum
eat	ate	eaten	swing	swung	swung
fall	fell	fallen	take	took	taken
fly	flew	flown	tear	tore	torn
freeze	froze	frozen	throw	threw	thrown
give	gave	given	use	used	used
go	went	gone	wear	wore	worn
grow	grew	grown	write	wrote	written

Note that the past tense and the past participle of the verbs *ask, suppose,* and *use* are regularly formed by the addition of *-ed* (or *-d*) to the present tense. Possibly because the *d* is not always clearly sounded in the pronunciation of the past tense and the past participle of these verbs, people frequently make the mistake of writing the present-tense form when one of the other forms is required:

I have *asked* (not *ask*) him to go with me.

I was *supposed* (not *suppose*) to do that job.

He *used* (not *use*) to be my best friend.

Another problem verb is *hang*, which in its transitive form has two sets of principal parts, although the meaning of the word is essentially the same for both. When the direct object of *hang* is an inanimate thing, (*I will hang the picture in the hall*), the past tense and the past participle are *hung* and *hung,* making it an irregular verb (*I hung the picture in the hall* and *I have hung the picture in the hall*). However, when the verb refers to the hanging of a human being (*The posse will probably hang the cattle thief*), its past tense and past participle are *hanged* and *hanged* (*The posse hanged the cattle thief* and *The cattle thief was hanged at sundown*). Be sure to remember this distinction in your writing.

■ 8b Two Troublesome Pairs of Verbs

Lie and *lay* and *sit* and *set* are frequent stumbling blocks to correct writing. These verbs need not be confusing, however, if the following points are remembered:

1. Each verb has a distinguishing meaning. *Lay* and *set,* for instance, are clearly distinguished from *lie* and *sit* by their meanings: both *lay* and *set* usually mean *place* and are correctly used when the verb *place* can be substituted for them.

2. *Lay* and *set* are always transitive verbs; that is, they require an object to complete their meaning when they are used in the active voice. *Lie* and *sit* are intransitive verbs and hence do not take an object.

3. Although *lay* and *lie* share the form *lay,* they use it in different tenses. The remaining principal parts are clearly distinguishable.

These three points may be graphically shown:

Principal parts	
Intransitive (takes no object)	Transitive (takes an object)
lie lay lain, *recline, remain in position*	lay laid laid, *place*
sit sat sat, *be in a sitting position*	set set set, *place*

Look at a few sentences that illustrate these distinguishing characteristics. Is it correct to say *I set the box on the table* or *I sat the box on the table*? To answer the question, try substituting *placed* for *set* and also see whether a direct object follows the verb. You can see at once that *placed* can be substituted for *set* and that *box* is the direct object of the verb; therefore, the first sentence, employing *set,* is the correct one. But in the sentence *I left the box sitting on the table,* the correct form is *sitting,* not *setting,* since *placing* cannot be substituted for *sitting* and since there is no direct object after *sitting:*

I *laid* (that is, *placed*) the book by the bed and *lay* (past tense of *lie*) down to rest.

Do not make the error of thinking that only animate things can stand as subjects of intransitive verbs. Note the following sentences in which inanimate objects are used as subjects of the intransitive verbs:

The book *lies* on the table.

The house *sits* near the road.

■ 8c Tense Sequence

Tense sequence demands that a logical time relationship be shown by the verbs in a sentence. Through force of habit we generally indicate accurate time relationships. A few cautions, however, should be stressed:

1. Use the present tense in the statement of a timeless universal truth or a customary happening:

   I wonder who first discovered that the sun *rises* (not *rose*) in the east. [The fact that the sun rises in the east is a universal truth.]

   Joe said that the class *begins* (not *began*) at 10:30. [The clause *that the class begins at 10:30* states a customary happening.]

2. Use the present tense of an infinitive or the present participle if the action it expresses occurs at the same time as that of the governing verb:

   Yesterday I really wanted *to go*. [Not *to have gone*. The governing verb *wanted* indicates a past time. At that past time I wanted to do something *then* — that is, yesterday — not at a time prior to yesterday.]

   Skipping along, she hummed a merry tune. [The skipping and the humming occur at the same time.]

3. When necessary for clarity, indicate time differences by using different tenses:

   INCORRECT: I told him that I *finished* the work just an hour before.

   CORRECT: I told him that I *had finished* the work just an hour before. [The verb *told* indicates a past time. Since the work was finished before the time indicated by *told*, the past perfect tense *had finished* must be used.]

   INCORRECT: *Making* my reservations, I am packing to go to Cape Cod.

   CORRECT: *Having made* my reservations, I am packing to go to Cape Cod. [The perfect participle *having made* must be used to denote an action before the time indicated by the governing verb *am packing*.]

■ 8d Voice

Transitive verbs always indicate whether the subject is acting or is being acted upon. When the subject is doing the acting, the verb is said to be in the **active voice:**

   I *laid* the book on the table. [*Laid* is in the active voice because the subject *I* is doing the acting.]

   When the subject is being acted upon or receiving the action, the verb is in the **passive voice:**

   The book *was laid* on the table. [*Was laid* is in the passive voice because the subject *book* is being acted upon.]

Note: The passive-voice verb always consists of some form of the verb *to be* plus a past participle: *is seen, was laid, have been taken.*

In general, the active voice is more emphatic than the passive and therefore should normally be used in preference to the passive voice:

WEAK: The automobile *was driven* into the garage.

MORE EMPHATIC: She *drove* the automobile into the garage.

When, however, the receiver of the action should be stressed rather than the doer, or when the doer is unknown, the passive voice is appropriate.

Class officers *will be elected* next Thursday. [The receiver of the action should be stressed.]

The dog *was found* last night. [The doer is unknown.]

Generally speaking, one should not shift from one voice to the other in the same sentence:

AWKWARD: John *is* the best athlete on the team, and the most points *are scored* by him.

BETTER: John *is* the best athlete on the team and also *scores* the most points.

AWKWARD: After Dr. Lovett *was conferred* with, I *understood* the assignment.

BETTER: After I *had conferred* with Dr. Lovett (OR After *having conferred* with Dr. Lovett), I *understood* the assignment.

■ 8e Mood

In Chapter 1, Section 1d defined the indicative, imperative, and subjunctive moods. Through force of habit we usually select the correct verb forms for the first two moods but sometimes have difficulty choosing the correct forms for the subjunctive mood.

The **subjunctive mood** is most frequently used today to express a wish or to state a condition contrary to fact. In both types of statement the subjunctive *were* is used instead of the indicative *was*. Tenses in the subjunctive do not have the same meaning as they do in the indicative mood. For example, the past subjunctive form points toward the present or future, as seen in the sentence *If I WERE you, I would give his suggestion strong consideration.* The present subjunctive form usually points toward the future with a stronger suggestion of hopefulness than does the past subjunctive. (*I move that John Marshall BE named chairman of our committee.*) The present subjunctive form of the verb *to be* is invariably *be* for all persons, and the past subjunctive form of the verb *to be* is invariably *were*. In all other verbs the subjunctive form varies from the indicative only in that in the present tense the third person singular ending is lost, as in *I suggest that he TAKE the subway to his friend's house.* Note the following examples of verbs in the subjunctive mood:

I wish that I *were* (not *was*) going with you to Hawaii this summer.

If I *were* (not *was*) king, I couldn't be happier.

The subjunctive mood may also be used in the following instances:

> If the report *be* true, we will have to modify our plans. [To express a doubt or uncertainty.]
>
> She commanded that the rule *be* enforced. [To express a command.]
>
> Even though he *disagree* with me, I will still admire him. [To express a concession.]
>
> It is necessary that he *see* his parents at once. [To express a necessity.]
>
> I move that the proposal *be* adopted. [To express a parliamentary motion.]

Exercise 36   Tense and Mood

A. In the space at the right, write the correct form of the verb that appears in parentheses.

Example: Have any of you (*fly*) kites since coming to the beach?   *flown*

1. Watch out for those wasps in the toolshed; one of them (*sting*) me yesterday.   _____

2. My sister is coming from New York on the train that is (*suppose*) to arrive at 4:05 this afternoon.   _____

3. The tremors during last week's earthquake only rattled the windows and (*shake*) the doors.   _____

4. The prevailing folklore (*lead*) us to believe that we would have a long, cold winter.   _____

5. On Christmas Day we gathered in the Rankins' living room and (*sing*) carols while Mimi played the piano.   _____

6. The college swim team has (*swim*) before breakfast every morning this week.   _____

7. Has everyone heard the news that Sara Sessions has (*ask*) to exchange her shorts for cut-offs?   _____

8. Although the Dow-Jones average (*dive*) sharply just before the market closed on Friday, it seems to be recovering this morning.   _____

9. After Dad had told us for the third time to go to bed, we turned off the television and (*drag*) the sleeping bags from the closet.   _____

10. Never having (*drink*) espresso before, Harvey was somewhat surprised at its strength.   _____

11. It was after midnight, but Milton (*steal*) down the stairs, counting on finding the caramel cake on the kitchen table.   _____

12. Although spring has been slow in coming, the dogwood trees in our woods have finally (*burst*) into bloom.   _____

13. Since the price war among the airlines began, the telephones at our travel agency have (*ring*) off the hook.

    _____

14. Cynthia has (*choose*) *War and Peace* for the subject of her research paper in English 102.

    _____

15. I certainly hope that she has not (*bite*) off more than she can chew.

    _____

B. Underline all verbs in the following sentences. Then write the past tense of the underlined verbs in the space at the right.

Example: Invariably Louis <u>drowns</u> his pancakes in melted butter and maple syrup.   *drowned*

1. In the summer we buy vegetables at the farmers' market and then freeze them to enjoy later.

    _____

2. Naturally she always wears a helmet when she rides her motorcycle.

    _____

3. When the temperature falls below freezing, this old house becomes difficult to heat.

    _____

4. Each morning just before the sun rises, the birds begin to stir in the trees outside my window.

    _____

5. The storyteller weaves such wonderful tales that the children never grow tired of hearing them.

    _____

C. Select the correct form of the verb in parentheses, and write it in the space at the right.

Example: If I (*were, was*) living in Montreal, I would have to improve my French.   *were*

1. When I was in Chicago last summer, I wanted to (*meet, have met*) Suzie for lunch.

    _____

2. (*Working, Having worked*) in the lab since supper, Bruce decided to shut down his computer and look for human company.

    _____

3. It is necessary that we (*are, be*) at the golf course by eight o'clock Saturday morning.

    _____

4. Marcia wishes that she (*were, was*) able to find an apartment away from traffic but near a shopping center.

      _____

5. He consulted an atlas and discovered that Izmir (*is, was*) a port on the Aegean Sea.

      _____

Exercise 37   Tense and Mood

In the space at the right write the correct form of the verb that appears in parentheses.

Example: Who (*leave*) that handsome umbrella in the
foyer yesterday?   *left*

1. I haven't (*begin*) to read all that has been written by
   or about Walker Percy.   _____

2. The meeting of the strategic planning committee
   (*take*) much longer than she had anticipated.   _____

3. Have you and Reba (*bring*) your ferns in for the
   winter?   _____

4. The painting by the obscure impressionist has (*sell*)
   for an unbelievable price.   _____

5. (*Putting*) on his bathing suit, George hurried down
   to the pool.   _____

6. Has anyone (*get*) the morning paper?   _____

7. It (*use*) to come before I had time to make the
   coffee.   _____

8. Recently, however, I have (*know*) it to arrive just as
   I am leaving to catch the bus.   _____

9. Although we had (*eat*) at Rudolph's often, we
   looked forward to having dinner there Friday night
   with Josh and his fiancée.   _____

10. Each morning after three of the children had (*raise*)
    the flag, the school day officially began.   _____

11. (*Walking*) his beat, the police officer often stopped
    to visit with the children playing on the steps or
    along the sidewalk.   _____

12. It soon became obvious that my new roommate
    was not (*accustom*) to studying without the benefit
    of her stereo.   _____

13. The local weather is (*forecast*) several times an hour
    on Channel 12.   _____

14. The throw was not in time, and the runner, who
    had (*slide*) home, was declared safe.   _____

15. A portrait of a signer of the Declaration of Independence has been (*hang*) in the lobby of the courthouse.   _____

16. William, it is essential that we (*be*) at the dock thirty minutes before the ferry leaves.   _____

17. The state trooper pressed down on his accelerator and (*speed*) after the long, sleek sports car.   _____

18. (*Watching*) the soap opera for years, Mrs. Treadwell knew instinctively what the next crisis would be.   _____

19. During the first half of Saturday's game the quarterback had (*throw*) the ball for three completions.   _____

20. The physical therapist said that the hospital's exercise program (*begin*) at five in the morning, even on weekends.   _____

21. According to today's *Wall Street Journal,* the U.S. dollar has (*rise*) against most foreign currencies.   _____

22. If I (*be*) you, I would not begin putting that bicycle together before reading the instructions.   _____

23. To reach the crystal pitcher, Ms. Joliette climbed the ladder and (*stand*) precariously on its top step.   _____

24. Drew inherited his Volkswagen from his brother, who had (*drive*) it for at least ten years.   _____

25. I must admit that I haven't even (*begin*) to learn my part for *The Glass Menagerie.*   _____

26. In the bottom of the ninth we were all on our feet by the time the pitcher had (*strike*) out the last batter.   _____

27. The wind, which had (*blow*) from the east most of the day, brought a downpour of cooling rain.   _____

28. My friend Jo has (*wear*) her hair in the same style ever since I have known her.   _____

29. However, she has not (*feel*) obliged to keep it the same color.   _____

30. Mr. Findlay has been (*ask*) to deliver a lecture at the next meeting of the historical society.   _____

31. Because my cousin has (*grow*) tired of commuting, she has asked to be transferred to a branch bank.   _____

32. Disgusted with his first effort, Scot (*tear*) up the printout and turned the computer back on. _____

33. In August of last year several of us from school (*go*) rafting in Colorado. _____

34. This winter we are (*suppose*) to go back over New Year's for skiing. _____

35. The audience was sure that the cattle rustler would be (*hang*) as soon as the marshal caught him. _____

36. Surprisingly, all was (*forgive*), and the reformed rustler married the rancher's daughter. _____

37. I understand that these sketches were (*draw*) by the art class that Ms. Fernandez teaches. _____

38. During the party Alan (*drag*) his chair over next to mine and gave me a lengthy account of his latest trip to Alaska. _____

39. Martha never (*dream*) that the day would come when she and her family would move to Puerto Rico. _____

40. Ned went to bed early and (*sleep*) soundly. _____

41. When he finally (*wake*) up, he stared at his strange surroundings. _____

42. Hearing the rain on the cabin roof, he wished fervently that he (*be*) anywhere but Camp Flowing Brook. _____

43. Aunt Flo has never (*ride*) on a Ferris wheel and doesn't intend to begin now. _____

44. Before the meeting was adjourned, Dick Giovanni was (*give*) time to outline the plans for the Clean and Green Campaign. _____

45. Last month Charlie hoped to (*buy*) a new car or at least a new used one. _____

46. It's hard to say how much oil Boo, his old rattletrap, has (*drink*) over the years. _____

47. Nevertheless, Boo possesses a certain charm that has (*come*) only with age. _____

48. Having arrived late at the station, the boys (*run*) the length of the platform to catch the train. _____

49. As they clambered aboard, the conductor (*blow*) his
final whistle.   _____

50. They made their way through the cars and (*swing*)
their duffle bags onto the rack above a pair of
empty seats.   _____

Name _____   Score _____

Exercise 38   Two Troublesome Pairs of Verbs

Select the correct form of the verbs in parentheses, and write it in the space at the right.

Example: I'm going to (*sit, set*) this basket of geraniums in the kitchen window.   *set*

1. I think that you'll find Morris (*lying, laying*) on the deck taking a sunbath.   _____

2. Yesterday we (*lay, laid*) our plan concerning job sharing before the department manager.   _____

3. Anna (*sat, set*) the saucepan of onion soup on the back of the stove.   _____

4. While the soup was simmering, she began (*sitting, setting*) the house in order.   _____

5. Then she got out two of her red-checked mats and (*lay, laid*) them on the table, along with soup bowls and spoons.   _____

6. Shortly before six o'clock she (*sat, set*) down in her favorite chair, picked up her novel, and listened for a familiar step on the stair.   _____

7. Once Michael had gathered the pears, he (*sat, set*) them on the back porch to ripen.   _____

8. Then it wasn't long before I found him (*sitting, setting*) on the back steps in the October sun eating a pear.   _____

9. I don't think that Mrs. Simpkins wants to be disturbed: she is (*lying, laying*) in the sunroom reading one of her romance novels.   _____

10. We had been (*sitting, setting*) on the hard seats in the drafty gymnasium for longer than seemed reasonable.   _____

11. We were greatly encouraged when the speaker glanced at the watch that he had (*lain, laid*) on the lectern.   _____

12. After the children had carefully carved a face on the best side of the pumpkin, they (*sat, set*) it on the front steps for all the world to see.   _____

13. The cold rain running down the window pane encouraged Tish to (*lie, lay*) in bed a while longer.   _____

14. The child who lives next door was (*lying, laying*) on the grass, closely examining a dandelion.   _____

15. I had (*sat, set*) my dripping umbrella in the stand by the door before looking for a place to hang my coat.   _____

16. Nick brought a large log from the shed and (*lain, laid*) it on the fire.   _____

17. His hat, always (*sitting, setting*) squarely on his head, identifies Dudley in any crowd.   _____

18. Clare, serving the wassail will be easier if you will (*sit, set*) the mugs on this tray.   _____

19. That pine tree has (*lain, laid*) across the path since last week's ice storm.   _____

20. Taylor is a forthright person: he always (*lies, lays*) his cards on the table.   _____

21. We got up with the sun so we would be among the first to claim the sand dollars (*lying, laying*) on the beach.   _____

22. Although I was early, several people were already (*sitting, setting*) in the tour bus by the time I arrived.   _____

23. Once we were under way, the guide explained how the city was (*lain, laid*) out and what stops we would make before lunch.   _____

24. The trappers stood on the steep bank, staring at the wilderness that (*lay, laid*) across the river.   _____

25. We don't know whose Siamese cat that is, but it frequently (*sits, sets*) in our gazebo.   _____

26. Joe had (*sit, set*) the breakfast dishes on the counter when he heard his taxi in the driveway.   _____

27. Having just (*lain, laid*) down in the hammock, I was annoyed when the telephone rang.   _____

28. You would be wise, Harriet, to employ a brickmason to (*lie, lay*) the walk from your house to the street.   _____

29. From the end of the pier he could see the fishing boats (*lying, laying*) on the horizon.   _____

30. A new globe (*sits, sets*) by the reference desk on the first floor of the library.   _____

Exercise 39 Voice

Revise the following sentences, using verbs in the active voice and eliminating unnecessary verbs.

Example: Every month one of the company cars is taken by my father to visit the offices in Ithaca and Syracuse.

Every month my father takes one of the company cars to visit the offices in Ithaca and Syracuse.

1. The award for outstanding sportsmanship was given to Steve at the banquet that was sponsored by the Touchdown Club.

2. One day last week the oak tree that had been uprooted in April was chopped up by Jesse and one of his friends.

3. Our bicycles were ridden by the three of us to the end of the island where clams are dug.

4. The two Irish setters were taken by my brothers to the Westside Clinic so they could be given their annual rabies shots by Dr. Abram.

5. The long black convertible was washed and polished for the parade by Nick, and then "Vote for Nora" posters were taped to its doors.

6. The bright red sweaters that had been knitted by Helen during the fall were given to her nieces for Christmas.

7. The article on fruit flies that had been written by Professor Boggs was faithfully read and photocopied by those of us in the biology class.

8. Her embroidered jacket, which had been brought from Mexico by her grandmother, was worn by Lynn with black velvet pants.

9. *The Optimist's Daughter*, which for many years has been considered a favorite novel of mine, was written by Eudora Welty.

10. My belt was fastened, and my seat was returned to an upright position even before we were requested to do so by the flight attendant.

11. The boys were asked by Mr. Proctor to rake the leaves in both the front and back yards.

12. The money that had been earned by the boys during the summer was invested by their father in a few shares of stock.

13. The small plane was brought to a stop by the novice pilot, who was being instructed by an experienced friend.

14. Although the cottage roof had recently been repaired by Luke, it was damaged again by last week's northeaster.

15. The song that was sung as an encore by the youthful soprano was first published as a lyric poem in the seventeenth century.

9

Agreement of Subject and Verb

The verb in every independent or dependent clause must agree with its subject in person and number. (There are **three persons;** the **first person** is the speaker, the **second person** is the person spoken to, and the **third person** is the person or thing spoken about. There are **two numbers:** the **singular,** denoting one person or thing, and the **plural,** denoting more than one person or thing.) A careful study of the conjugation of the verb in Chapter 1 will show you that a verb can change form not only in *tense* but also in *person* and *number.* If you can recognize the subject and the verb, you should have no trouble making the two agree. Although there is ordinarily no problem in doing so, certain difficulties need special attention.

■ 9a Intervening Expressions

The number of the verb in a sentence is not affected by any modifying phrases or clauses standing between the subject and the verb but is determined entirely by the number of the subject:

> The *evidence* that they submitted to the judges *was* [not *were*] convincing. [*Evidence* is the subject of the verb *was.*]
>
> The new *library* with its many books and its quiet reading rooms *fills* [not *fill*] a long-felt need. [*Library* is the subject of the verb *fills;* the phrase *with its many books . . .* has nothing to do with the verb.]
>
> A list of eligible candidates *was* [not *were*] posted on the bulletin board. [*List* is the subject of the verb *was posted.*]

Our big pine tree as well as a small oak *was* [not *were*] damaged by the high winds. [*Tree* is the subject of the verb *was damaged;* the intervening phrase *as well as a small oak* is not a part of the subject.]

The famous golfer along with his many fans *was* [not *were*] heading toward the ninth green. [*Golfer* is the subject of the verb *was heading; along with his many fans* is not a part of the subject.]

My father, together with my two brothers, *is* [not *are*] planning to build a cabin at the lake. [*Father* is the subject of the verb *is planning.* The phrase that comes between the subject and the verb is not a part of the subject.]

■ 9b Verb Preceding the Subject

In some sentences the verb precedes the subject. This reversal of common order frequently leads to error in agreement:

There *is* [not *are*] in many countries much *unrest* today. [*Unrest* is the subject of the verb *is.*]

There *are* [not *is*] a *table,* two *couches,* four *chairs,* and a *desk* in the living room. [*Table, couches, chairs,* and *desk* are the subjects of the verb *are.*]

Where *are* [not *is*] *Bob* and his *friends going*? [*Bob* and *friends* are subjects of the verb *are going.*]

■ 9c Indefinite Pronouns

The indefinite pronouns or adjectives *either, neither,* and *each;* the adjective *every;* and such compounds as *everybody, anybody, everyone, anyone* are always singular. *None* may be singular or plural. The plural usage is more common:

Each of the plans *has* [not *have*] its advantages.

Everyone who heard the speech *was* [not *were*] impressed by it.

Every bud, stalk, flower, and seed *reveals* [not *reveal*] a workmanship beyond the power of man.

Is [not *Are*] *either* of you ready for a walk?

None of the men *have* brought their wives.

None of the three is [*are*] interested.

None — no, not one — *is* prepared.

■ 9d Compound Subjects

Compound subjects joined by *and* normally require a plural verb:

Correctness and *precision are* required in all good writing.

Where *are* the *bracelets* and *beads*?

Note: When nouns joined by *and* are thought of as a unit or actually refer to the same person or thing, the verb is normally singular:

The *sum* and *substance* of the matter *is* [not *are*] hardly worth considering.

My *friend* and *coworker* Mr. Jones *has* [not *have*] gone abroad.

■ 9e Subjects Joined by *Or* and *Nor*

Singular subjects joined by *or* or *nor* take a singular verb. If one subject, however, is singular and one plural, the verb agrees in number and person with the nearer one:

Either the *coach* or the *player was* [not *were*] at fault.

Neither the *cat* nor the *kittens have* been fed. [The plural word *kittens* in the compound subject stands next to the verb *have been fed.*]

Neither the *kittens* nor the *cat has* been fed. [The singular subject *cat* stands next to the verb, which is therefore singular.]

Neither my *brothers* nor *I am* going. [Note that the verb agrees with the nearer subject in person as well as in number.]

■ 9f Nouns Plural in Form

As a general rule use a singular verb with nouns that are plural in form but singular in meaning. The following nouns are usually singular in meaning: *news, economics, ethics, physics, mathematics, gallows, mumps, measles, shambles, whereabouts:*

The *news is* reported at eleven o'clock.

Measles is a contagious disease.

The following nouns are usually plural: *gymnastics, tactics, trousers, scissors, athletics, tidings, acoustics, riches, barracks:*

Athletics attract him.

The *scissors are* sharp.

Riches often *take* wing and *fly* away.

Plural nouns denoting a mass, a quantity, or a number require a singular verb when the subject is regarded as a unit.

Five *dollars is* too much for her to pay.

Fifty *bushels was* all the bin would hold.

Though usage is mixed, phrases involving addition, multiplication, subtraction, and division of numbers preferably take the singular:

Two and two is [are] four.

Two times three is six

Twelve divided by six is two.

■ 9g Determining Modifiers

In expressions like *some of the pie(s)*, *a percentage of the profit(s)*, *all of the money*, *all of the children*, the number of *some*, *percentage*, and *all* is determined by the number of the noun in the prepositional phrase:

> *Some* of the pie *is* missing.
>
> *Some* of the pies *are* missing.

Whether to use a singular or plural verb with the word *number* depends on the modifying article. *The number* requires a singular verb; *a number*, a plural one.

> *The number* of students at the art exhibit *was* small.
>
> A small *number* of students *were* at the art exhibit.

■ 9h Subject, *To Be* Forms, and Predicate Nouns

When one noun precedes and another follows some form of the verb *to be*, the first noun is the subject, and the verb agrees with it and not with the complement (i.e., the predicate noun) even if the complement is different in number:

> The only *fruit* on the market now *is* peaches.
>
> *Peaches are* the only fruit on the market now. [In the first sentence *fruit* is the subject; in the second, *peaches*.]

■ 9i Relative Pronoun as Subject

When a relative pronoun (*who, which,* or *that*) is used as the subject of a clause, the number and person of the verb are determined by the antecedent of the pronoun, the word to which the pronoun refers:

> This is the student *who is* to be promoted. [The antecedent of *who* is the singular noun *student*; therefore, *who* is singular.]
>
> These are the students *who are* to be promoted. [The antecedent of *who* is the plural noun *students*.]
>
> Should I, *who am* a stranger, be allowed to enter the contest? [*Who* refers to *I*; *I* is first person, singular number.]
>
> She is one of those irresponsible persons *who are* always late. [The antecedent of *who* is *persons*.]

If sentences such as the last one give you trouble, try beginning the sentence with the "of" phrase, and you will readily see that the antecedent of *who* is *persons* and not *one*:

> Of those irresponsible *persons who are* always late she is one.

■ 9j Collective Nouns

Some nouns are singular in form but plural in meaning. They are called **collective nouns** and include such words as *team, class, committee, crowd,* and *crew.* These nouns may take either a singular or a plural verb: if you are thinking of the group as a unit, use a singular verb; if you are thinking of the individual members of the group, use a plural verb:

> The *crew is* striking for higher pay. [The crew is acting as a unit.]
>
> The *crew are* writing reports of the wreck. [The members of the crew are acting as individuals.]

■ 9k Nouns with Foreign Plurals

Some nouns retain the plural forms peculiar to the languages from which they have been borrowed: *alumni, media, crises.* Still other nouns occur with either their original plural forms or plural forms typical of English: *aquaria* or *aquariums, criteria* or *criterions.* If you are in doubt as to the correct or preferred plural form of a noun, consult a good dictionary.

Note: Be careful not to use a plural form when you refer to a singular idea. For instance, write *He is an alumnus of Harvard,* not *He is an alumni of Harvard.*

Name _____   Score _____

Exercise 40   Subject-Verb Agreement

Write the correct form of the *italicized* verb in the space at the right.

Example: Arranged in the pine cupboard (*were, was*) a
set of dishes belonging to my grandmother.   *was*

1. The media (*seem, seems*) to know exactly what will
capture our interest and what won't.   *seems*

2. A list of the amendments that will be on Tuesday's
ballot (*are, is*) on the front page of the morning
paper.   *is*

3. Each of the tankards she brought from Germany
(*bear, bears*) a different design.   *bears*

4. Not every boat in the marina (*are, is*) participating
in the regatta this weekend.   *is*

5. Somewhere in the stadium (*are, is*) my father and
my brother Joe.   *are*

6. Evidently neither of them (*are, is*) aware that I have
a serious problem.   *is*

7. Either Joe or my father (*have, has*) my ticket to the
game tucked safely in some pocket or other.   *has*

8. The tote bag, which contained not only library
books but the key to my apartment and my lunch
as well, (*were, was*) nowhere to be found.   *was*

9. I decided to retrace my steps, and there at the bike
rack (*were, was*) my tote bag along with my bicycle. *was*

10. Like many of us, the McGuire family (*go, goes*) in a
dozen different directions from morning till night.   *goes*

11. The stage crew (*are, is*) having a party at Maggie's
after rehearsal.   *is*

12. There (*are, is*) a personal computer in each of the
study rooms at the back of the library.   *is*

13. "The New Explorers" (*are, is*) an engrossing series
of programs appearing on PBS.   *is*

14. The clouds were so dark and heavy that none of the astronauts (*were, was*) surprised when the liftoff was postponed.

were

15. It could not be I who (*am, is*) responsible for this flat tire.

_am is_

16. Ice cream and cake (*seem, seems*) to be essential for any child's birthday party.

seem

17. The data from the San Francisco store (*are, is*) needed for us to make an intelligent decision.

is are

18. She is one of those commentators who (*are, is*) able to extract the essence of complex issues.

is are

19. Eight cups of coffee (*are, is*) all that we can make in this old percolator.

is are

20. Green beans (*are, is*) the only vegetable that Millie will eat.

is is are

Name _____   Score _____

Exercise 41   Subject-Verb Agreement

Write the correct form of the *italicized* verb in the space at the right.   18/20

Example: A team of ecologists (*are, is*) to present reports at
this evening's seminar.   ___are___

1. At the beginning of the movie the sheriff along with his
   chief deputy (*are, is*) confronted with a dilemma.   ___is___

2. A series of bank robberies (*have, has*) occurred during the
   past several months.   ___have___

3. Naturally every drifter and ne'er-do-well (*are, is*) suspected.   ~~are~~'s

4. However, neither the portly president nor the beautiful
   teller (*are, is*) willing to account for his or her time the
   night the local bank was robbed.   ~~are~~'s

5. Where these two (*were, was*) on that night has become, of
   course, the principal concern of the lawmen.   ___were___

6. Could it be that none of the drifters and ne'er-do-wells
   (*are, is*) guilty?   ___are___

7. Could it be that both the president and the teller (*are, is*)
   responsible for the crime?   ___are___

8. Could it be that economics (*are, is*) not the only interest of
   the bachelor banker and the widowed teller?   ___is___

9. Neither of the child's parents was surprised that the doctor's diagnosis (*were, was*) mumps.   ___was___

10. The percentage of gainers on the New York Stock Exchange
    (*were, was*) greater this week than last.   ___Was___

11. The scissors that we use to clip coupons (*are, is*) in one of
    the kitchen drawers.   ___is___

12. J. R. R. Tolkein is the author of *The Lord of the Rings*, a tril-
    ogy that (*include, includes*) *The Fellowship of the Ring, The Two
    Towers*, and *The Return of the King*.   ___includes___

13. Every electronic index in the library (*are, is*) updated
    regularly.   ___is___

14. The number of women running in last week's road race
    (*were, was*) unusually high.   ___was___

15. A number of them (*were, was*) from neighboring states.   _were_

16. The alumnus raising the most money for the college's scholarship fund (*are, is*) recognized at the Spring Fling.   _is_

17. In the *Statistical Abstract of the United States* one can find statistics that (*apply, applies*) to everything from national defense to population to trade.   _apply_

18. My calculator indicates that I am correct: $650.33 minus $75.20 (*equal, equals*) $575.13.   _equals_

19. Most of the Sunday newspaper (*are, is*) in a chair on the deck.   _is_

20. In our city most of the newspapers (*are, is*) delivered not by boys on bicycles but by adults driving automobiles.   _are_

Exercise 42 Subject-Verb Agreement

Write the correct form of the *italicized* verb in the space at the right.

Example: (*Are, Is*) neither of the freshman forwards dressed
out today?   *Is*

1. The sum and substance of the doctor's advice (*are, is*) that
   Dad must decrease calories and increase exercise.   is

2. Every dollar, mark, and yen (*were, was*) affected by yesterday's news from the Middle East.   was

3. The phenomenon of UFO's (*continue, continues*) to engage
   the imagination.   continues

4. There (*are, is*) a remarkable number of persons whose interest in the subject is as keen as ever.   are

5. The purse's contents, which (*were, was*) spread out on the
   bed, failed to reveal the missing credit card.   were

6. German measles (*are, is*) different from and milder than the
   measles that John has now.   is

7. Everybody from the head coach to the crowd in the stands
   (*were, was*) incensed by the referee's call.   was

8. The crises in Mabel's life (*are, is*) surpassed only by those
   of the star in my favorite soap opera.   is

9. That humid afternoon every dryer and washing machine in
   the laundromat (*were, was*) going full tilt.   was

10. The pair of lazy ceiling fans (*were, was*) doing little to cool
    the long, narrow room.   were

11. The riches of the Queen of Sheba (*were, was*) reported to in-
    clude "spices, and very much gold, and precious stones." were

12. Indexes such as the *Reader's Guide to Periodical Literature*
    (*are, is*) published on paper and on data discs.   are

13. An exhibition of fifty paintings, the work of several contem-
    porary artists, (*open, opens*) at our local gallery this week. opens

14. Not one of us who knew the Brians well (*were, was*) at all
    aware of their plans to move to Juneau.   was

15. Mathematics (*are, is*) a science whose truth is admired by
    philosophers of every age.   is

16. A number of books by Peter Drucker (*are, is*) included in
    the bibliography for the management class.   _is_

17. My former roommate and longtime friend (*have, has*) joined
    a spelunking club.   _has_

18. Neither the manager nor the players (*are, is*) ready to settle
    for second place in the standings.   _is_

19. A collection of letters, bills, and advertisements (*were, was*)
    waiting for me when I finally got back from my tour of
    Quebec.   _was_

20. The barracks, which (*have, has*) just been built, will house
    the new recruits.   _have_

Exercise 43 Subject-Verb Agreement

Write the correct form of the *italicized* verb in the space at the right.

Example: There (*are, is*) either sleet or snow in the forecast.   *is*

1. The alumnae (*have, has*) published a cookbook, whose sales will help maintain the archives of the college.   *have*

2. I'm afraid that my breakfast (*are, is*) usually a cup of black coffee and a bagel.   *is*

3. Jesse glanced across the aisle, and there (*were, was*) the same American couple he had seen earlier in the hotel lobby.   *was*

4. Some may consider politics an art or a science, but according to Will Rogers, "all politics (*are, is*) applesauce."   *are*

5. Al is one of those managers who immediately (*infuse, infuses*) a team with optimism.   *infuse*

6. Our team (*are, is*) unanimous in acknowledging this fact.   *is*

7. The medium used to paint these landscapes (*was, were*) acrylic.   *was*

8. I have difficulty appreciating the fact that one billion dollars (*are, is*) the equivalent of one thousand million dollars.   *is*

9. Each of the baskets submitted by the weavers from Cherokee (*were, was*) intricately designed.   *was*

10. Electronics, according to the dictionary, (*are, is*) a branch of physics, dealing with "the emission, behavior, and effects of electrons."   *is*

11. Even though they may not understand all the implications of this definition, the faculty and the staff (*enjoy, enjoys*) the convenience of electronic mail.   *enjoy*

12. Peanut butter and jelly (*are, is*) a time-honored combination at this house.   *is*

13. Ray says that there (*have, has*) never been a more satisfying snack than a peanut-butter-and-jelly sandwich along with a glass of milk.   *has*

14. According to the international flag code, every one of these pennants (*represent, represents*) a numeral or a letter of the alphabet.   *represents*

15. Where (*are, is*) the sheik and his entourage staying tonight?   *are*

16. The small auditorium with its stained-glass windows and worn murals (*were, was*) as intriguing as the play itself.   *was*

17. Because the dice that came with the Parcheesi game (*have, has*) been lost, we'll have to play checkers tonight.   *has*

18. Most of the T-shirts with the university's seal (*are, is*) navy blue.   *are*

19. On the other hand, none of the sweatshirts (*come, comes*) in any color but crimson.   *come*

20. Neither the owner of the shop nor the two of us who worked for her on the weekends (*were, was*) able to explain what Miss Minnie Mauldin did with all the doughnuts she bought.   *were*

Agreement of Pronoun and Antecedent

Pronouns, as you saw in Chapter 1, are words that are used in the place of nouns when repetition of a noun would be awkward. *The dog hurt the dog's foot* is clearly an unnatural expression. Usually a pronoun has a definite, easily recognized *antecedent* (the noun or pronoun to which it refers), with which it agrees in *person, number,* and *gender.* The *case* of a pronoun, however, is not dependent on the case of its antecedent.

■ 10a Certain Singular Antecedents

Use singular pronouns to refer to singular antecedents. The indefinite pronouns *each, either, neither, anyone, anybody, everyone, everybody, someone, somebody, no one, nobody* are singular, and pronouns referring to them should be singular:

> *Each* of the girls has *her* own car.
>
> *Neither* of the boys remembered *his* poncho.
>
> Does *everyone* have *his* or *her* ticket?
>
> Does *everyone* have *his* ticket?

Note: The last two sentences illustrate a current usage dilemma prompted by a limitation of English: the language has no third person singular form of the personal pronoun that refers to persons of either sex. By definition a dilemma has no satisfactory solution; nevertheless, you will need to be aware of and sensitive to the different viewpoints. Some writers use *he or she, his or her,* and *him or her,* although such expressions are awkward. Others use the masculine pronouns (or possessive adjectives) in a universal sense, a practice based on long tradition but one objected to by those who perceive it to be sexist. The best practice nowadays is to avoid the problems of both awkwardness and sexism by rephrasing the sentence:

> Does *everyone* have *a* ticket?
>
> Do *we* all have *our* tickets?
>
> *Who* doesn't have *a* ticket?

■ 10b Collective Nouns as Antecedents

With *collective nouns* use either a singular or a plural pronoun according to the meaning of the sentence. Since collective nouns may be either singular or plural, their correct usage depends upon (1) a decision as to meaning (see Chapter 9, Section 9j) and (2) consistency:

> The *team* has elected Jan as *its* captain. [The team is acting as a unit and therefore requires the singular possessive pronoun *its*.]
>
> The *team* quickly took *their* positions on the field. [Here each member of the team is acting individually.]

Exercise 44 — Agreement of Pronoun or Possessive Adjective and Antecedent

From the *italicized* forms in parentheses choose the correct pronoun or possessive adjective for each sentence and write it in the space at the right. In a sentence where you choose the singular pronoun and you have the *he / she, his / her, him / her* option, you may select either the masculine or the feminine form as your answer, avoiding the awkward *he or she* expression.

Example: Did either of the auditors discuss (*their, his / her*) findings with the comptroller?   *his / her*

1. We took the train because neither of us wanted to drive (*their, his / her*) car downtown. _____

2. The field was so muddy that the team had to change (*their, its*) jerseys at the half. _____

3. According to my grandmother, neither Rob nor Andy seems to be able to find (*himself, themselves.*) _____

4. The board of directors affirmed (*their, its*) unqualified support of the innovative chief executive officer. _____

5. The stockholders of the company, however, divided (*their, its*) support among several candidates for the position. _____

6. Immediately after the census data had been published, city officials questioned (*their, its*) validity. _____

7. Every Labor Day each family in the neighborhood brought (*their, its*) own picnic basket to the block party. _____

8. Ed, wear the navy slacks; with the plaid jacket (*they, it*) will look better than those khaki ones. _____

9. Is either of the sopranos ready to have (*their, her*) makeup put on? _____

10. Miraculously, one and all had found (*their, his / her*) way to the Walkers' lake house. _____

11. The plan is for every dog and cat in Windcrest to have (*their, its*) rabies shot next Saturday morning. _____

12. The League of Women Voters decided to make voter registration (*their, its*) principal project for the year. _____

13. Consequently, last week members of the League were asking every prospective voter at the mall whether (*they, he / she*) had registered. _____

159

14. I have all of five dollars left in my wallet, and I don't want to spend (*them, it*) on a ticket to a grade-B western. _____

15. We all knew the coach's chief criterion for membership on the soccer team, but every year we saw (*them, it*) posted outside his office. _____

16. The crisis caused by Mary Nell's words proved so earth-shaking that (*they, it*) affected everyone in the office. _____

17. Someone at last night's game left (*their, his*) coat and tie on the bleachers in the gym. _____

18. With (*their, its*) years of experience the ring of computer hackers had no difficulty infecting the program with a virus. _____

19. As the intermittent drizzle turned into pouring rain, neither of the middle-aged matrons could help thinking of (*their, her*) carefully arranged hair. _____

20. Either of those boys will be glad to lend us (*their, his*) history notes if we return them tomorrow. _____

Name _____ Score _____

	Agreement of Pronoun or Possessive Adjective
Exercise 45	**and Antecedent**

From the *italicized* forms in parentheses choose the correct pronoun or possessive adjective for each sentence and write it in the space at the right. In a sentence where you choose the singular pronoun and you have the *he / she, his / her, him / her* option, you may select either the masculine or the feminine form as your answer, avoiding the awkward *he or she* expression.

Example: The class wanted to see the play before writing (*their, its*) papers. _____*their*_____

1. There was no need to argue with David: his statistics spoke for (*themselves, itself*). _____themselves_____

2. Because the media had not met with the President since his trip to Canada, (*they, it*) anticipated Monday's press conference. _____they_____

3. That morning I thought that every student in the school had arrived, with (*their, his / her*) skis in hand, to catch the northbound train. _____their his_____

4. Everyone with a seat on the train had made (*their, his / her*) reservation days ahead. _____his/her_____

5. All who had procrastinated in doing so could now repent at (*their, her*) leisure. _____their_____

6. Marcia is one of those persons who enjoy (*themselves, herself*) from first to last at any party. _____her themselves_____

7. Athletics had interested my Uncle George when he was a boy growing up in Cleveland, and (*they, it*) continued to do so despite his eighty years. _____they_____

8. First in one part of the sky and then in another, the fireworks suddenly exploded and then burned (*themselves, itself*) out in moments. _____themselves_____

9. The news of the archaeological discovery was so significant that (*they, it*) appeared in press releases around the world. _____it_____

10. Once the club secretary had made copies of the agenda for the meeting, she placed (*it, them*) on the rostrum. _____them_____

11. Both the tall, skinny boy and his younger brother appeared to have enough money to pay (*their, his*) way to the game. _____their his_____

12. Neither Dad's car nor mine should need (*their, its*) tires rotated yet.

       its

13. A crowd of men, women, and children lined the streets, hoping that (*they, it*) could catch a glimpse of the Queen or perhaps the Queen Mother.

       they

14. Because the experienced teacher anticipated our delaying tactics, she was prepared to deal with (*them, it*).

       them

15. Both of the men who witnessed the accident had been asked to give (*their, his*) accounts to the state patrol officer.

       their / his

16. Although Fran must take statistics to graduate, she doesn't think that she will register for (*them, it*) this quarter.

       it

17. Every woman enrolled in the exercise class received (*their, her*) own progress report.

       her

18. The hotel was attractive enough, but none of the tourists looked forward to carrying (*their, his or her*) luggage up the long flight of stairs.

       his or her

19. Physics had never attracted Morton, and time had not increased (*their, its*) appeal.

       its

20. Although election night brought good tidings, none of us had expected (*them, it*) to be so overwhelmingly good.

       them

       18/20

| Exercise 46 | Agreement of Subject, Verb, and Pronoun or Possessive Adjective |

From the *italicized* forms in parentheses choose the correct verb and the correct pronoun or possessive adjective. Write them in the spaces at the right. In a sentence where you choose the singular pronoun and you have the *he/she, his/her, him/her* option, you may select either the masculine or the feminine form as your answer, avoiding the awkward *he or she* expression.

Example: Neither of the cars we just met (*have, has*) (*their, its*) lights on.

has,
its

1. Although the volcanic phenomena (*were, was*) a natural occurrence, (*they, it*) continued to attract tourists year after year.

were, they

2. Everybody who (*want, wants*) to apply for the position must submit (*their, his/her*) résumé by the first of January.

wants, his

3. The criteria for becoming a chef seemed reasonable, but (*they, it*) (*were, was*) not easily met.

they, were

4. The grand jury (*were, was*) unanimous in (*their, its*) decision to hand down indictments against the drug dealers.

_____

5. The young man and driver of the car (*were, was*) creeping along River Road as if (*they, he*) could not find a particular address.

_____

6. The acoustics in the small auditorium (*were, was*) so superb that (*they, it*) overrode all other considerations.

_____

7. In the first half of the course the emphasis (*were, was*) on the causes of the war; in the second half (*they, it*) shifted to the effects.

_____

8. Neither Nathan nor his brothers (*have, has*) denied (*their, his*) part in breaking Mrs. Carr's kitchen window.

_____

9. The alumni who (*attend, attends*) the Saturday afternoon games can enjoy seeing (*their, his*) long-time friends as well as the football team.

_____

10. None of the candidates for mayor (*have, has*) made (*their, his or her*) views clear on the school-bond issue.

_____

11. The memoranda (*were, was*) waiting for Janice on her desk, and she keyed (*them, it*) into her computer immediately.

_____

12. The audience (*were, was*) almost indifferent during the
    first act, but (*they, it*) became warm and responsive after
    intermission.   _____

13. It is one of the miracles of nature that larvae (*are, is*) able
    to transform (*themselves, itself*) into something so beauti-
    ful as butterflies.   _____

14. Every one of the condominiums (*have, has*) (*their, its*)
    own deck with a marvelous view of the ocean.   _____

15. The House of Representatives (*were, was*) at odds: (*they,
    it*) could not reach cloture on the arms debate.   _____

16. The brass candelabra on the altar (*were, was*) tall and
    handsome; (*they, it*) had been a gift of one of the
    parishioners.   _____

17. The flock of snow geese (*were, was*) flying south, heading
    for (*their, its*) winter home.   _____

18. Either my father or my grandfather (*are, is*) quite willing
    to let the umpire know (*their, his*) opinion of a call.   _____

19. Gymnastics (*were, was*) her passion, and she participated
    in (*them, it*) at every opportunity.   _____

20. The shambles following this hurricane (*are, is*) as nothing
    when compared with (*those, that*) of last season's.   _____

Reference of Pronouns

The word to which a pronoun refers should always be clear to the reader; that is, a **pronoun** and the **antecedent** to which it refers must be instantly identified as belonging together. Even when a pronoun agrees properly with its antecedent in person and number, it may still be confusing or misleading if there is more than one possible antecedent. Therefore, it is sometimes necessary to repeat the antecedent or to reword the whole sentence for the sake of clarity.

■ 11a Ambiguous Reference

Sometimes a sentence contains more than one word to which a pronoun may grammatically refer (the term *ambiguous* means "capable of more than one interpretation"). The sentence should be written in such a way that the reader has no doubt which word is the antecedent:

> Albert told his uncle that his money had been stolen. [The first *his* is clear, but the second *his* could refer to either *Albert* or *uncle*.]

> Albert told his uncle that Albert's money had been stolen. [The meaning is clear, but the sentence is unnatural and awkward.]

To avoid the ambiguous reference of the first sentence and the awkward repetition of the second, reword the sentence:

> Albert said to his uncle, "My money has been stolen."

Another kind of ambiguous reference (sometimes called *divided* or *remote* reference) occurs when a modifying clause is misplaced in a sentence:

INCORRECT: The colt was almost hit by a car that jumped over the pasture fence.

CORRECT: The colt that jumped over the pasture fence was almost hit by a car.

Note: A relative pronoun should always be placed as near as possible to its antecedent. (See Chapter 15.)

11b Broad Reference

Usually a pronoun should not refer broadly to the whole idea of the preceding clause:

She avoided using slang, which greatly improved her speech. [*Which* has no clearly apparent antecedent but refers broadly to the whole idea in the first clause.]

She talked endlessly about her operation, and this was tiresome.

A method often used to improve such sentences is to supply a definite antecedent or to substitute a noun for the pronoun:

She avoided using slang, a practice that greatly improved her speech.

She talked endlessly about her operation, and this chatter was tiresome.

As you can see, these sentences are awkward, adding unnecessary words. A better method is to get rid of the pronoun and make a concise, informative sentence that says everything in one clause:

By avoiding slang, she greatly improved her speech.

Her endless talk about her operation was tiresome.

11c Weak Reference

A pronoun should not refer to a word merely implied by its context. Nor, as a common practice, should the pronoun refer to a word used as a modifier:

INCORRECT: My father is a chemist. *This* is a profession I intend to follow. [The antecedent of *This* should be *chemistry*, which is implied in *chemist* but is not actually stated.]

CORRECT: My father is a chemist. Chemistry is the profession I intend to follow.

ALSO CORRECT: My father's profession of chemistry is the one I intend to follow.

INCORRECT: When she thrust a stick into the rat hole, it ran out and bit her. [*Rat* in this sentence is the modifier of *hole*.]

CORRECT: When she thrust a stick into the rat hole, a rat ran out and bit her.

■ 11d Impersonal Use of the Personal Pronoun

Remember that pronouns are frequently used impersonally and when so used do not have antecedents. Notice the correct impersonal use of *it* in statements about *weather, time,* and *distance:*

> *It* looks like rain. [Reference to weather.]
>
> *It* is now twelve o'clock. [Reference to time.]
>
> How far is *it* to the nearest town? [Reference to distance.]

Avoid the use of *you* and *your* unless you are directing your statement specifically to the reader. Instead, use an impersonal word like *one* or *person.* Also note that the pronoun *you* can never refer to an antecedent in the third person:

> INCORRECT: If *you* want to excel in athletics, *you* should watch your diet. [Incorrect when referring to athletes in general.]
>
> CORRECT: If *one* wants to excel in athletics, *he* should watch his diet.
>
> INCORRECT: When a woman marries, *you* take on new responsibilities. [Here *you* refers incorrectly to *woman,* an antecedent in the third person.]
>
> CORRECT: When a woman marries, *she* takes on new responsibilities.
>
> INCORRECT: All those planning to attend the meeting should get *your* registration fees in on time. [Here *your* incorrectly refers to the third person plural antecedent *those.*]
>
> CORRECT: All those planning to attend the meeting should get *their* registration fees in on time.

A rewording of the sentence often produces a clearer and more emphatic sentence while eliminating the problem of the correct pronoun to use:

> CORRECT: Those who wish to excel in athletics should watch their diets.
>
> CORRECT: To marry is to take on new responsibilities.
>
> CORRECT: Registration fees must be in on time for those who plan to attend the meeting.

Exercise 47 Reference of Pronouns

Write **R** after each sentence that contains an error in the reference of a pronoun. Then rewrite the sentence correctly. Notice that some sentences may be corrected in more than one way. Write **C** if the sentence is correct.

Example: Most of the convention delegates were pleased with its outcome. _____*R*_____

Example: *Most of the delegates were pleased with the convention's outcome.*

1. Her denim jacket was no longer in the closet, which she had promised to lend her sister. _____

2. Martin told Tony that everyone in the neighborhood knew about his latest skydiving maneuvers. _____

3. It turned cold in the night, and I finally had to get up to look for a blanket. _____

4. I rummaged through the closet, and this helped me find the plaid blanket from Scotland. _____

5. If mother would lower the blinds every afternoon, it would prevent the sun from fading her hooked rug. _____

6. I never dreamed that Alicia wanted to be a drummer, but they do intrigue her.   _____

7. On the Fourth of July children gathered on the Ashlands' lawn to watch the fireworks; this was followed by home-made ice cream.   _____

8. When a writer has finished her first draft of a paper, then you need to edit that draft carefully.   _____

9. The prints that my brother sent me from Japan testified to their great artistic gifts.   _____

10. The car was scheduled to be serviced, but I wanted to meet Stacy's plane; that was my dilemma.   _____

11. The yellow day lilies were planted by the members of the Men's Garden Club that are growing along the exit ramp.   _____

12. The ride to work this morning was stop-and-go, which frayed and frazzled everyone's nerves.   _____

Exercise 48   Reference of Pronouns

Write **R** after each sentence that contains an error in the reference of a pronoun. Then rewrite the sentence correctly. Notice that some sentences may be corrected in more than one way. Write **C** if the sentence is correct.

Example: If you want to look your best, a woman needs to
plan her wardrobe carefully.   _____R_____

Example: *If a woman wants to look her best, she needs to plan her*
wardrobe carefully.

1. My neighbor, a well-known architect, frequently enjoyed
discussing it with me.   _____

2. Huddled around the campfire, the boys sang one song
after another, which kept their spirits up.   _____

3. We arranged the Queen Anne's lace in Mother's blue
pitcher, which we had picked by the road to the cabin.   _____

4. It is nearly as far to the Mexican border from Pete's house
as it is from mine.   _____

5. Marvin told Grandfather that he certainly needed to think
about something other than his new motorcycle.   _____

6. The sky in the west became darker and the thunder louder, which was the reason that the lifeguard cleared the pool.   _____

7. We enjoyed watching the program about life in a space station, but none of us could imagine living in one.   _____

8. The computer was eating up the text of J. T.'s English paper, and nobody in the lab knew what to do about it.   _____

9. The sound of the music spilled out over the town square, which was coming from someone's second-floor studio.   _____

10. The race-car driver miraculously escaped injury when it crashed into a wall.   _____

11. When I read about changes in the earth's climate, this invariably alarms me.   _____

12. We had no idea what to do with the outlandish gift that Elsie and Joe had brought to the housewarming.   _____

Exercise 49   Reference of Pronouns

Write **R** after each sentence that contains an error in the reference of a pronoun. Then rewrite the sentence correctly. Notice that some sentences may be corrected in more than one way. Write **C** if the sentence is correct.

Example: She always orders a pepperoni pizza because it is
              her favorite topping.   _____R_____

Example: *She always orders a pizza with pepperoni, her favorite*
              topping.

1. All along the coast the fog was heavy, which made it difficult for the bus driver to see the road.   _____

2. The trapeze artist told me about her life in the circus, and
   this occupied most of our trip.   _____

3. Dr. Irvin's article is optimistic about the future use of solar
   energy, which I think everyone should read.   _____

4. If swimmers use this suntan lotion, you don't have to
   worry about sunburn.   _____

5. After climbing Mt. Mitchell, the hikers were hungry, which
   made the pancakes taste all the better.   _____

6. Because the rare-book room is climate-controlled, they were housed in ideal conditions. _____

7. It was after midnight, all the votes in the governor's race had been counted, and both winners and losers went to bed. _____

8. Oyster stew is a favorite at this restaurant, which is absolutely filled with oysters and is well seasoned too. _____

9. Her hat suggested that she was a small-town girl, and I suspected that she missed it. _____

10. The recreation council has voted to buy new swings and slides for the park, and everyone in the neighborhood is delighted with that. _____

11. His telephone number in Cincinnati was unlisted, which made calling him impossible. _____

12. The Washington correspondent for this newspaper finds it a stimulating but frustrating place. _____

Case of Pronouns

Nouns and pronouns have three case functions: the **nominative,** the **objective,** and the **possessive.** Except in the possessive, nouns do not show case by change of form and consequently do not present any problems of case. The chief difficulties are in the correct use of personal and relative pronouns.

■ 12a The Nominative Case

The **nominative case** is used (1) as the subject of a verb (*I* shall come); (2) as the complement after *is, are,* and the other forms of the verb *to be* (It is *I*); or (3) as an appositive of the subject or of the complement after forms of the verb *to be* (Two of us — *he* and *I* — called). Ordinarily the case of a pronoun that comes before a verb presents no difficulties, for we naturally write "I am going," not "Me am going." But not all constructions requiring the nominative cases are so simple as this one. Study carefully the following more difficult constructions:

1. A clause of comparison introduced by *as* or *than* is often not written out in full; it is elliptical. The verb is then understood. The subject of this understood verb is in the nominative case:

No one can do the work as well as *he* (can).

He knows more about the subject than *she* (does).

2. After forms of the linking verb *to be,* nouns and pronouns used to identify the subject agree in case with the subject. Nouns and pronouns used in this way are called **predicate nominatives** and are in the nominative case:

It was *they* [not *them*].

The persons mentioned were *she* and Rob [not *her*].

He answered, "It could not have been *I* [not *me*]."

3. Pronouns are frequently combined with a noun or used in apposition with a noun. If they are thus used in the subject of the sentence or with a predicate nominative, they are in the nominative case:

We boys will be responsible for the equipment.

Two photographers — *you* and *he* — must attend the convention.

My friend and *I* went to town. [Not *Me* and my friend went to town.]

If you read these sentences omitting the nouns, you will see at once the correct form of the pronoun.

4. The position of the relative pronoun *who* often causes confusion, especially if it follows a verb or a preposition. The role of the relative pronoun within the dependent clause determines its case. Thus if *who* is the subject of the verb in the dependent clause, it is in the nominative case:

You know *who* sent the money. [Since *who* is the subject of the verb *sent* and not the object of *know*, it must be in the nominative case. The whole clause *who sent the money* is the object of *know*.]

Give the praise to *whoever* deserves it. [*Whoever* is the subject of *deserves*. The whole clause *whoever deserves it* is the object of the preposition *to*.]

5. Parenthetical expressions such as *you think, I believe, I suppose,* and *he says* often stand between a verb and the pronoun that is the subject. The pronoun must still be in the nominative case:

Who do you think called me last night? [The expression *do you think* has nothing to do with the case of *who*. Leave it out, or place it elsewhere in the sentence, and you will see that *who* is the subject of *called*.]

The man *who* Jim says will be our next governor is in the room. [Leave out or place elsewhere *Jim says*, and you will see that *who* is the subject of *will be*.]

■ 12b The Objective Case

The **objective case** of a pronoun is used when the pronoun is the direct or indirect object of a verb, the object of a preposition, or an appositive of an object:

1. Compound objects present a special difficulty:

He wrote a letter to Mary and *me*. [Both words *Mary* and *me* are objects of the preposition *to* and therefore in the objective case. Omit *Mary and* or shift *me* to the position of *Mary*, and the correct form is at once apparent.]

She gave George and *him* the list of names. [*Him* is part of the compound indirect object.]

They invited William and *me* to the barbecue. [*Me* is part of the compound direct object.]

2. You will also have to watch the case of a pronoun, in combination with a noun, that serves as an object or the appositive of an object.

The dean spoke candidly to *us* boys.

The chairman appointed three of us girls — Mary, Sue, and *me* — to the subcommittee.

Note: In the sentence *The Dean spoke candidly to us boys, boys* is an appositive of *us. Boys* renames *us.* Here both words are substantives. The following sentence may appear similar to this one, but actually its structure is different:

The dean spoke candidly to *them* boys.

This sentence mistakenly uses a personal pronoun when a demonstrative adjective is needed. First-person speakers do not need to point out themselves; a second person is spoken to directly and needs no pointing out. Only a noun or pronoun in the third person must be pointed out; therefore, use of a demonstrative adjective is called for to modify that noun or pronoun. *Those* is the word needed to modify *boys.* Once the correction is made, you can see that the prepositional phrase in this sentence contains a substantive and a demonstrative adjective, not two substantives.

3. *Whom,* the objective case of *who,* deserves special consideration. Its use, except after a preposition, is declining in colloquial or informal usage (see Chapter 21). Formal usage, however, still requires *whom* whenever the relative pronoun serves as an object:

Whom were you talking to? [To *whom* were you talking?]

He is the boy *whom* we met on the plane. [*Whom* is the object of the verb *met.* The subject of *met* is *we.* Remember that the case of the relative pronoun is determined by its role within the dependent clause.]

Whom do you think we saw last night? [The parenthetical expression does not change the fact that *whom* is the object of *saw.*]

◼ 12c Case of Pronouns Used with Infinitives

An infinitive phrase, as you have learned already, can have both an object and adverbial modifiers. In addition, an **infinitive** may have a subject. There are rules governing the case of pronouns when they are subjects or complements of infinitives:

1. When a pronoun is the subject of an infinitive, it will be in the objective case:

We want *him* to be elected.

2. If the infinitive is a form of the verb *to be* and if it has a subject, its complement will also be in the objective case:

She took him to be *me.*

3. If the infinitive *to be* does not have a subject, its complement will be in the nominative case:

The best player was thought to be *he.*

■ 12d The Possessive Case

Personal pronouns and the relative pronoun *who* have **possessive case** forms, which may be used with a noun or a gerund.

1. When the possessive forms *my, our, your, her, his, its,* and *their* modify nouns or gerunds, they are classified as **possessive adjectives:**

My book is on the table. [*My* is a possessive adjective, modifying *book.*]

We appreciate *your* giving to the United Way. [Not *you giving.* The object of the verb *appreciate* is the gerund *giving;* therefore, *your* is merely the possessive adjective modifying the gerund.]

2. Personal and relative pronouns form their possessives without the apostrophe:

The boy *whose* car is in the driveway works here.

The dog chewed *its* bone.

Note: Notice the difference between *its,* the possessive form, and *it's,* the contraction of *it is:*

It's time for your car to have *its* oil changed.

Exercise 50   Case of Pronouns

In the following sentences underline each pronoun that is used incorrectly, and then write the correct form in the space at the right. Write **C** if the sentence is correct.

Example: Mark works out at the gym more often than me.   _____*I*_____

1. We asked the whole staff, including he and Gerald, to help set up the computer lab.   _____

2. The woman with all the luggage really seemed to appreciate you helping her.   _____

3. Him and Mary wrote the lyrics for the songs we sang at the fundraiser.   _____

4. I know of no one who has as much drive and energy as her.   _____

5. The instructions given to we who were waiting to board the hydrofoil weren't at all clear.   _____

6. There is absolutely no contest: the best cook in the family is him.   _____

7. Furthermore, the person with the greenest thumb is also acknowledged to be he.   _____

8. I can't remember whether her or her assistant manager is to set up the exhibit.   _____

9. Of course we knew it was them the moment the yellow Miata pulled up to the curb.   _____

10. Every New Year's Eve, without fail, the two of us call he and Fran.   _____

11. Everyone now agrees that us flying out of Dulles airport is a good idea.   _____

12. In fact, Tony has already offered to drive us — Mike and I — to the airport right after breakfast.   _____

13. Between you and I, Millie ought not to wear those boots with a skirt that length.   _____

14. The only problem that I see with this old desk is that it's drawers stick. _____

15. Him and his friends from down the street spend most of their weekends at the beach. _____

16. It is difficult to see how you mistook the couple who just moved in upstairs for she and Stan. _____

17. Nevertheless, I did take the new tenants to be they. _____

18. Who wants to walk with Larry and I to the top of the trail? _____

19. Those three — Maria, Bill, and her — are outstanding students. _____

20. We two — you and I — should try to set a good example. _____

Exercise 51 Case of Pronouns

In the following sentences underline each pronoun that is used incorrectly, and then write the correct form in the space at the right. Write **C** if the sentence is correct.

Example: None of the bikers had brought as much equipment as <u>him</u>.　　　　　*he*

1. Instead of you and I, this year Albert and his date are going to be in charge of plans for the picnic.　　　　　_____

2. Grandfather often tells about him writing reviews for the *Observer* when he was a young reporter.　　　　　_____

3. Although Paul and her left home before noon, they did not reach the ranch until suppertime.　　　　　_____

4. I first met Ben when we went to see a *Star Wars* movie; he was standing in line just behind Susie and I.　　　　　_____

5. Then, because he sat next to me in the theater, we chatted about our both liking science fiction.　　　　　_____

6. The Grangers and them usually take their vacations together.　　　　　_____

7. That fact doesn't surprise me, but them riding motorcycles certainly does.　　　　　_____

8. Because the Trojans need height and speed, their first draft choice is reported to be him.　　　　　_____

9. Of course my brother should mow the lawn; he does a much better job than me.　　　　　_____

10. Not one of Carol's children looks very much like her.　　　　　_____

11. If you don't mind me saying so, I think we should take the Metro to the game.　　　　　_____

12. Because we could find no middle ground, the argument turned into a battle of wills between him and me.　　　　　_____

13. We both insisted that the disagreement had nothing to do with us supporting different candidates for mayor.　　　　　_____

14. Finally we decided that its important for old friends to agree simply to disagree. _____

15. Who would have imagined that that man in the gray flannel suit was him? _____

16. Martha, and women like her, somehow manage to work and raise children successfully. _____

17. The detective saw at once that the only ones left in the tavern were her and the waiter. _____

18. Father won't take no for an answer; you attending the wedding is mandatory. _____

19. Everyone will be there, except he and Mother, of course. _____

20. I'm afraid that no one but they will have an acceptable excuse. _____

Exercise 52 Case of Pronouns

In the space at the right, write the correct form of the pronoun *who* (*whoever*).

Example: (*Who, Whom*) did the salesperson ask for?   _**Whom**_

1. Have you decided (*who, whom*) should be our first choice for speaker at the kickoff breakfast?   _____

2. I know (*who, whom*) I think would make the most entertaining speech.   _____

3. All the parents of the children (*who, whom*) attend this day-care center are company employees.   _____

4. (*Who, Whom*) will we be competing against in the first debate?   _____

5. Ms. Steiner hasn't been told (*who, whom*) our first opponents will be.   _____

6. However, she maintains that our team is ready to debate (*whoever, whomever*) they are.   _____

7. The tennis players (*who, whom*) we saw in the clubhouse came in that red van.   _____

8. (*Who, Whom*) do you suppose selected the paintings hanging in Dr. Stewart's office?   _____

9. (*Who, Whom*) do you want to send these last three Christmas cards to?   _____

10. Mr. Alvarez is a well-organized person, (*who, whom*) I am confident is capable of bringing order out of our present chaos.   _____

11. Ask (*whoever, whomever*) is in the information booth whether men's shoes are on this floor.   _____

12. I have no idea (*who, whom*) the young woman is that drives Sarah's school bus.   _____

13. (*Whoever, Whomever*) she is, she needs to be reminded to stop for Sarah at the corner of Merton Drive and Franklin Place.   _____

14. The old comedian always responded warmly to (*whoever, whomever*) he found waiting at the stage door.   _____

15. The Canadian skiers (*who, whom*) we saw on the train are staying in that condominium.   _____

16. The quarterback (*who, whom*) Dad thought would start has sprained his ankle in practice.   _____

17. Invite (*whoever, whomever*) you please to the open house.   _____

18. We will be delighted to have (*whoever, whomever*) can come.   _____

19. (*Who, Whom*) is this basket of fruit intended for?   _____

20. And (*who, whom*) do you think could have sent it?   _____

Exercise 53   Review of Agreement and Case

Underline each verb or pronoun that is incorrectly used. Then write the correct word in the space at the right. Write **C** if the sentence is correct.

Example: The most outstanding chef in this city is
considered to be <u>him</u>.   *he*

1. The Boston Pops orchestra has more than regional
   appeal; their music is enjoyed throughout the country.   _____

2. Riding bikes all morning and swimming most of the afternoon is more than enough exercise for one day.   _____

3. We were good friends, but there was seldom agreement
   between James and I as far as cars were concerned.   _____

4. Statistics indicate that the economy is improving here
   and abroad.   _____

5. Mario is enthusiastic about you going with us to the
   rodeo.   _____

6. Are either of these steaks cooked the way you want?   _____

7. The committee charged with the environmental study
   did not issue their report yesterday.   _____

8. We have been told that Professor Horne's analyses of
   Eliot's poetry always occupies at least five class periods. _____

9. None of us knows who's book that is, but it contains
   fascinating stories about famous gems.   _____

10. There is quite a few cars parked in front of the Wards'
    house this afternoon.   _____

11. Did you realize that neither of her older sisters swims
    the backstroke as well as her?   _____

12. On Thursday those three — Dave, Lynn, and him — left
    San Antonio for Mexico City.   _____

13. The editor of the newspaper together with the bureau
    chief were at the senator's press conference.   _____

14. Although they proved demanding, Shirley enjoyed physics. _____

15. Obviously Uncle Andrew is older than her and his other sister. _____

16. I know that we were in a hurry, but I can't imagine us forgetting the forks and knives. _____

17. The girl whom Tom introduced me to last night is sitting over there with he and our friend Bud. _____

18. The panel of commentators has selected its topic for next Friday's political forum. _____

19. He is one of those rare humorists who is able to transcend time. _____

20. The number of shrimp boats going out each morning are not as great this month as last. _____

21. The media seemed at its best during this year's World Series. _____

22. Perhaps a dozen boys, including Fred and I, gathered on the courthouse steps to wait for the parade to form. _____

23. Could it have been her, the star of last night's play, whom I saw in the park at lunchtime? _____

24. Standing across the street in front of Norton's Drugstore was a small girl, clutching an even smaller terrier. _____

25. Early one morning I stood on the back porch and watched a covey of quail make their way toward the woods. _____

26. One of us has to go to the grocery store, either you or me. _____

27. It's up to we two to keep up with the food supplies; after all, Sam and Felix are doing the cooking. _____

28. Fortunately, the data that I lost when the computer went down was not of vital importance. _____

29. That boy in the parka and jeans is the one whom I think owns the malamute you were talking about. _____

30. Do either of those children playing ball in the parking lot live in this apartment complex? _____

31. The one student who can talk himself out of any difficulty is acknowledged by all to be him. _____

32. The slender girl, who's hair had been tied neatly with a red ribbon, easily outraced the two boys — him and his older brother. _____

33. A group of men gathers regularly at Dot's Diner to drink coffee and catch up on the news. _____

34. The ticket agent is sure that the woman with the baby have already boarded the plane. _____

35. Somebody has left their black sneakers on the front walk. _____

36. There's also a bike outside; its in the middle of the driveway. _____

37. The red carpet with the elaborate design as well as the plain blue one have already been shipped. _____

38. Neither her son nor her daughters has a disposition like Emma's. _____

39. After much debate everybody decided to make their own reservations for the trip to the lake. _____

40. The author and illustrator of the children's book were recognized recently at a party given by the publisher. _____

Adjectives and Adverbs

Adjectives and adverbs, as you saw in Chapter 1, are words that modify, describe, or add to the meaning of other words in a sentence. It is important to remember the special and differing functions of these two kinds of modifier; *adjectives* modify only nouns and other substantives; *adverbs* modify verbs, adjectives, adverbs, and certain phrases and clauses.

■ 13a Adjective and Adverb Forms

An adverb is frequently formed by adding *-ly* to the adjective form of a word: for example, the adjectives *rapid, sure,* and *considerate* are converted into the adverbs *rapidly, surely,* and *considerately* by this method. But there are numerous exceptions to this general rule. Many common adverbs, like *well, then,* and *quite,* do not end in *-ly;* moreover, there are many *adjectives* that do end in *-ly,* like *manly, stately, lonely, unsightly.*

Sometimes the same form is used for both adjective and adverb: *fast, long,* and *much,* for example. (There are no such words as *fastly, longly,* or *muchly.*) Certain adverbs have two forms, one being the same as the adjective and the other ending in *-ly: slow, slowly; quick, quickly; loud, loudly;* etc. The first form is often employed in short commands, as in the sentences *Drive slow* and *Speak loud.*

■ 13b Predicate Adjectives

In any sentence that follows a "subject-verb-modifier" pattern, you must be careful to determine whether the modifier is describing the subject or the verb:

John talks *intelligently.*

John is *intelligent.*

In the first sentence the modifier clearly describes how John talks — that is, it modifies the verb *talks;* consequently, the adverb *intelligently* is needed. But in the second sentence the modifier describes the subject *John;* therefore, an adjective is used. In this construction the adjective following the linking verb *is* is called the **predicate adjective.**

The term **linking verb,** as you learned from Chapter 1, refers to certain intransitive verbs that make a statement not by expressing action but by expressing a condition or state of being. These verbs "link" the subject of the sentence with some other substantive that renames or identifies it or with an adjective that describes it. Any adjective that appears after a subject-linking verb construction is called the predicate adjective. The verbs most commonly used as linking verbs are the following:

| appear | become | remain | stay |
| be | grow | seem | feel (as an emotion) |

Along with these are the five "sense" verbs, which are usually linking verbs:

| look | feel | smell | taste | sound |

The following sentences illustrate the use of predicate adjectives:

The little dog was *glad* to be out of his pen. [*Glad,* a predicate adjective, follows the linking verb *was* and describes *dog.*]

Father appeared *eager* to drive his new car.

Laurie became *angry* at being put to bed.

Jackie seems *happy* in her new job.

Remain *quiet,* and I will give you your seat assignments. [*Quiet,* the predicate adjective, describes the subject, *you,* understood.]

The day grew *dark* as the clouds gathered.

Peggy looks *sporty* in her new tennis outfit.

I feel *confident* that Ty will win his case.

That cinnamon bread smells *delicious.*

The rain sounds *dismal* beating on the roof.

Almond toffee ice cream tastes *marvelous.*

This warm robe feels *comfortable.*

A practical test to follow in determining whether to use an adjective or an adverb is to try to substitute some form of the verb *to be* for the verb in the sentence. If the substitution does not substantially change the meaning of the sentence, then the verb should be followed by an adjective. For instance, *She is smart in her new uniform* has essentially the same meaning as *She looks smart in her new uniform;* therefore, the adjective *smart* is the correct modifier.

Occasionally, one of the "sense" verbs is followed by an adverb because the verb is being used not as a *linking* verb but as an *action* verb: *He looked nervously for his keys. Nervously* describes the act of looking, so the adverb is used to express how the looking was done. The substitution test would show immediately that an adjective would be incorrect in the sentence.

■ 13c Misuse of Adjectives

Using an adjective to modify a verb is a common error but a serious one. The sentence *The doctor spoke to the sick child very kind* illustrates this error. *Kind* is an adjective and cannot be used to modify the verb *spoke;* the adverb *kindly* must be used.

Four adjectives that are frequently misused as adverbs are *real, good, sure,* and *some.* When the adverbial form of these words is needed, the correct forms are *really, well, surely,* and *somewhat:*

> The mountain laurel is *really* (or *very,* not *real*) colorful.

> You did *well* (not *good*) to stop smoking so quickly.

> I *surely* (not *sure*) hope to see him before he leaves.

> I feel *somewhat* (not *some*) better today.

Note: Remember that *well* can also be an adjective, referring to a state of health, as in *I feel well now, after my long illness.*

■ 13d Comparison of Adjectives and Adverbs

When you wish to indicate to what extent one noun has a certain quality in comparison with that of another noun, change the form of the modifying adjective that describes the quality: My dog is *bigger* than your dog. My dog is the *biggest* dog in town.

Descriptive adverbs, like adjectives, may also be compared:

> We awaited the holidays *more eagerly* than our parents did.

> The shrimp and the oysters were the foods *most rapidly* eaten at the party.

Adjectives and adverbs show or imply comparison by the use of three forms, called **degrees:** the **positive, comparative,** and **superlative degrees.**

Positive Degree

The **positive degree** of an adjective or adverb is its regular form:

> He is a *fine* man.

> Frances took notes *carefully.*

Comparative Degree

The **comparative degree** of an adjective or adverb compares two things, persons, or actions:

He is a *finer* man than his brother.

John took notes *more carefully* than Bob did.

Superlative Degree

The **superlative degree** compares three or more persons, things, or actions:

He is the *finest* man I know.

John took notes *most carefully* of all the boys in his class.

The comparative degree is regularly formed by adding *-er* to the positive form of an adjective or adverb or by using *more* or *less* before the positive form. The superlative degree is formed either by adding *-est* to the positive or by using *most* or *least* before the positive. The number of syllables in the word determines which of these forms must be used:

	Positive	Comparative	Superlative
	strong	stronger	strongest
Adj.	pretty	prettier	prettiest
	difficult	more difficult	most difficult
	quietly	more quietly	most quietly
Adv.	easily	more easily	most easily
	fast	faster	fastest

The comparison of some words is irregular, as of *good* (*good, better, best*) and *bad* (*bad, worse, worst*).

Be careful not to use the superlative form when only two persons, groups, objects, or ideas are involved:

Tom is the *healthier* (not *healthiest*) of the two brothers.

Certain adjectives and adverbs such as *perfect, unique, round, square, dead,* and *exact* cannot logically be used in the comparative or superlative degrees, and most should not be modified by words like *quite* or *very*. These words in their simplest forms are absolute superlatives, incapable of being added to or detracted from:

ILLOGICAL: Samuel is the *most unique* person I know.

LOGICAL: Samuel is a unique person.

ALSO LOGICAL: Samuel is an *almost unique* person.

ILLOGICAL: Beth's engagement diamond is the *most perfect* stone I've seen in years.

LOGICAL: Beth's engagement diamond is a *perfect* stone.

ALSO LOGICAL: Beth's engagement diamond is the *most nearly perfect* stone I've seen in years.

ILLOGICAL: The figures that Ben used in his report are *less exact* than they should be.

LOGICAL: The figures that Ben used in his report are *not exact*, though they should be.

■ 13e Incomplete Comparisons

When using the comparative degree of an adjective or adverb, be sure that both items being compared are included; for example, do not say, *Using a paint roller is quicker.* Your reader will ask, "Quicker than what?" The unknown answer might even be *Using a paint roller is quicker than daubing paint on with one's fingers.* Always complete a comparison by including both items: *Using a paint roller is quicker than using a brush.*

Exercise 54   Adjectives and Adverbs

Underline the word or words modified by the *italicized* adjective or adverb. Then in the space at the right, write **Adj** if the italicized word is an adjective, **Adv** if it is an adverb.

Example: The Friday newspaper includes reviews of the
most <u>recent</u> films.   *Adv*

1. The car was almost *too* small for their luggage and the Christmas presents.   _____

2. It was *entirely* too small for them to consider taking their golf clubs.   _____

3. The soup had simmered *slowly* most of the morning.   _____

4. Now it smelled so *tempting* that we decided to eat an early lunch.   _____

5. The hurricane's momentum gradually increased, and the storm's power was *awesome*.   _____

6. *Never* have I seen a road so narrow and steep as this one.   _____

7. However, even though we must drive *cautiously*, we should reach the camp by dark.   _____

8. Despite his seventy years my Uncle Charles seems *quite* vigorous.   _____

9. In fact he is as *energetic* as his sons.   _____

10. The train inched along, gaining speed only after it had left the city *behind*.   _____

11. In the open country it traveled *faster* than any train we had ever ridden.   _____

12. Furthermore, the trip proved not only *fast* but also exceedingly smooth.   _____

13. My sister Mae walked *confidently* onto the stage and sat down at the piano.   _____

14. Despite the size of the audience she remained *confident* throughout the performance.   _____

15. Even as a little girl, she had played *well* at recitals.   _____

16. With talent such as hers the family felt *good* about her decision to be a professional musician.   _____

17. At first glance the recipe for the trifle looked *difficult*.   _____

18. However, it seemed *rather* easy after Nita showed me how to combine the ingredients.   _____

19. Our roommates agreed that the results were well *worth* the effort.   _____

20. Ben has *just* called the garage to see when his old clunker will be ready.   _____

21. With that car's problems I do *not* anticipate its being ready tomorrow or even the next day.   _____

22. I *really* struggled with the accounting problem we had for homework.   _____

23. Once the sun rose, the day turned very *warm*.   _____

24. The headache that I had when I finally went to bed was *real*, not imaginary.   _____

25. Everyone going to the rodeo was *quite* excited to hear that two of the riders were from this area.   _____

26. It was a cold January morning, and the church bells sounded especially *loud* and clear.   _____

27. I grew *sleepy* during the twelfth inning and missed that controversial call.   _____

28. The hot, dry summer meant that the corn would grow *slowly*.   _____

29. Long before eight o'clock the auditorium was *full* of hundreds of fans, waiting eagerly for the trio to appear.   _____

30. The moment they walked out on the stage the crowd went absolutely *wild*.   _____

Exercise 55   Adjectives and Adverbs

Underline any modifier that is incorrectly used. Then write the correct form at the right. Write **C** if the sentence is correct.

Example: Bert <u>sure</u> doesn't relish going back to a nine-to-five job.   *surely*

1. All of us feel some better now that we're warm and have had a good supper.   _____

2. My Aunt Alice wears hats; furthermore, she wears most unique ones.   _____

3. Spring had come, and the cold mountain streams ran more rapid than ever.   _____

4. Thank you muchly, George, for helping me move the piano again.   _____

5. Late in the afternoon the wind came up sudden; we were glad that we had brought our jackets.   _____

6. Professor Franks looked directly at you, Marge, when he asked for someone to identify Byzantium.   _____

7. The sky was leaden, snow was in the forecast, and I decided that it was absolutely a most perfect time to listen to the CD's I had received for Christmas.   _____

8. As we approached the cruise ship, we could see its lights, shining bright and clear, reflected in the dark sea.   _____

9. Ask Chris about "M*A*S*H"; he watches the reruns regular.   _____

10. Dad feels quite good now that he has recovered from his annual bout with bronchitis.   _____

11. After they get off the expressway at Exit 9, they should turn sharp to the right, and our house is the first on the left.   _____

12. Grandmother doesn't think that she is deaf, but for years she has told the boys to speak more distinct. _____

13. I can tell that you have a miserable cold, so I know that you feel too badly to play bridge. _____

14. This very circular staircase is typical of the architecture of an early period in American history. _____

15. Although he has a fine batting average this season, he hit very poor during the playoffs because of a sore shoulder. _____

16. The hollandaise sauce I made for the asparagus doesn't seem as smooth as yours. _____

17. She knew that Marvin was wearing his new boots: his footsteps sounded heavily on the stairs. _____

18. Of the two apartments this one is surely the roomiest. _____

19. Moreover, it is somewhat nearer the bus stop than the other one. _____

20. Everyone readily agrees that Farley passes a football as skillful as a professional. _____

21. Shirley, you should take your truck to my mechanic; he's real reliable. _____

22. The florist worked steady all morning, hoping to have the tables decorated by noon. _____

23. A bicyclist rounded the curve so unexpected that I had to swerve my car onto the shoulder to avoid hitting him. _____

24. He seemed sure that I was at fault. _____

25. Nevertheless, I know that I sure was on my side of the road. _____

26. The worse day of my life happened when I was thirteen years old. _____

27. As a caddy at the local golf course, I had worked long and hard to make the five dollars I thought was stuffed safely in my pocket. _____

28. Once I got home, it plain wasn't there.   _____

29. The teacher asked the children who had completed
    their art projects to play quiet in the back of the
    classroom.   _____

30. Exams are over, spring holidays begin tomorrow, and
    I feel very well about life in general!   _____

Exercise 56   Adjectives and Adverbs

Select the correct form of the two choices in parentheses, and write it in the space at the right.

Example: My Brazilian friend says that I speak too
(*rapid, rapidly*) for her to understand me.   _____*rapidly*_____

1. The second segment of the documentary seemed
(*some, somewhat*) lighter and more interesting than
the first.   _____

2. My grandmother insists that when she was a girl,
our spring weather came (*more early, earlier*) than it
does now.   _____

3. Ron called this morning to say that we should
dress (*casual, casually*) for his party Saturday night.   _____

4. Do you like this wooden picture frame or that brass
one (*better, best*)?   _____

5. I think that your sister's picture will look (*well,
good*) in the wooden frame, and Jack's is right for
the brass one.   _____

6. Have you noticed that your new neighbor speaks
(*confident, confidently*) on any number of subjects?   _____

7. In fact, he has become downright (*bold, boldly*) in
stating his views on the rezoning issue.   _____

8. One wonders whether he will remain (*fearless, fear-
lessly*) after he is confronted by Mrs. Worthington.   _____

9. The small boys held on (*tight, tightly*) as the roller
coaster made its wild descent.   _____

10. At the final turn the car swung (*sharp, sharply*).   _____

11. Needless to say, the screams sounded (*alarming,
alarmingly*) to those of us waiting in line for the
next ride.   _____

12. Time was running out, and Joe worked the last
algebra problem (*hurried, hurriedly*).   _____

13. In the late afternoons the crowds on the streets appear more (*hurried, hurriedly*) now that the days are
short and cold.   _____

14. The decorator in the shop next door has a flair for color, and she uses it in a (*unique, most unique*) way.   _____

15. Why clowns look (*sad, sadly*) when they intend to amuse is a question worth pondering.   _____

16. The paralegal dug (*deep, deeply*) into the records at the courthouse before finding the information she was looking for.   _____

17. Of all the silk scarves your friend brought from Singapore, this magenta one is surely the (*loveliest, lovelier*).   _____

18. Rita, if you will season your deviled eggs with this mustard, I guarantee that they will taste (*delicious, deliciously*).   _____

19. Uncle Horace has no intention of following the doctor's orders, so one wonders how long it will be before he feels (*well, good*) again.   _____

20. Nan is a competitor: she never fails to do (*well, good*) under pressure.   _____

21. The local newspaper gave (*most exact, exact*) accounts of the basketball team's performances in the regional playoff.   _____

22. The candidate for governor stood (*firm, firmly*) in his support of a policy designed to preserve the barrier islands.   _____

23. He (*firm, firmly*) rejected those proposals that weakened his policy of expanded protection.   _____

24. Jeff is quite a remarkable father: he appears (*calm, calmly*) in the midst of every crisis.   _____

25. No matter what the noise level, he seems (*cool, coolly*) and collected.   _____

26. Even though it was May, the water was still cold enough for us to approach it (*cautious, cautiously*).   _____

27. My old friend looked (*questioning, questioningly*) at me when I suggested that we inquire into the schedules of tramp steamers.   _____

28. On the other hand, I (*sure, surely*) was surprised when she suggested that we look into the possibility of riding a train across Siberia.   _____

29. Your ginger lilies smell so (*sweet, sweetly*) that I noticed them when I first came into the living room.   _____

30. I can think of no flower that smells (*sweeter, more sweetly*).   _____

Dangling Modifiers

A **modifier** must always have a word to modify. This fact seems almost too obvious to warrant discussion. And yet we frequently see sentences similar in construction to this one: "Hearing a number of entertaining stories, our visit was thoroughly enjoyable." *Hearing a number of entertaining stories* is a modifying phrase. But where in the sentence is there a word for it to modify? Certainly the phrase cannot logically modify *visit:* it was not our visit that heard a number of entertaining stories. Who did hear the stories? *We* did. Since, however, the word *we* does not appear in the sentence for the phrase to modify, the phrase is said to "dangle." Any modifier dangles, or hangs unattached, when there is no obvious word to which it is clearly and logically related. (Note the similarity of this problem of modifiers and the problem of pronouns and their antecedents.)

■ 14a Recognizing Dangling Modifiers

It is important that you recognize dangling modifiers when you see them. Such modifiers usually appear as two types of constructions — as *verbal phrases* and as *elliptical clauses*. (An elliptical clause, as applicable to this lesson, is a dependent clause in which the subject and/or verb are omitted.)

> *Hearing a number of entertaining stories*, our visit was thoroughly enjoyable. [Dangling participial phrase.]
>
> *On entering the room*, refreshments were being served. [Dangling gerund phrase.]
>
> *To play tennis well*, the racket must be held properly. [Dangling infinitive phrase.]
>
> *When only three years old*, my father took me to a circus. [Dangling elliptical clause.]

In each of the examples on p. 205, the dangling modifier stands at the beginning of the sentence. If the modifier were *not* dangling — that is, if it were correctly used — it would be related to the subject of the sentence. In none of these sentences, however, can the introductory modifier logically refer to the subject. If the error is not immediately apparent, try placing the modifier just after the subject. The dangling nature of the modifier becomes easily recognizable because of the illogical meaning that results when you say, "Our visit, *hearing a number of entertaining stories,* . . ." or "Refreshments, *on entering the room,* . . .".

Dangling modifiers frequently appear at the end as well as at the beginning of sentences. The participial phrase dangles in the sentence "The dog had only one eye, *caused by an accident.*"

At this point an exception to the rules governing the recognition of dangling modifiers should be noted: some introductory verbal phrases are general or summarizing expressions and therefore need not refer to the subject that follows:

CORRECT: *Generally speaking,* the boys' themes were more interesting than the girls'.

CORRECT: *To sum up,* our vacation was a disaster from start to finish.

■ 14b Correcting Dangling Modifiers

Sentences containing dangling modifiers are usually corrected in one of two ways. One way is to leave the modifier as it is and to reword the main clause, making the subject a word to which the modifier logically refers. Remember that when modifiers such as those discussed in this lesson stand at the beginning of the sentence, they must always clearly and logically modify or be related to the subject of the sentence:

Hearing a number of entertaining stories, *we* thoroughly enjoyed our visit.

On entering the room, *I* found that refreshments were being served.

To play tennis well, *one* must hold the racket properly.

When only three years old, *I* was taken to a circus by my father.

You may test the correctness of these sentences, as you tested the incorrectness of the others, by placing the modifier just after the subject. Then see whether the sentence reads logically; if it does, the modifier has been correctly used. The following sentence, though awkward, is clear and logical: "We, hearing a number of entertaining stories, thoroughly enjoyed our visit."

The other way to correct sentences containing dangling modifiers is to expand the modifiers into dependent clauses:

Since we heard a number of entertaining stories, our visit was thoroughly enjoyable.

When I entered the room, refreshments were being served.

If Maria wishes to play tennis well, she must hold the racket properly.

When I was only three years old, my father took me to a circus.

Dangling Modifiers

Rewrite in correct form all sentences containing dangling modifiers. Write **C** if a sentence is correct.

Example: By shopping early in the morning, it is not difficult to find fresh tomatoes.

By shopping early in the morning, Gwen has no difficulty finding fresh tomatoes.

1. When discovered in the back of the toy store, I didn't know whether the mother or the child was more relieved.

2. Stripped of several layers of green paint, I was delighted with my mother's old kitchen table.

3. Having just missed the shuttle bus to the hotel, an hour's wait was a real possibility.

4. Before listening to this new recording of *Appalachian Spring*, Aaron Copeland's music had not appealed to her.

5. Our scheduling problems were resolved after considering two or three alternative time frames.

6. Discovered in a box under the bed, Aunt Lou was delighted to find her long-lost silk pajamas.

7. After catching still another bulletlike pass, the coach decided to leave Cyril in as wide receiver.

8. While driving into town, it suddenly occurred to Mamie that she had forgotten her briefcase.

9. Invariably expecting the worst, the worst seemed invariably to descend on Mr. Tumley.

10. To maintain a productive discussion, there must be an effort by all of us to understand the history behind this restoration plan.

11. Cooked over slow-burning coals, José knew that his hamburgers would be irresistible to the whole crowd.

12. Generally speaking, the news at eleven is the last program my father watches at night.

13. If lost, one can always replace travelers' checks.

14. Having driven home with half of the population of Houston, the prospect of going out to a movie held little appeal.

15. Elected by an overwhelming majority, no one could doubt that the legislator had the confidence of his constituency.

16. Standing on the curb, the two men were so busy discussing the Super Bowl that I was certain they would miss their bus.

17. To make a really good peanut-butter-and-jelly sandwich, each ingredient must be chosen carefully.

18. Delivered every morning by six, Pete usually had time before class to check the box scores in the newspaper.

19. After staring for a long moment at the key in the ignition of the locked car, there was nothing left to do but call a locksmith.

20. In talking to Ms. Dunster, the thought occurred to me that she had no idea that her calico cat was terrorizing the neighborhood.

Exercise 58   Introductory Modifiers

Using the following phrases and elliptical clauses as introductory modifiers, write complete sentences.

Example: Turned at top volume, *the radio could be heard in every room along the hall.*

1. After reading about the workshop for beginning playwrights, _____

   _____

2. Having ordered our pizza for eight o'clock, _____

   _____

3. Seated on a top row of the opera house, _____

   _____

4. When cut in two, _____

   _____

5. Driving to Texas last spring, _____

   _____

6. Without saying another word to Dr. Watson, _____

   _____

7. Although considered striking by many of my friends, _____

   _____

8. To volunteer to work for Congressman Rosenburg's election, _____

   _____

9. Not completely satisfied with her weaving, _____

   _____

10. Gripping the steering wheel tighter by the minute, _____

    _____

11. Since learning to use a word processor, _____

    _____

12. To sum up, _____

    _____

13. Before waxing these pine floors, _____

    _____

14. Strung across the front of the building, _____

    _____

15. Never having seen the film, _____

    _____

16. Forgotten for a moment, _____

    _____

17. Without first reading the annual report, _____

    _____

18. Having reached nearly the end of her rope, _____

    _____

19. To get a new license tag, _____

    _____

20. In responding to our questions, _____

    _____

21. To continue with his job at the warehouse, _____

_____

22. Once hung, _____

_____

23. By getting up early, _____

_____

24. Careening around the corner, _____

_____

25. Upon arriving at the White House, _____

_____

Misplaced Modifiers

Modifiers must always be so placed that there will be no uncertainty about the words they modify. A modifier should, in general, stand as close as possible to the word that it modifies. This does not mean, however, that in every sentence there is only one correct position for a modifier. The following sentence, in which the adverb *today* is shifted from one position to another, is equally clear in any one of these three versions:

> *Today* she arrived in Chicago.
>
> She arrived *today* in Chicago.
>
> She arrived in Chicago *today*.

The position of the modifier *today* can be shifted because, no matter where it is placed, it clearly modifies the verb *arrived*.

■ 15a Misplaced Phrases and Clauses

When, however, a modifier can attach itself to two different words in the sentence, the writer must be careful to place it in a position that will indicate the meaning intended:

> They argued the subject while I tried to study *at fever pitch*.

This sentence is illogical as long as the phrase *at fever pitch* seems to modify *to study*. The phrase must be placed where it will unmistakably modify *argued:*

> CORRECT: They argued the subject *at fever pitch* while I tried to study.
>
> ALSO CORRECT: *At fever pitch* they argued the subject while I tried to study.

A relative clause — that is, a clause introduced by a relative pronoun — should normally follow the word that it modifies:

ILLOGICAL: A piece was played at the concert *that was composed of dissonant chords.*

CORRECT: A piece *that was composed of dissonant chords* was played at the concert.

■ 15b Ambiguous Modifiers

When a modifier is placed between two elements so that it may be taken to modify either element, it is **ambiguous.** These ambiguous modifiers are sometimes called **squinting modifiers:**

The girl who had been dancing *gracefully* entered the room.

Does the speaker mean that the girl had been dancing gracefully or that she entered the room gracefully? Either of these meanings may be expressed with clarity if the adverb *gracefully* is properly placed:

The girl who had been *gracefully* dancing entered the room. [*Gracefully* modifies *had been dancing.*]

The girl who had been dancing entered the room *gracefully.* [Here *gracefully* modifies *entered.*]

■ 15c Misplaced Words like *Only, Nearly,* and *Almost*

Words such as *only, nearly,* and *almost* are frequently misplaced. Normally these modifying words should immediately precede the word they modify. To understand the importance of properly placing these modifiers, consider the different meanings that result in the following sentences when *only* is shifted:

Only I heard John shouting at the boys. [*Only* modifies *I.* Meaning: I was the only one who heard John shouting.]

I *only* heard John shouting at the boys. [*Only* modifies *heard.* Implied meaning: I heard but didn't see John shouting.]

I heard *only* John shouting at the boys. [*Only* modifies *John.* Meaning: John was the only one whom I heard shouting.]

I heard John *only* shouting at the boys. [*Only* modifies *shouting.* Possible implied meaning: I didn't hear John hitting the boys — I heard him only shouting at them.]

I heard John shouting at the boys *only.* [*Only* modifies *boys.* Possible implied meaning: The boys were the ones I heard John shouting at — not the girls.]

Misplacing *only, nearly,* or *almost* will frequently result in an illogical statement:

ILLOGICAL: The baby *only* cried until he was six months old.

CORRECT: The baby cried *only* until he was six months old.

ILLOGICAL: Since his earnings amounted to $97.15, he *nearly* made a hundred dollars.

CORRECT: Since his earnings amounted to $97.15, he made *nearly* a hundred dollars.

ILLOGICAL: At the recent track meet Ralph *almost* jumped six feet.

CORRECT: At the recent track meet Ralph jumped *almost* six feet.

■ 15d Split Infinitives

A **split infinitive** is a construction in which the sign of the infinitive *to* has been separated from the verb with which it is associated. *To vigorously deny* and *to instantly be killed* are split infinitives. Unless emphasis or clarity demands its use, such a construction should be avoided:

AWKWARD: He always tries *to efficiently and promptly do* his work.

CORRECT: He always tries *to do* his work *efficiently and promptly*.

CORRECT: We expect *to more than double* our sales in April. [Placing the modifiers *more than* anywhere else in this sentence would result in ambiguity or changed meaning.]

Exercise 59   Misplaced Modifiers

Place **M** or **C** in the space at the right to indicate whether each sentence contains a misplaced modifier or is correct. Underline the misplaced word or words and indicate the proper position by means of a caret ($\wedge$). Use additional carets if there is more than one correct position.

Example: Bob said that he has <u>hardly</u> read$_\wedge$any of the newest
biography of Harry Truman.   *M*

1. To reach our seats, we had to climb a steep flight of stairs,
   which were surprisingly comfortable.   _____

2. Nina is a spunky woman who has almost had every problem
   that one can imagine.   _____

3. He gazed from the window of the train at the girl in the lavender suit with great interest.   _____

4. The ballerina acknowledged the applause of the audience, holding an armful of spring flowers.   _____

5. At the shareholders' meeting Mr. Thurston used a bar graph to
   clearly and succinctly explain the company's rate of growth.   _____

6. My cousin Horace and I used to enjoy countless double features
   with a good supply of popcorn.   _____

7. Every Saturday afternoon we crowded into the old State Theater
   to see good triumph over evil with our friends.   _____

8. Moreover, it seems as though we nearly saw every cartoon
   Hollywood had produced.   _____

9. My father used to say that one needed great stamina to from beginning to end see all that the old movie houses had to offer.   _____

10. A gold necklace was the groom's gift to the bride, found in an
    antique shop in New Orleans.   _____

11. The girls sat around the pool, sipping soft drinks in bathing
    suits.   _____

12. Brian took the athletic department's van to the mechanic that
    needed a brake inspection.   _____

13. As most of us remember, a great deal was written and said about Columbus's discovery of America in 1992. _____

14. We had scarcely driven two miles before seeing the exit for the science museum. _____

15. The two small boys were riding bikes wearing bright green helmets. _____

16. The man walked along the river bank carefully looking for specimens of wild flowers. _____

17. Brad has called the travel agent about booking a flight to Portugal more than once. _____

18. In the latest census the population in that metropolitan county appears to have more than doubled. _____

19. Maureen almost packed everything she owned for a week's trip to Costa Rica. _____

20. The landscape company has pruned the hollies recently planted behind my apartment building. _____

Exercise 60   Misplaced Modifiers

Place **M** or **C** in the space at the right to indicate whether each sentence contains a misplaced modifier or is correct. Underline the misplaced word or words and indicate the proper position with a caret ($_\wedge$). Use additional carets if there is more than one correct position.

Example: Mick has <u>just</u> jogged$_\wedge$twice this week.   *M*

1. Finchley tripped and almost fell on the scatter rug.   _____

2. The stories in Homer's *Odyssey* may well have first been recited to small groups of listeners, introduced to many of us in English 201.   _____

3. The trumpet player who uses this practice room regularly appears with a small jazz band on weekends.   _____

4. To once and for all settle the dispute over the land line, my neighbors agreed to have the property surveyed.   _____

5. The hikers had nearly climbed two miles when they remembered their lunches, left behind in the back of the van.   _____

6. That man hurrying up the escalator now is looking for his wife and daughters who were in the sportswear department a few minutes ago.   _____

7. We walked across the narrow footbridge with the other tourists swinging above the river.   _____

8. Mary stood on the curb, waiting for the bus lost in thought.   _____

9. Before finding the pewter bracelet, Kim had only looked in one store in Westlake Mall.   _____

10. My grandmother is a long-time admirer of A. E. Housman, who still attends poetry readings.   _____

11. We could count on a crowded bus at the end of the day when people were eager to get home.   _____

12. After the cold front passed through, the thermometer dropped almost twenty degrees.   _____

13. Mother wants to put the new plaid sofa in front of the fireplace, which is to arrive any minute.   _____

14. She says that we barely have enough time to clear a path for the delivery men from the furniture store.   _____

15. This old sofa could tell many a tale about the family, obviously beyond repair.   _____

16. We are looking forward to visiting the cottage where Franklin Roosevelt stayed over spring break.   _____

17. My favorite personality who appears on Channel 10 in the mornings forecasts the weather.   _____

18. Tina just bought enough doughnuts for each of us to have one with a cup of coffee.   _____

19. It was good of Clarence to take the small terrier to the veterinarian that he found in the park.   _____

20. We merely saw a trace of snow on the mountaintops despite the earlier predictions.   _____

Parallelism

Frequently in writing and speaking you need to indicate equality of ideas. To show this equality, you should employ **parallel** grammatical constructions. In other words, convey parallel thought in parallel language; and conversely, use parallel language only when you are conveying parallel thoughts.

■ 16a Coordinate Elements

In employing parallelism, balance nouns against nouns, infinitives against infinitives, prepositional phrases against prepositional phrases, adjective clauses against adjective clauses, etc. Never make the mistake of saying, "I have always liked swimming and to fish." Because the object of *have liked* is two parallel ideas, you should say:

> I have always liked *swimming* and *fishing*. (*And* joins two gerunds.)
>
> OR
>
> I have always liked *to swim* and *to fish*. (*And* joins two infinitives.)

Parallel prepositional phrases are illustrated in the following sentence. The parallel elements appear immediately after the double bar:

> Government ‖ of the people,
> by the people,
> and ‖ for the people   shall not perish from the earth.

Next we see an illustration of parallel noun clauses:

> He said ||| that he would remain in the East,
> ||| that his wife would travel through the Northwest,
> and ||| that his son would attend summer school in the South.

The following sentence contains parallel independent clauses:

> ||| I came;
> ||| I saw;
> ||| I conquered.

Parallel elements are usually joined either by simple coordinating conjunctions or by correlative conjunctions. The most common coordinating conjunctions used with parallel constructions are *and, but, or*. Whenever one of these connectives is used, you must be careful to see that the elements being joined are coordinate or parallel in construction:

> FAULTY: Ann is a girl with executive ability and who therefore should be elected class president.

This sentence contains faulty parallelism, since *and* is used to join a phrase (*with executive ability*) and a dependent clause (*who therefore should be elected class president*). To correct the sentence, (1) expand the phrase into a *who*-clause, or (2) make an independent clause of the *who*-clause:

> CORRECT: Ann is a girl ||| who has executive ability
> and ||| who therefore should be elected class president.

Note: A safe rule to follow is this: *And who* or *and which* should never be used unless preceded by another *who*- or *which*-clause.

> ALSO CORRECT: ||| Ann is a girl with executive ability;
> ||| she therefore should be elected class president.

A common error results from making a construction appear to be parallel when actually it is not:

> Mr. Lee is honest, intelligent, and works hard.

The structure of the sentence suggests an *a, b,* and *c* series; yet what we have is not three parallel elements but two adjectives (*honest, intelligent*) and a verb (*works*). The sentence can be corrected in two ways: we can use three adjectives in a series or two independent clauses in parallel construction, thus:

> CORRECT: Mr. Lee is ||| honest,
> ||| intelligent,
> and ||| industrious.
> ALSO CORRECT: ||| Mr. Lee is honest and intelligent,
> and ||| he works hard.

■ 16b Use of Correlative Conjunctions

Correlative conjunctions are used in pairs: *either . . . or . . . ; neither . . . nor . . . ; both . . . and . . . ; not only . . . but also . . . .* When these conjunctions are used in a sentence, they must be followed by parallel constructions:

INCORRECT: I hope *either* to spend my vacation in Mexico *or* Hawaii. [In this sentence *either* is followed by an infinitive, *or* by a noun.]

CORRECT: I hope to spend my vacation either ‖ in Mexico
or ‖ in Hawaii.

ALSO CORRECT: I hope to spend my vacation in either ‖ Mexico
or ‖ Hawaii.

INCORRECT: She knew *not only* what to say, *but also* she knew when to say it.

CORRECT: She knew not only ‖ what to say
but also ‖ when to say it.

■ 16c Repetition of Certain Words

In order to make parallel constructions clear, you must sometimes repeat an article, a preposition, an auxiliary verb, the sign of the infinitive (*to*), or the introductory word of a dependent clause. Three of these types of necessary repetition are illustrated in the sentences that follow:

OBSCURE: He must counsel all employees who participate in sports and also go on recruiting trips throughout the Southwest.

CLEAR: He must counsel all employees who participate in sports and *must* also go on recruiting trips throughout the Southwest.

OBSCURE: The instructor wants to meet those students who enjoy barbershop harmony and organize several quartets.

CLEAR: The instructor wants to meet those students who enjoy barbershop harmony and *to* organize several quartets.

OBSCURE: He thought that economic conditions were improving and the company was planning to increase its dividend rate.

CLEAR: He thought that economic conditions were improving and *that* the company was planning to increase its dividend rate.

■ 16d *Than* and *As* in Parallel Constructions

Than and *as* are frequently used to join parallel constructions. When these two connectives introduce comparisons, you must be sure that the things compared are similar. Don't compare, for instance, a janitor's salary with a teacher. Compare a janitor's salary with a teacher's salary:

INCORRECT: A janitor's salary is frequently larger than a teacher.

CORRECT: ‖ A janitor's salary is frequently larger
          than ‖ a teacher's (salary).

■ 16e Incorrect Omission of Necessary Words

A very common kind of faulty parallelism is seen in the following sentence:

> I always have and always will *remember* to send my first-grade teacher a Christmas card.

In this sentence *remember* is correctly used after *will*, but after *have* the form needed is *remembered*. Consequently, *remember* cannot serve as the understood participle after *have:*

CORRECT: I ‖ always have *remembered*
           and ‖ always will remember   to send my first-grade teacher
              ‖ a Christmas card.

Other sentences containing similar errors are given below:

INCORRECT: I *was* mildly surprised, but all of my friends gravely shocked. [After *all of my friends* the incorrect verb form *was* seems to be understood.]

CORRECT: I was mildly surprised, but all of my friends *were* gravely shocked.

INCORRECT: He gave me an apple and pear. [Before *pear* the incorrect form *an* seems to be understood.]

CORRECT: He gave me an apple and *a* pear.

INCORRECT: I was interested and astounded *by* the story of his latest adventure.

CORRECT: I was ‖ interested *in*
           and ‖ astounded by   the story of his latest adventure.

INCORRECT: She is as tall if not taller *than* her sister.

CORRECT: She is as tall *as* her sister, if not taller. [The reader understands *than her sister.*]

ALSO CORRECT: She is as tall *as,* if not taller than, her sister.

■ 16f Correct Use of "Unparallel" Constructions

A caution should be added to this lesson. Parallelism of phraseology is not always possible. When it is not, do not hesitate to use natural, "unparallel" constructions:

CORRECT THOUGH "UNPARALLEL": He spoke *slowly* and *with dignity.*

Here *slowly* and *with dignity* are parallel in a sense: they are both adverbial modifiers.

Exercise 61   Parallelism

Rewrite in correct form all sentences that contain faulty parallelism. Note that some sentences may be corrected in more than one way. Write **C** if a sentence is correct.

Example: Lee has sent résumés both to interior design firms in San Francisco and in Los Angeles.

Lee has sent résumés to interior design firms in both San Francisco and Los Angeles.

1. The boys stood in line, bought their tickets, and then they headed straight for the concession stand.

2. The flavor of the Dutch chocolate yogurt is better than the white chocolate.

3. Stuffed in the overhead compartment were a carry-on bag, briefcase, and two garment bags.

4. The sun was shining, the sky was blue, but thunder rumbled in the distance.

5. Of course pollution of the food chain not only is a threat to wildlife but also to human beings.

6. The historical society will open the restored courthouse on weekends for those who wish to see the exhibits and make it available for community meetings during the week.

7. No one's enthusiasm can match Sandy.

8. I neither know what kind of coffee he likes nor where one might buy it.

9. Clearly qualified for the job, she was competent, diligent, and she knew her way around the organization.

10. We always have and always will support your efforts to invent a perpetual-motion machine.

11. Jamie hoped to fly to Columbus and that she could rent a car to use while she was there.

12. Mr. Candler, I can assure you that my brother and I are grateful and almost overwhelmed by your offer of jobs in Alaska.

13. This summer is as hot, if not hotter than, any I remember since moving here in 1985.

14. My friend can tutor students who need English as a second language and lead orientation sessions for foreign students.

15. I am hot, tired, and I wish I had something to drink.

16. We want to have a vegetable garden, but we don't know when to begin, how to proceed, or the vegetables we should plant.

17. The town is quite excited but somewhat overawed by the news that the President will stop for lunch at Wesley's Diner.

18. The senator congratulated Mr. Goodwin for his analysis of the issues facing the state and Mrs. Laurel for organizing the meeting.

19. Pete wanted to see one of the *Star Trek* movies again, but the rest of us in favor of finding something new.

20. Green River is a mall flooded with light and which consequently has an air of spaciousness.

Exercise 62   Parallelism

Complete each of the following sentences by adding a construction that is parallel to the *italicized* construction.

Example: When he was a child, his lunchbox always contained fruit: *a*

banana, an apple, or ***an orange.*** _____

1. I was neither *for painting the walls bright pink* nor _____

   _____

2. Ed's idea was *to get up early, to stop at a fast-food restaurant for breakfast,* and

   _____

3. Even though I have thought about cleaning out the storage closet, I dread

   having to decide *what to keep, what to give away,* and _____

   _____

4. Eric found what he needed in the glove compartment: *a flashlight, a map,*

   and _____

   _____

5. The square was crowded with young tourists *studying their guidebooks, eating*

   lunches from their knapsacks, or _____

   _____

6. We looked for a café where we could *discuss tomorrow's sales meeting* and

   _____

   _____

7. Not only *did the building contain an auditorium for plays and concerts,* but also

   _____

   _____

8. After much deliberation all of us agreed that we either had to *paint the fence*

   or _____

   _____

9. Throckmorton's bright new subcompact car was *snug* but _____

   _____

10. *I am amazed at the number of mail-order catalogs I receive;* furthermore, _____

    _____

17

Subordination

Parallelism enables you to indicate equality of ideas. More often, however, your writing will include sentences in which some ideas are more important than others. The main device for showing the difference between major and minor emphasis is **subordination:** reserve the independent clause for the main idea and use dependent clauses, phrases, and single words to convey subordinate ideas:

> In our garden there is a birdbath *that is carved from marble.* [Subordinate idea placed in a dependent clause.]
>
> In our garden there is a birdbath *carved from marble.* [Subordinate idea reduced to a participial phrase.]
>
> In our garden there is a *marble* birdbath. [Subordinate idea reduced to a one-word modifier.]

■ 17a Primer Style

It is necessary to understand the principle of subordination, for without subordination you would be unable to indicate the relative importance of ideas or their various shades of emphasis in your thinking. The following group of sentences is both childish and monotonous because six dissimilar ideas have been presented in six simple sentences and thus appear to be of equal importance:

> A pep meeting was held last Friday night. Memorial Stadium was the scene of the meeting. The meeting was attended by thousands of students. Over a hundred faculty members were there too. It rained Friday night. There was also some sleet.

As you know, coordinating conjunctions are used to join ideas of equal importance; consequently, the six sentences given above would not be improved if
they were joined by such conjunctions. As a matter of fact, a type of sentence
that you should avoid is the long, stringy one tied together by *and, but, so,* or
and so. Instead of using this kind of sentence, weigh the relative importance of
your several ideas, and show their importance by the use of main and subordinate sentence elements. Notice how the six ideas can be merged into one clear
sentence:

> Despite rain and some sleet the pep meeting held last Friday night at Memorial
> Stadium was attended by thousands of students and over a hundred faculty
> members.

In combining the six sentences, the writer has chosen to use the fact about
student and faculty attendance as the main idea. Another writer might have
chosen otherwise, for there will not always be complete agreement as to which
idea can be singled out and considered the most important. You may be sure,
however, that if your sentence reads with emphasis and effectiveness you have
chosen a correct idea as the main one.

■ 17b Upside-down Subordination

When there are only two ideas of unequal rank to be considered, you should
have no difficulty in selecting the more important one:

1. He showed some signs of fatigue.
2. He easily won the National Open Golf Tournament.

Of these two sentences the second is undoubtedly the more important. Hence,
when the two sentences are combined, the second should stand as the independent clause, and the first should be reduced to a dependent clause or even a
phrase. If you made an independent clause of the first sentence and a subordinate
element of the second, your sentence would contain upside-down subordination:

> FAULTY (upside-down subordination): Though he easily won the National Open Golf
> Tournament, he showed some signs of fatigue.

> CORRECT: Though he showed some signs of fatigue, he easily won the National Open
> Golf Tournament.

■ 17c Choice of Subordinating Conjunctions

In introducing a subordinate element, be sure that you choose the right subordinating conjunction. The following sentences illustrate the correct use of certain
conjunctions:

I don't know *whether* (or *that;* not *as* or *if*) I can see you tomorrow.

Although (not *while*) she isn't a genius, she has undeniable talent.

I saw in the autobiography of the actor *that* (not *where*) there is a question about the exact date of his birth.

(See Glossary of Faulty Diction in Chapter 22 for further discussion of accurate word choice.)

Exercise 63 Subordination

Combine the ideas in the following groups of sentences into one effective simple or complex sentence.

Example: Ho Chi Minh City is the largest city in Vietnam.
It has a population of approximately four million people.
It was formerly known as Saigon.

With a population of approximately four million people, Ho Chi Minh City, formerly known as Saigon, is the largest city in Vietnam.

1. *The World Almanac and Book of Facts* has been in publication since 1868.
It contains an enormous amount of detailed information.
There one can find everything from a list of common abbreviations to a summary of Zoroaster's teachings.

2. *Hippies* is a word first used to denote some young Americans of the 1960's.
They often rejected society's traditional sources of authority.
Above everything they prized individual expression in thought and behavior.

3. Tara's Hall was located in County Meath, Ireland.
Here the High Kings of early Irish history delivered proclamations and judged disputes.
The High Kings also enjoyed the entertainment of bards.

4. Sisters in Crime is an organization that promotes the works of women mystery writers.
   It is also known by the acronym SinC.
   It was founded in 1987.
   Sara Paretsky spearheaded its creation.

5. Circe is a sorceress in Greek mythology.
   In Homer's *Odyssey* she turns some of Odysseus' companions into swine.
   Her spell was broken by Odysseus with the help of Hermes.

6. Bill Mauldin was a cartoonist.
   During World War II he served with the 45th Infantry Division.
   He was awarded a Pulitzer Prize for his series of cartoons titled "Up Front with Mauldin."

7. Mauldin's most memorable characters were two infantrymen named Willie and Joe.
   Willie and Joe had keen insights into the foibles of their superiors and of their peers.

8. In 1990 Octavio Paz won the Nobel Prize in literature.
   He is recognized as a poet and an essayist.
   His work reflects a deep interest in his native Mexico.

9. Sacajawea was a Shoshone woman who served as a guide and an interpreter. Along with her husband she accompanied Lewis and Clark in the exploration of the Northwest.
   They remained with the group from 1804 until 1806.

Exercise 64 Subordination

Combine the ideas in each of the following groups of sentences into one effective simple or complex sentence.

Example: My brother and sister are ardent fans of "The Far Side" cartoons. They declare that they always get cartoonist Gary Larson's point. However, I am still not sure that they do.

Ardent fans of "The Far Side" cartoons, my brother and sister declare that they always get cartoonist Gary Larson's point, though I'm still not sure that they do.

1. Henri Matisse is now recognized as a gifted painter.
   He was born in Le Cateau, France, in 1869.
   Today in Le Cateau one may visit the Matisse Museum in the town hall.

2. In November, 1992, a retrospective exhibit of Matisse's work opened at the Museum of Modern Art.
   The Museum of Modern Art is a famous gallery in New York.
   More than three hundred of the artist's paintings were on display.

3. Long lines of people waited to see Matisse's paintings.
   According to the *New York Times*, about 900,000 people attended the exhibit.
   The exhibition closed in January, 1993.

4. The history of women's fashions is marked by constant change.
   One season women may favor tailored pantsuits.
   The next season they may prefer brief miniskirts.

5. The name Charles Babbage is noteworthy in the history of computer technology.
   His calculating machines were early forerunners of modern computers.
   Babbage was an English mathematician who lived from 1792 to 1871.

6. Augusta Ada was the child of Lord Byron.
   She was the first programmer for one of Babbage's machines.
   The high-level computer language Ada is named for her.

7. My sister's favorite reading is science fiction, and mine is fantasy.
   There is a difference between the two.
   Science fiction is set in a world that might be, fantasy in one that can never be.

8. I worked at our library's annual used-book sale.
   I came across three copies of *The Rubáiyát of Omar Khayyám*.
   The author, Omar Khayyám, was a Persian mathematician, an astronomer, and a poet.

9. *The Rubáiyát* is a book of poetry on the mysteries of life.
   It was freely translated into English by Edward FitzGerald.
   The translation beautifully preserves the spirit of the original.

Exercise 65   Subordination

The following sentences contain upside-down subordination or too much coordination. Rewrite each sentence to make it an effective simple or complex sentence.

Example: It's pouring rain, and I've left my umbrella in the car, and I hope that Dan will lend me his.

Because it's pouring rain and I've left my umbrella in the car, I hope that Dan will lend me his.

1. Mary and I graduated in June, and we found jobs in Charlotte, and we decided to share an apartment off Sugar Creek Road.

2. Courageously rescuing the beautiful maiden trapped on the railroad tracks, the hero was applauded by the audience.

3. Jim left the office early, and he caught a taxi to the Fourteenth Street station, and he met Lisa at the newsstand.

4. Before throwing his full weight against the door, the sheriff had found it locked.

5. Making his way down the aisle and up the stairs to the stage, the winner of the Oscar grinned broadly.

6. The water had begun to boil, and I had opened the package of spaghetti, and I suddenly remembered that I had forgotten to reheat the sauce.

7. Before describing the complexities of the economic situation within the European Community, the visiting lecturer paused to take a drink of water.

8. Late that afternoon it began raining, and the temperature dropped during the night, and we woke up to a world covered with ice.

9. Waiting for the sun to rise out of the dark ocean, the photographer carefully set up his camera.

10. While stripping the iron bed of a thick coat of white enamel, Max whistled cheerily.

Exercise 66   Subordination

The following sentences contain upside-down subordination or too much coordination. Rewrite each sentence to make it an effective simple or complex sentence.

Example: It's just a week before Christmas, and I have packages to wrap, but I must address the rest of my cards first.

Even though it's just a week before Christmas and I have packages to wrap, I must address the rest of my cards first.

1. When the huge new map of Africa had been hung on the far wall in the seminar room, we gathered to admire it.

2. While thanking the editor for the kind words with which he had received her feature story, Janice tried to hide her surprise.

3. It was Saturday morning, and the fast-food restaurant on the corner was crowded, and Bob had to wait in line for almost ten minutes to order his sausage biscuit.

4. George read the newspaper regularly, but he did not find his job with the airline in the want ads, but he found it through a friend.

5. New Year's Day was bright and beautiful, and Terry and I decided to load up our bikes, and we headed for the trails in the hill country.

6. Acknowledging his no-hitter his last time out, the cheering crowd stood as Steve walked to the mound.

7. As the boatman steered the raft toward the churning rapids, he cautioned his passengers.

8. Yesterday a young man sat next to me on the train, and he told me more than I wanted to know about professional wrestling, and he simply would not let me enjoy my usual nap.

9. As confident and accomplished a skater as we had ever seen, the young man had begun performing in public as a child.

10. I needed to be on time for my dental appointment, and I had gotten a late start, but fortunately traffic was unusually light on the freeway.

18

Illogical Comparisons and Mixed Constructions

Correctness and clarity are essential to good writing. To reach these goals, you must know the rules of grammar and punctuation. But further, you must think logically and find the exact words in which to express your thoughts. Nothing is more bothersome to a reader than inexact, illogical, or confusing sentences. Some of the lessons that you have already studied have shown how to avoid errors that produce vagueness or confusion in writing; among these errors are faulty reference of pronouns, dangling or misplaced modifiers, and upside-down subordination. This lesson will consider certain other errors that obstruct clarity of expression.

■ 18a Illogical Comparisons

When you make comparisons, you must be sure not only that the things compared are similar (a matter considered in the lesson on parallelism) but also that all necessary elements of the comparison are included.

Note the following sentence:

Harold is taller than any boy in his class.

Since *Harold*, the first term of the comparison, is included in the classification *any boy in his class*, the comparison is obviously illogical: the sentence might be interpreted to mean *Harold is taller than Harold*. The first term of the comparison must, therefore, be compared with a second term or classification that excludes the first term, thus:

CORRECT: Harold is taller than any *other* boy in his class.

ALSO CORRECT: Harold is taller than any *girl* in his class.

When the superlative is followed by *of,* the object of *of* must be plural:

> ILLOGICAL: Harold is the tallest of any other boy in his class.
>
> CORRECT: Harold is the tallest of *all the boys* in his class.
>
> ALSO CORRECT: Harold is the *tallest boy* in his class.

Ambiguity results from a comparison like this one:

> I helped you more than Jim.

Does the sentence mean *I helped you more than I helped Jim* or *I helped you more than Jim did*? The writer should use one sentence or the other, according to whichever meaning is intended.

The type of incomplete comparison illustrated by the following vague sentences is particularly popular with writers of advertising copy and with careless speakers:

> VAGUE: Eastern Rubber Company makes a tire that gives 20 percent more mileage.
>
> CLEAR: Eastern Rubber Company makes a tire that gives 20 percent more mileage *than any tire it made ten years ago.*
>
> ALSO CLEAR: Eastern Rubber Company makes a tire that gives 20 percent more mileage *than any other tire made in the United States.*
>
> VAGUE: Litter is more of a problem in cities.
>
> CLEAR: Litter is more of a problem in cities *than in small towns.*
>
> ALSO CLEAR: Litter is more of a problem in cities *than it used to be.*

■ 18b Mixed or Confused Constructions

Mixed constructions are frequently the result of some sort of shift in a sentence. Through ignorance or forgetfulness the writer starts a sentence with one type of construction and then switches to another. Notice the shift of construction in the following sentence:

> She bought an old, dilapidated house, which having it extensively repaired converted it into a comfortable home.

The sentence reads correctly through the relative pronoun *which.* The reader expects *which* to introduce an adjective clause, but is unable to find a verb for *which.* Instead, the reader finds that the sentence is completed by a construction in which a gerund phrase stands as the subject of the verb *converted.* The sentence may be corrected in various ways. Two correct versions follow:

> She bought an old, dilapidated house, which after extensive repairs was converted into a comfortable home.
>
> By means of extensive repairs she converted an old, dilapidated house that she had bought into a comfortable home.

Other examples of mixed constructions are given below:

MIXED: Bob realized that during the conference how inattentive he had been. [This sentence is confusing because *that* as used here is a subordinating conjunction and should introduce a noun clause. However, the *that*-construction is left incomplete. Further on, *how* introduces a noun clause. What we find then is only one noun clause but two words, *that* and *how*, used to introduce noun clauses. Obviously, only one such word should introduce the one dependent clause.]

CORRECT: Bob realized that during the conference he had been inattentive.

ALSO CORRECT: Bob realized how inattentive he had been during the conference.

MIXED: Because she had to work in the library kept her from attending the party. [A dependent clause introduced by *because* is always adverbial; hence such a clause can never be used as the subject of a sentence.]

CORRECT: Having to work in the library kept her from attending the party.

ALSO CORRECT: Because she had to work in the library, she could not attend the party.

MIXED: He pulled a leg muscle was why he failed to place in the broad jump. [He *pulled a leg muscle* is an independent clause used here as the subject of *was*. An independent clause, unless it is a quotation, can never be used as the subject of a sentence.]

CORRECT: Because he pulled a leg muscle, he failed to place in the broad jump.

MIXED: By attending the reception as a guest rather than as a butler was a new experience for him. [The preposition *by* introduces a modifying phrase, and a modifying phrase can never be used as the subject of a sentence.]

CORRECT: Attending the reception as a guest rather than as a butler was a new experience for him.

ALSO CORRECT: By attending the reception as a guest rather than as a butler, he enjoyed a new experience.

MIXED: A pronoun is when a word is used in the place of a noun. [Never use *is when* or *is where* in defining a word. Remember that an adverbial *when-* or *where*-clause cannot be used as a predicate nominative.]

CORRECT: A pronoun is a word used in the place of a noun.

MIXED: I was the one about whom she was whispering to my father about. [To correct this sentence, omit either *about*.]

MIXED: We know that if he were interested in our offer that he would come to see us. [To correct this sentence, omit the second *that*. The first *that* introduces the noun clause *that . . . he would come to see us. If he were interested in our offer* is an adverbial clause within the noun clause.]

MIXED: The reason I didn't play well at the recital was because I had sprained my little finger. [This very common error again illustrates the incorrect use of a dependent adverbial clause, introduced by *because*, as a predicate nominative. To correct the mistake, use a noun clause, introduced by *that*.]

CORRECT: The reason I didn't play well at the recital was that I had sprained my little finger.

Exercise 67   Illogical Comparisons and Mixed Constructions

The following sentences contain illogical or ambiguous comparisons or mixed constructions. Rewrite each sentence in a correct form. (Notice that some sentences permit more than one correct interpretation.)

Example: After I hurt my leg was when I decided to drop out of our softball team.

After I hurt my leg, I decided to drop out of our softball team.

1. Margaret Ann is much the most sympathetic of my two cousins.

2. Anxiety is when one is uneasy or distressed about future uncertainties.

3. Mr. Edwards says that his homegrown tomatoes are better than Mr. Austin.

4. The reason that I am happy is because I have won a scholarship to Georgetown University.

5. I cannot believe that Ted thinks Harry is the strongest of any other boy on the wrestling team.

6. Maria's lasagna is delicious because by using her grandmother's recipe is how she learned to make it.

7. Grindelwald, Switzerland, is a beautiful village, which by being high in the Alps, it has snow on the mountaintops even in summer.

8. I am aware that Robin trusts you more than Laura.

9. Eudora Welty's short stories, about which we were talking about yesterday, are mostly set in the South.

10. Of the three contestants on the "Jeopardy" College Tournament, the one who can press the button faster has a big advantage.

11. The meteorologist said that if we have another six inches of rain this summer, that we will no longer have a rainfall deficit.

12. It looks as though the Atlanta Braves are going to have a better year.

13. Because our pine trees have been infested with beetles is why so many of the trees are dying.

14. John and Helen found that after six years how hard it was to locate the path that led to the waterfall.

15. Marcia wore a red linen dress to the party, and she looked the prettiest of any other girl there.

16. Because he had been wasting his money and forgetting to make regular bank deposits was the reason why Jack couldn't keep up his car payments.

17. The inconsistencies in his story about a shifty-eyed man were how the real thief gave himself away.

18. Once the bell had rung for classes to begin was when Tim sauntered into the room.

19. Jo has a better accent than any member of her French class.

20. The discount store at the mall advertises that it has cheaper prices.

21. We found an arrowhead on our mountain property, and trying to learn its history was when an old man told us that a Cherokee trading post had once been in the area.

22. A pinch hitter in baseball is when someone bats in place of the scheduled batter, especially when a run is badly needed.

23. I keep telling Ray that my brand of toothpaste is better, but he will not listen.

24. Mother thinks that Jenny's hair is the same color as Aunt Gloria.

25. Yesterday I drove to Columbus, which, driving at the legal speed limit, I reached there by dark.

Punctuation

Punctuation depends largely upon the grammatical structure of a sentence. In order to punctuate correctly, you must therefore understand grammatical elements. For this reason, rules of punctuation in this text have been correlated, whenever applicable, with your study of grammar and sentence structure. You learned, for instance, how to punctuate certain phrases when you studied the phrase as a sentence unit.

In order that this chapter may present a reasonably complete treatment of punctuation, you will find on the pages that follow a summary of the rules already studied, as well as reference by chapter to additional rules. The rules given below have become to a large extent standardized; hence they should be clearly understood and practiced. Following the principle of punctuating "by ear" or of using a comma wherever there is a vocal pause results in an arbitrary and frequently misleading use of punctuation.

■ 19a Terminal Marks

The terminal marks of punctuation — that is, those marks used to end a sentence — are the period, the question mark, and the exclamation mark.

Use a period after a declarative sentence, an imperative sentence, or an indirect question:

DECLARATIVE: John answered the telephone.

IMPERATIVE: Answer the telephone.

INDIRECT QUESTION: She asked whether John had answered the telephone.

Note: A request that is stated as a polite question should be followed by a period. Such a request frequently occurs in business correspondence:

Will you please send me your special summer catalog.

Use a period also after most abbreviations:

Mr., Ms., Dr., B.S., Jr., i.e., viz., etc., A.D., B.C., A.M., P.M.

Use three periods to indicate an omission of a word or words within a quoted sentence, three periods plus a terminal mark to indicate an omission at the end of a quoted sentence:

"Fourscore and seven years ago our fathers brought forth . . . a new nation . . . ."

Use a question mark after a direct question:

Did John answer the telephone?

"Have you finished your work?" she asked.

Use an exclamation mark after an expression of strong feeling. This mark of punctuation should be used sparingly:

"Halt!" he shouted.

How disgusting!

There goes the fox!

19b The Comma

1. Use a comma to separate independent clauses when they are joined by the coordinating conjunctions *and, but, or, nor, for, so,* and *yet.* (See Chapter 5.)

The game was over, but the crowd refused to leave the park.

If the clauses are long or are complicated by internal punctuation, use a semicolon instead of a comma. (See 19c, Rule 3.)

2. Use a comma to separate words, phrases, and clauses written as a series of three or more coordinate elements. This rule covers short independent clauses when used in a series, as shown in the third example sentence below.

A trio composed of Marie, Ellen, and Frances sang at the party.

Jack walked into my office, took off his hat, and sat down.

I washed the dishes, I dried them, and I put them away.

3. Use a comma to separate two or more coordinate adjectives that modify the same noun:

The noisy, enthusiastic freshman class assembled in Section F of the stadium. [*Noisy* and *enthusiastic* are coordinate adjectives; therefore they are separated by a comma.

But *freshman,* though an adjective, is not coordinate with *noisy* and *enthusiastic;* actually *noisy* and *enthusiastic* modify not just *class* but the word group *freshman class.* Hence no comma precedes *freshman.*]

To determine whether adjectives are coordinate, you may make two tests: if they are coordinate, you will be able (1) to join them with *and* or (2) to interchange their positions in the sentence. You can certainly say *the noisy and enthusiastic freshman class* or *the enthusiastic, noisy freshman class;* thus *noisy* and *enthusiastic* are clearly coordinate. However, to say *the noisy and freshman class* or *the freshman noisy class* would be absurd; thus *freshman* is not structurally parallel with *noisy:*

a blue wool suit [Adjectives not coordinate.]

an expensive, well-tailored suit [Adjectives coordinate.]

a new tennis court [Adjectives not coordinate.]

a muddy, rough court [Adjectives coordinate.]

4. Use a comma to separate sharply contrasted coordinate elements:

He was merely ignorant, not stupid.

5. Use commas to set off all nonessential modifiers. Do not set off essential modifiers. (See Chapter 4 for a discussion of essential and nonessential phrases; see Chapter 6 for a discussion of essential and nonessential clauses.)

NONESSENTIAL CLAUSE: Sara Sessions, *who is wearing red shorts today,* was voted the most versatile girl in her class.

NONESSENTIAL PHRASE: Sara Sessions, *wearing red shorts today,* was voted the most versatile girl in her class.

ESSENTIAL CLAUSE: The girl *who is wearing red shorts today* is Sara Sessions.

ESSENTIAL PHRASE: The girl *wearing red shorts today* is Sara Sessions.

6. Use a comma after an introductory adverbial clause, verbal phrase, or absolute phrase. (See Chapter 6 for a discussion of dependent clauses, Chapter 4 for a discussion of phrases.)

INTRODUCTORY ADVERBIAL CLAUSE: *When he arose to give his speech,* he was greeted with thunderous applause.

INTRODUCTORY PARTICIPIAL PHRASE: *Being in a hurry,* I was able to see him only briefly.

INTRODUCTORY GERUND PHRASE: *On turning the corner,* Tom ran squarely into a police officer.

INTRODUCTORY INFINITIVE PHRASE: *To get a seat,* we have to arrive by 7:30 P.M.

INTRODUCTORY ABSOLUTE PHRASE: *My schedule having been arranged,* I felt like a full-fledged college freshman.

7. Use commas to set off nonessential appositives. (See Chapter 4.)

Tom, *the captain of the team*, was injured in the first game of the season.

Sometimes an appositive is so closely "fused" with its preceding word that it constitutes an essential element in the sentence and thus is not set off by commas:

William *the Conqueror* died in 1087.

The poet *Keats* spent his last days in Italy.

The word *bonfire* has an interesting history.

8. Use commas to set off items in dates, geographical names, and addresses and to set off titles after names:

July 22, 1977, was a momentous day in his life.

Birmingham, Alabama, gets its name from Birmingham, England.

Do you know who lives at 1600 Pennsylvania Avenue, Washington, D.C.?

Alfred E. Timberlake, Ph.D., will be the principal speaker.

9. Use commas to set off words used in direct address:

It is up to you, *Dot*, to push the campaign.

I think, *sir*, that I am correct.

You, *my fellow Americans*, must aid in the fight against inflation.

10. Use a comma after a mild interjection and after *yes* and *no:*

Oh, I suppose you're right.

Yes, I will be glad to go.

11. Use a comma to separate an independent clause from a question dependent on the clause:

You will try to do the work, won't you?

12. Use commas to set off expressions like *he said* or *she replied* when they interrupt a sentence of direct quotation. (But see Rule 1 under The Semicolon, below.)

"I was able," *she replied*, "to build the bookcase in less than an hour."

13. Use commas to set off certain parenthetical elements:

I was, *however*, too tired to make the trip.

My hopes, *to tell the truth*, had fallen to a low ebb.

14. Use a comma to prevent the misreading of a sentence:

Above, the mountains rose like purple shadows.

To John, Harrison had been a sort of idol.

19c The Semicolon

1. Use a semicolon to separate independent clauses when they are not joined by *and, but, or, nor, for, so,* or *yet.* (See Chapter 5.)

> Wade held the ball for an instant; then he passed it to West.
>
> "He is sick," she said; "therefore, he will not come."

2. Use a semicolon to separate coordinate elements that are joined by a coordinating conjunction but that are internally punctuated:

> His tour included concert appearances in Austin, Texas; Little Rock, Arkansas; Tulsa, Oklahoma; and Kansas City, Kansas.

3. Use a semicolon to punctuate independent clauses that are joined by a coordinating conjunction in sentences that are heavily punctuated with commas internally:

> Having invited Sara, Susan, and Leon to my party, I began, at long last, to plan the menu; but I could not decide on a dessert.

19d The Colon

1. Use a colon after a clause that introduces a formal list. Do not use a colon unless the words preceding the list form a complete statement:

> INCORRECT: The poets I like best are: Housman, Yeats, and Eliot.
>
> CORRECT: The poets I like best are these: Housman, Yeats, and Eliot.
>
> ALSO CORRECT: The poets I like best are Housman, Yeats, and Eliot.
>
> INCORRECT: The basket was filled with: apples, oranges, and bananas.
>
> CORRECT: The basket was filled with the following fruits: apples, oranges, and bananas.
>
> ALSO CORRECT: The basket was filled with apples, oranges, and bananas.

2. Use a colon after a statement that introduces an explanation or amplification of that statement:

> One characteristic accounted for his success: complete honesty. [A dash, which is less formal than the colon, may be substituted for the colon in this sentence.]
>
> There was only one way to solve the mystery: we had to find the missing letter.

3. Use a colon after expressions like *he said* when they introduce a long and formal quotation:

> The speaker rose to his feet and said: "Students and teachers, I wish to call your attention to . . . ."

4. Use a colon after the formal salutation of a letter, between the hour and minute figures in time designations, between a chapter and verse reference from the Bible, and between a title and subtitle:

Dear Sir:

8:40 P.M.

John 3:16

Victorian England: Portrait of an Age

■ 19e The Dash

1. Use a dash to indicate an abrupt shift or break in the thought of a sentence or to set off an informal or emphatic parenthesis:

Harvey decided to go to — but you wouldn't be interested in that story.

Mary told me — would you believe it? — that she preferred a quiet vacation at home.

At the age of three — such is the power of youth — Judy could stand on her head.

2. Use dashes to set off an appositive or a parenthetical element that is internally punctuated:

Her roommates — Jane, Laura, and Ruth — are spending the weekend with her.

■ 19f Quotation Marks

1. Use quotation marks to enclose direct quotations, but do not use them to enclose indirect quotations:

INCORRECT: He said that "I was old enough to know better."

CORRECT: He said, "You are old enough to know better."

ALSO CORRECT: He said that I was old enough to know better.

If a direct quotation is interrupted by an expression like *he said,* use quotation marks to enclose only the quoted material. This necessitates the use of two sets of quotation marks:

INCORRECT: "It's just possible, Mary responded, that I'll get up before six in the morning."

CORRECT: "It's just possible," Mary responded, "that I'll get up before six in the morning."

If there are two or more consecutive sentences of quoted material, use only one set of quotation marks to enclose all the sentences, not one set for each sentence:

INCORRECT: Ruby shouted, "Wait for me." "I'll be ready in two minutes."

CORRECT: Ruby shouted, "Wait for me. I'll be ready in two minutes."

Use single marks to enclose a quotation within a quotation:

The instructor asked, "Who said, 'Change the name of Arkansas? Never!'?"

Place the comma and the period inside the quotation marks, the semicolon and colon outside. Place the question mark and exclamation mark inside the quotation marks when they apply to the quoted material, outside when they apply to the entire sentence:

"Of course," he replied, "I remember you." [Comma and period inside the quotation marks.]

Her favorite poem was Kipling's "If."

Several times the witness said, "I swear to the truth of my statement"; yet the jury remained unconvinced. [Semicolon outside the quotation marks.]

He asked, "Where are you going?" [The question mark comes within the quotation marks because only the quoted material is a question.]

Did she definitely say, "I accept your invitation"? [The question mark comes outside the quotation marks because the entire sentence is a question.]

2. Use quotation marks to enclose the titles of short works (short stories, short poems, articles, one-act plays, songs, speeches, and television programs) and of smaller units of books. (See Rule 3 under Italics, Chapter 20, Section b.)

Benét's story "The Devil and Daniel Webster" was first published in the *Saturday Evening Post*.

The kindergarten children sang "America" for us.

"Who Will Be the New Bishop?" is the title of the first chapter of *Barchester Towers*.

3. Use quotation marks to enclose words taken from special vocabularies or used in a special sense:

All the money he had won on the quiz program was invested in "blue chips."

In certain sections of the United States a man who is both honest and good-natured is known as a "clever man."

■ 19g Parentheses

Use parentheses to enclose certain parenthetical elements. From a study of the preceding marks of punctuation you will remember that commas and dashes are also used to set off parenthetical material. There are no clearly defined rules by which you can always determine which marks to use. In general, however, commas are used to set off a parenthetical element that is fairly closely connected with the thought of the sentence. Dashes are used to set off a loosely connected element such as an abrupt break in the thought of the sentence; they tend to emphasize the element set off. Parentheses are used to enclose (1) material that is supplementary or explanatory and (2) figures repeated to ensure accuracy or used to designate an enumeration. An element enclosed by parentheses is usually even more loosely connected with the sentence than one set off by dashes; and parentheses, unlike dashes, tend to minimize the element set off:

> The *Ville de Nantes* (see Plate 5) is a large, semidouble, red and white camellia.
>
> I am enclosing a check for thirty-five dollars ($35.00).
>
> Please write on the card (1) your full name, (2) your home address, and (3) a parent's or guardian's full name.

■ 19h Brackets

Use brackets to enclose any interpolation, or insertion, that you add to material being quoted. (You will note that in this text brackets are used to enclose explanations that follow illustrative sentences.)

> In September, 1793, Robert Burns wrote a letter that included this sentence: "So may God ever defend the cause of truth and liberty as he did that day [the day of Bruce's victory over Edward II at Bannockburn]."

If one parenthetical expression falls within another, then brackets replace the inner parentheses:

> Thomas Turner, a member of the class of 1991 (Mr. Turner was his class valedictorian [See Athens *Banner-Herald* story, May 16, 1991] and class president), has been named a Rhodes scholar.

Exercise 68   The Comma

In the following sentences insert commas wherever they are needed or remove them if they are not needed, replacing them with other marks of punctuation when necessary. If a sentence is correctly punctuated, mark it **C**.

Example: While I was having my breakfast I watched the birds at the feeder outside the window.

While I was having my breakfast, I watched the birds at the feeder outside the window.

1. Although I was not really hungry, the aroma of the spice cake Amanda was baking certainly made my mouth water.

2. Our eldest brother, Frank, plans to study architecture at the University of Florida.

3. Sonia's becoming, pink taffeta dress was the envy of all the other girls at the party.

4. "My, how you have grown," Mrs. Sanford-Bailey told me, as she had every year since I was six years old.

5. From the plane window we could see the distant mountains; below, the river looked like a long, twisting snake.

6. Memphis, Tennessee, is the location of Elvis Presley's famous mansion, Graceland.

7. It is you, Doris, who can take credit for the success of our science project.

8. The tremendous oak tree, that stands at the corner of First Avenue and Brandon Drive, was split down the length of its trunk in last night's lightning storm.

9. It is laziness, not lack of intelligence, that causes Joe to do poorly in college.

10. Hoping to escape his father's embarrassing questions, Fred decided to leave early for work.

11. The word *cryptogram* is derived from the Greek word *kruptos,* meaning *hidden;* a cryptogram is something written in code or cipher.

12. We enjoyed seeing a manatee come up to our dock on the river; the poor thing had scars on its back from encounters with motorboats.

13. Florence said, that she and David plan to hike the entire length of the Appalachian Trail this summer.

14. The Appalachian Trail begins in Georgia at Springer Mountain, and ends in Maine at Mount Katahdin.

15. The defiant, screaming mob seemed determined to break down the door if Mr. Smith refused to come outside.

16. Miriam, I hear that you are going to the meeting tonight; I would like to ride with you.

17. The woman, wearing the gray slacks, is my history professor.

18. My father was born in New Orleans, Louisiana in 1942. C

19. When it was time for him to select a college he had trouble deciding between Tulane and Louisiana State University.

20. I was amazed by Kitty's unhappy appearance for I did not know that she had just received bad news.

21. Kitty's bad news was, that she had failed her chemistry final.

22. When we had finished giving the dog its bath Ed and I were soaking wet and thoroughly exhausted.

23. After all, it's not easy to wrestle with an English sheep-dog, that wants no part of the washing process.

24. In order to be sure that we would have seats we arrived for the basketball game an hour before starting time.

25. On entering the house Mrs. Bartholomew heard a faint moaning sound from the upstairs.

26. She immediately whirled slammed the door behind her and went racing down the front steps.

27. Mrs. Bartholomew as she frankly told us later had been frightened out of her wits.

28. "I was certain " she exclaimed "that that dilapidated old house was the hideout for the wounded burglar we had heard about!"

29. Ivan, the Terrible was a Russian czar during the sixteenth century.

30. Ken is planning to be a counselor at Camp Brevard next summer isn't he?

31. Jo and Marian who were born on the same day are going to have a joint birthday party this year.

32. To make sure that he had all his equipment Tom took everything out of his bag and checked it again.

33. The lonely, old man sat in his easy chair, and watched television all day and most of the night.

34. The dangerously rocking boat was hard to control and it took every ounce of my strength to keep it from capsizing.

35. Angelina whose parents were born in Italy will spend this winter with her grandparents in Venice.

Exercise 69   The Comma

In the following sentences insert commas wherever they are needed or remove them if they are not needed. If a sentence is correctly punctuated, mark it **C**.

Example: We were truly surprised Mary Lou when you and Fred announced your engagement.

We were truly surprised∧ Mary Lou∧ when you and Fred announced your engagement.

1. The Alabama Shakespeare Festival an annual event is held in Montgomery Alabama every summer.

2. Uncle Thad told me that the Latin phrase *habeas corpus* is a term used by the legal profession.

3. Mimi Janet Don and I hiked to the top of Burnt Mountain; we were hot and footsore when we got home.

4. Vicki has been cast as Ophelia in the Town and Gown production of *Hamlet* and she says that she is looking forward to playing the "mad scene."

5. Slamming the door with a loud bang Terry stalked out of the house got into his car and drove away.

6. "Slamming the door was a childish thing to do " said Aunt Sara.

7. Alicia's hat all things considered has too many roses on it.

8. Though I was tired and discouraged the high spirits of my nieces and nephews were a wonderful diversion.

9. Looking east we could see the lovely curve of Crescent Beach, so aptly named, just two hundred yards away.

10. Richard, the Lion-Hearted a famous king of England, was a character in Sir Walter Scott's novel *Ivanhoe*.

11. The word, *camaraderie* has its origin in an Old French word that means "roommate."

12. I stayed indoors, trying to keep cool by running the air conditioner at full speed; outside the patio was blistering hot.

13. Patty, and Michael were swimming in the lake when they heard Frank calling to them from the dock.

14. "It is hard for me " said Oliver "to believe that weird story that Roger told me about his brother's adventures in Tibet."

15. Dr. Frederick told Mrs. Entwistle, that she must lose forty pounds.

16. "Coming from you Dr. Frederick," she said, "that is a strange request."

17. In baseball a rhubarb is a heated quarrel among players on opposing teams sometimes erupting into physical violence.

18. Our Physics 125 professor told us that there would be a midterm test next Wednesday.

19. Judy's hot pink, chiffon dress complemented her dark complexion and black hair.

20. The woman, who is taking tickets at the auditorium door, is my Aunt Gertrude.

21. Lucy Franklin wearing an engagement ring and a big smile is sitting there at the corner table with her fiancé.

22. Seeing Harry come into the room, I went to his table sat down across from him and told him the big news.

23. "I've already heard," Harry said, "that Lucy and Don are engaged, and that you will be the best man at their wedding."

24. Yesterday our outdoor thermometer registered eighteen degrees and I am afraid the cold weather has killed our early-blooming azaleas.

25. I got up at seven, I ate a hurried breakfast, and I jogged for an hour before going to work.

26. Next year I am going to enter art school or I am going to find a job.

27. I hope that I can finish reading my English assignment, before my roommate wants to turn off the light.

28. Theo, you cannot hope to reach Cleveland before dark nor should you try.

29. Having ruined my new shoes by wearing them out in the rain I dejectedly went to the closet, and got out my old loafers.

30. There was not enough time to eat breakfast before catching my bus so I grabbed a stale doughnut and took it with me.

Exercise 70   The Colon and the Dash

In the following sentences insert colons and dashes wherever they are needed or remove them if they are not needed. If a sentence is correctly punctuated, mark it **C**.

Example: Their plane was due to arrive at 6 48 P.M., but it was over an hour late.

Their plane was due to arrive at 6⦂48 P.M., but it was over an hour late.

1. Marty, please be careful with that porcelain vase because it oh, goodness, I spoke too late!

2. Here is Dr. Harriman's suggested list of books I should read this semester *Little Dorrit, The Essays of Elia, The Sun Also Rises,* and *The Sound and the Fury.*

3. The best way to get Henry's attention is to utter these simple words "Let's eat."

4. I believe I see a parking place just to the right of well, now we have passed it.

5. Fred's latest book will probably not have a wide appeal; its title is *Snakes History of a Reptilian Species.*

6. Dot made the announcement that : she will receive her degree in June and will spend next year in France.

7. The woman's basket was so full of vegetables beets, squash, potatoes, corn, and beans that she could hardly carry the load to her car.

8. Bobby declares that his favorite television shows are : "Batman," "Superman," and "The Flintstones."

9. Bobby is you've probably guessed only four years old.

10. Our club officers Frances, Marilyn, and Joel are going to post announcements on campus to advertise our Saturday-morning car wash.

11. Kitty has finally told me how she makes her delicious — I can't believe it is so simple — chicken casserole.

12. The letter to all alumni from the college president began as follows "Dear Former Students It is with great pleasure that I issue you a cordial invitation to visit our campus for Alumni Day."

13. Toni, I wish that you would stop and think before you but maybe this is not the time or place to discuss it.

14. Nita's preparations for her dinner party include: baking a ham, making a spinach soufflé, and tossing a salad.

15. The four of us Grace, Bob, Margaret, and I are going to Atlanta for the new Piedmont Theater production on Wednesday night.

16. I'll expect all of you yes, you too, Jessica to help me clean up the kitchen after our barbecue tonight.

17. The worst things about cleaning up are: scrubbing the greasy pans, scraping the plates, and putting away the clean dishes.

18. At exactly 5 30 A.M. now don't complain we will get up and begin the Chattahoochee Road Race.

19. The students who will report to Dr. Masters' office after class are Tom Fields, Marcia Hunt, and Joe Gomez.

20. Dad said, "Here's good news Barry will be home tomorrow."

Exercise 71   Quotation Marks

In the following sentences insert quotation marks wherever they are needed. Remove those not needed and replace them with the proper marks of punctuation or mechanics where necessary. If a sentence is correctly punctuated, mark it **C**.

Example: Was it The Stars and Stripes Forever that the band played at the end of the concert last night?

Was it "The Stars and Stripes Forever" that the band played at the end of the concert last night?

1. Jean said that "she had really wanted to water-ski with us yesterday."

2. My pocket-size dictionary contains an erroneous definition for the word "masterful."

3. "I am sorry to tell you, said Dr. Malone, that you have very little chance of passing this course."

4. Wouldn't you say that "Romeo and Juliet" is perhaps the best known of all Shakespeare's plays?

5. Franklin announced loudly to the group, "I am going to work out every morning from now on;" he lived up to that vow, however, for only one week.

6. Mother called to Tommy, "Please close my car windows." "It is going to rain."

7. Wasn't it Edgar Allan Poe who wrote that eerie short story "The Pit and the Pendulum"?

8. Mary Louise said, "Joan told me, "I am going to quit the soccer team," but I hope that she was only joking."

9. My cousin Marvin, because of his appetite, has been nicknamed Starvin' Marvin.

10. The poems that she memorized last summer include "Pippa Passes, Crossing the Bar, and Dover Beach."

11. When I read "David Copperfield" for the first time, I thought that it was the best novel I had ever read.

12. Gus and Dan both say that "Ms. Garrison's history assignments are too long and hard."

13. Anna Suarez disagrees with the boys, saying, I really enjoy reading every one of those assignments.

14. Have you ever heard the Beach Boys' recording of "California Girls ? "

15. "I am sure," said Frances, that Norma will be late again for our lunch date."

16. Only in the final chapter, titled A Villain Unmasked, does the author of the mystery novel reveal the identity of the criminal.

17. Mr. Logan asked, "Wasn't it Patrick Henry who spoke those famous words 'Give me liberty or give me death! ?"

18. The grocery clerk assured me that the asparagus was "nice and fresh."

19. I learned in English class today that the word " charity " comes from a Latin word that refers to affection.

20. Most people cannot remember the words to the second stanza of "The Star-Spangled Banner ".

Exercise 72   Review of Punctuation

In the following sentences insert all marks of punctuation; remove all unnecessary or incorrect marks, replacing them with the proper ones wherever needed. If a sentence is correctly punctuated, mark it **C**.

Example: Mr   Norris   went   to   Dr   Jones's   office   yesterday   to   have his   cholesterol   checked.

Mr⊙ Norris   went   to   Dr⊙ Jones's   office   yesterday   to   have his   cholesterol   checked.

1. During   the   second   semester   Ms.   Freeman   will   take   us   on : botany   field   trips,   art   museum   visits,   and   excursions   of historical   interest.

2. Millie   asked   Sam   "if   he   were   the   one   who   had   left   an umbrella   on   her   porch   the   other   day ?"

3. "That   Chicargo   *sic*   restaurant   that   you   told   me   about   has gone   out   of   business,"   Frank's   letter   said.

4. To   Albert   Foster   was   a   real   hero   after   the   daring   rescue on   the   mountainside.

5. Mrs.   Lanier   by   the   way,   is   your   first   name   Sue?   I   hear that   you   are   moving   into   the   house   next   door   to   me.

6. Jasper   lived   in   Cody,   Wyoming   for   about   fourteen   years before   moving   east.

7. "My   organic   chemistry   lab   is   scheduled   for   8   15   A.M. ,   I hope   that   I   won't   oversleep   and   miss   it,"   Hal   remarked.

8. The   newspaper's   managing   editor   Eugene   Kelly   has   written a   strong   editorial   that   denounces   television   violence.

9. "Be   careful   on   the   ice!   cried   Mike.   It   may   be   too   thin for   skating."

10. Our   high   school   reunion   included   alumni   who   came   from the   following   cities: Enid,   Oklahoma ,   Santa   Ana,   California , Albany,   New   York ,   and   Dallas,   Texas.

11. Please   follow   these   steps   in   setting   the   clock   on   your microwave   oven   (1)   Push   the   button   marked   "Clock   set"; (2)   Push   the   correct   numbers   to   show   the   exact   time;   and (3)   Push   the   button   marked   "Start."

12. Kevin Carey, a champion swimmer (Carey swam in the 1992 Summer Olympics [See *Time,* July 19, 1992] in Barcelona, Spain), recently participated in a swimming meet in Argentina.

13. A child, who is not disciplined early in life, may be irresponsible as an adult.

14. Mother was out shopping; so I decided to cook supper for the family.

15. The cold, forbidding, manor house looked as though it had been vacant for years.

16. The hurricane's force having finally abated we set about assessing the damage it had caused.

17. John McShane, Ph.D. will lead a discussion on Gerard Manley Hopkins at the seminar next week.

18. The young boy looked innocent and timid, yet I detected an impish gleam in his eyes.

19. Dear Sir: I wish to order one dozen *Tropicana* rose bushes, for which I enclose my check for eighty-six dollars $86.00

20. Jed told us at breakfast that the concert last night was, in his words, totally awesome.

21. If you've never read Charles Lamb's humorous essay A Dissertation upon Roast Pig, I recommend that you read it.

22. "Why " asked Mrs. Hanson "do you insist on calling me by my sister's name " ?

23. Thomas Wolfe's novel "Of Time and the River" is considered to be semiautobiographical.

24. The Braves had been leading by five runs until the bottom of the ninth inning, when would you believe it? the Padres scored six runs and won the game.

25. I think the success of Bill's spaghetti sauce is due to two ingredients oregano and mushrooms.

Exercise 73   Review of Punctuation

In the following sentences insert all necessary punctuation marks; remove all incorrectly used marks, replacing them with the proper ones wherever needed. If a sentence is correctly punctuated, mark it **C**.

Example: Trying hard to keep a straight face, Randy wickedly told Mary Anne that he was leaving for Nome, Alaska the next day.

Trying hard to keep a straight face, Randy wickedly told Mary Anne that he was leaving for Nome, Alaska‸ the next day.

1. Margie walked all the way home from the supermarket and she was carrying a heavy bag of groceries.

2. Aunt Roberta who wears heavy woolen sweaters in ninety-degree weather is the most cold-natured person I know.

3. In our catalog see page 149 you will find listed several models of the type of television set you desire.

4. The Secretary of State was quoted as saying, "The situation [in the Middle East] seems somewhat improved."

5. My lovely, new, blue warm-up suit shrank when I foolishly washed it in hot water.

6. Did Natalie say, "I am going to watch a rerun of 'I Love Lucy' tonight?"

7. Frankly, Dorothy, I think you should give up this idea of buying oh, have you already bought it?

8. Pocahontas daughter of an American Indian chief is popularly believed to have rescued Captain John Smith when her father threatened to kill him.

9. The person, who invented the electric can opener has a place in the hearts of a host of homemakers.

10. No, Martin, it was Tom not his brother who helped Father change the flat tire.

11. Did you know that Home on the Range was President Franklin D. Roosevelt's favorite song?

12. "Be very careful", whispered Sara Jane, "not to awaken the baby."

13. Last month's issue of *Consumer Reports* (a magazine that assesses the quality of various products March, 1995) has rated our new refrigerator a best buy.

14. To Florence Dwight seemed cold and unfriendly so she moved away as soon as she tactfully could.

15. I'm afraid I don't have the amount of money you want to borrow; I can however let you have half of what you need.

16. The teacher's list of requirements for acceptable term papers included: neatness, accuracy, and correct spelling.

17. While I answered the telephone, I left my bait bucket on the dock, someone must have taken it.

18. Andy, have you seen my bait oh, there it is in the boat!

19. Rachel, what do you think of Flannery O'Connor's short story "A Good Man Is Hard to Find"?

20. His excuse for missing class was tried and true his alarm clock had failed to go off.

21. I received birthday cards from Lee, Tommy, Ricardo, and Anna, but Jenny must have forgotten the big day.

22. Lamar's latest book is titled *Among My Souvenirs Memories of a Happy Youth.*

23. Lawrence tells me that your family is moving to Tyler, Texas the first of next year.

24. The Irish poet, William Butler Yeats, was born in Dublin, and was the son of a noted painter.

25. She divided the ice cream equally among the children, then she cut the birthday cake.

20

Mechanics:
Capital Letters, Italics,
the Apostrophe,
the Hyphen, Numbers

■ 20a Capital Letters

1. Capitalize the first word of a sentence, of a line of traditional poetry, and of a direct quotation:

All the students attended the meeting.

"Under the spreading chestnut tree / The village smithy stands."

He said, "She does not wish to see you."

2. Capitalize proper nouns, words used as proper nouns, and adjectives derived from proper nouns:

Great Britain, William, the Bible

President, Senator, Captain, University (when these are used with or substituted for the name of a particular president, person of high rank, or university), and similarly

Mother, Grandfather, Uncle (as in *We told Mother to go to bed, We bought Grandfather a bicycle*, and *We buried Uncle in Arlington Cemetery*, but not in *My mother is ill, His grandfather is eighty-two*, and *Our uncle was wounded at Gettysburg*)

British, Shakespearean, Scandinavian

3. Capitalize the names of days, months, and holidays:

Monday, February, Fourth of July, Ash Wednesday, Veterans Day

4. Capitalize the names of historical periods and events:

the Middle Ages, the French Revolution, the Battle of the Bulge, the Reformation

5. Capitalize the first word in the titles of books, chapters, essays, short stories, short poems, songs, and works of art. Capitalize also all other words in these titles except articles, prepositions, and conjunctions:

> *The Last of the Mohicans,* "Without Benefit of Clergy," "Ode to the West Wind," "Only a Bird in a Gilded Cage," El Greco's *View of Toledo*

6. Capitalize names of the Deity, religions, and religious organizations:

> Jehovah, God, the Redeemer, Buddhism, Church of England, Society of Jesus, Order of St. Francis

7. Capitalize the names of governing bodies, political parties, governmental agencies, and civic and social organizations:

> The House of Commons, the Senate, the Democratic Party, the Internal Revenue Service, the Chamber of Commerce, Daughters of the American Revolution

8. Capitalize the points of the compass when they refer to a specific region but not when they indicate direction:

> He lived in the East all his life.
>
> They traveled west for about a hundred miles and then turned south.

9. Capitalize the names of studies only if they are derived from proper nouns or are the names of specific courses of instruction:

> He was studying physics, chemistry, and German.
>
> He failed Mathematics 101 and Human Biology 1.

10. Capitalize personifications:

> O wild West Wind, thou breath of Autumn's being.
>
> Daughters of Time, the hypocritic Days.
>
> Be with me, Beauty, for the fire is dying.

■ 20b Italics

1. Italicize words that you wish to emphasize. (In manuscript indicate italics by underlining.)

> Do you mean to say that she ate them *all*?
>
> He could hardly have been *the* Robert Frost.

Note: Use this device sparingly. Frequent use of italics for emphasis is a sign of an immature style.

2. Italicize numbers, letters, and words referred to as such:

He made his *7* and his *9* very much alike.

She has never yet learned to pronounce *statistics*.

In his handwriting he uses the old-fashioned *s*.

3. Italicize the names of books, magazines, newspapers, major musical works, and movies. (Smaller units of books, such as chapters, stories, essays, and poems, are usually set in quotation marks.)

A Tale of Two Cities, the *Atlantic Monthly*, the Atlanta *Journal*

Note: In the names of newspapers or magazines it is not always necessary to italicize the definite article or the name of a city.

4. Italicize the names of ships, trains, and airplanes:

the *Queen Elizabeth*, the *Twentieth-Century Limited*, the *Spirit of St. Louis*

5. Italicize foreign words and phrases in an English context, unless they have become so familiar that they are no longer considered foreign.

The *coup d'état* led to his becoming emperor.

We served tamales on the patio.

6. Italicize the titles of paintings, statues, and other works of art:

Gainsborough's *Blue Boy*, Rodin's *The Thinker*

■ 20c The Apostrophe

1. Use the apostrophe and *s* to form the possessive case of singular nouns:

the boar's head, Mary's lamb, the boss's orders

Note: Proper names ending in *s* may form the possessive by adding *'s* if the resulting word is not unpleasant or difficult to sound:

Keats's poems, Charles's work, *but* Ulysses' return

2. Use an apostrophe without *s* to form the possessive of plural nouns ending in *s:*

Soldiers' quarters, boys' clothes

3. Use an apostrophe and *s* to form the possessive of plural nouns not ending in *s:*

Men's coats, children's shoes, the alumni's contributions

4. The possessive of words indicating time is formed like the possessive of other nouns:

A week's delay, a day's journey, *but* a two days' visit

5. The apostrophe is frequently omitted in the names of organizations and institutions:

The Farmers Hardware Company, Boys High School, State Teachers College

6. In forming the possessives of compounds, use the apostrophe according to the meaning and the logic of the construction:

Beaumont and Fletcher's plays [Plays written by Beaumont and Fletcher jointly.]

Smith's and Jones's children [The children of Smith and the children of Jones.]

John and Mary's house [The house belonging to John and Mary.]

Somebody else's business [The business of somebody else.]

7. Use an apostrophe to indicate the omission of letters in contractions and of digits in numerals:

Isn't, don't, 'tis

Martha's been sunbathing.

the class of '23

Note: Be sure that the apostrophe is placed at the exact point where the letter or digit is omitted. Do not write *is'nt, do'nt.*

8. Use an apostrophe and *s* to indicate the plural of letters, numerals, signs, and words used as such:

Dot your *i*'s and cross your *t*'s.

His telephone number contains four *8*'s.

In your next theme omit the *&*'s.

He uses too many *so*'s.

■ 20d The Hyphen

In English, compounds are made in three ways:

   (1) by writing the words solid (*bedroom, watchmaker, starlight*),

   (2) by writing them separately (*ice cream, motion picture, mountain lion*), or

   (3) by separating the words with a hyphen (*name-caller, ne'er-do-well, finger-paint*).

The resulting confusion, like so much confusion in English, lies in the fact that the language is constantly changing. A compound may begin as two words. As the expression develops into a familiar term, a hyphen appears. Finally it may end as a solid formation — its destiny accomplished, so to speak. Thus we write *bedroom* (one word) but *dining room* (two words). We have the noun *bluepoint* to refer to an oyster, but we use the two words *blue point* to describe a Siamese cat. A decision may be *far-reaching*, but a forecaster is *farseeing*. The only solution to this confusing problem is to consult a dictionary. But this authority is not always satisfactory because many compounds are made for the occasion and are not in the dictionary — and dictionaries may disagree. Furthermore, a compound with a hyphen may be correct in one part of a sentence and incorrect in another, or it may be correct as a noun and incorrect as a verb. The stylebook of one publisher says, "If you take hyphens seriously, you will surely go mad." Nevertheless, there is a sort of logic in the use of the hyphen, as well as a kind of common sense; furthermore, one can learn some of the pitfalls to avoid.

Consider the following sentences:

He is a great admirer of Henry Kissinger, the ex-Republican Secretary of State. [Is Mr. Kissinger no longer a Republican? The phrase should read *the former Republican Secretary of State.*]

The parents enjoyed their children's recreation of the first Thanksgiving. [In this sentence *re-creation* is the appropriate word, and the hyphen distinguishes it from *recreation.*]

I would think that your sixteen year old brother could scramble an egg. [In this sentence *sixteen, year,* and *old* form a compound modifier and should be hyphenated. The phrase should read *your sixteen-year-old brother.*]

He introduced me to his uncle, an old car enthusiast. [Is his uncle old? Or is his uncle interested in old cars? The phrase is clarified with a hyphen: *an old-car enthusiast.*]

Did you hear the reporter's interview with the singing whale authority? [Did the reporter interview a whale authority who sings or an authority on singing whales? Appropriate hyphenation clears up the confusion; the phrase should read *with the singing-whale authority.*]

The following rules indicate common practice and are fairly reliable:

1. Compound numerals (*twenty-one* through *ninety-nine*) are always written with a hyphen:

twenty-six, forty-eight, fifty-two

2. Fractions are written with a hyphen if they are adjectival:

His speech was one-third fact and two-thirds demagoguery.

But Three fourths of the apples are rotten.

3. Compounds with *self* are written with a hyphen:

self-styled, self-taught, self-centered

Note the exceptions *selfsame, selfhood, selfless.*

4. The hyphen is used in certain expressions of family relationship:

great-grandfather, great-aunt

5. Most compounds beginning with *ex* and *pro* are written with a hyphen. *Pre* is followed by a hyphen only when this prefix is used with a proper noun or adjective.

ex-president, pro-British, pre-Christian [*but* prerequisite]

Do not hyphenate after *ex* unless it means *former*.

6. The hyphen is commonly used in compounds with prepositional phrases:

mother-in-law, stick-in-the-mud, heart-to-heart

7. One of the commonest uses of hyphens is to form compound modifiers for nouns and pronouns:

An eight-year-old child, a well-done steak, a blue-green sea

Note: Such compounds are hyphenated when they immediately precede the word they modify, but frequently they are not hyphenated when they are used predicatively:

His well-spoken words pleased the audience [*but* His words were well spoken].

She made a number of off-the-record comments [*but* Her comments were made off the record].

8. Hyphens are used in coined or occasional compounds:

She gave him a kind of "you-ought-to-know-better" look.

Her bird-on-the-nest hat was sensational.

9. The hyphen is used in compound nouns that name the same person in two different capacities:

Author-publisher, musician-statesman, tycoon-playboy

10. The hyphen is frequently used to avoid confusion between words:

Re-claim [to distinguish from *reclaim*]

Re-cover [to distinguish from *recover*]

11. Hyphens are used to avoid clumsy spellings:

Bull-like, semi-independent, ante-election, pre-empt

Note: *Cooperate* and *coordinate* are common enough to be accepted.

12. The hyphen is used at the end of a line of writing to indicate the division of a word continued on the next line. The division must always come at the end of a syllable. Do not divide words of one syllable:

PROPER DIVISIONS: con-tin-ued, in-di-cate, au-di-ence

IMPROPER DIVISIONS: wo-rd, laugh-ed, comp-ound

Note: If you are uncertain about the division of a word, consult your dictionary.

■ 20e Numbers

1. Numbers that can be expressed in one or two words should be written out: five girls; seventeen giraffes; twenty-five books; four hundred tickets; ten thousand people.

2. Numbers of more than two words should be written as numerals: 9,425; 650; 700,000.

3. Numbers that start a sentence should be written out, even though they would ordinarily be written as numerals: *Four hundred and forty* dollars is a good price for that cashmere coat.

Exercise 74   Capitals

In the following sentences change small letters to capital letters wherever necessary and vice versa. If a sentence is correct as it stands, mark it **C.**

Example: My father was six years old when aunt Louise

was born.

My father was six years old when ₳unt Louise

was born.

1. On the Eastern horizon I could see a line of pelicans skimming the surface of the Atlantic ocean.

2. I enjoyed my french course last quarter; I may decide to spend next summer in France.

3. David asked, "are you planning a trip to the mountains this weekend?"

4. "Yes," Fran replied, "We love hiking the Appalachian trail."

5. Jim is having a fine time this summer; he is engrossed in Hall and Nordhoff's wonderful novel *Mutiny On The Bounty*.

6. Dad has a mahogany desk that once belonged to his Grandfather.

7. What poet wrote the lines "And malt does more than Milton can | to justify God's ways to man"?

8. I believe that A. E. Housman wrote those lines in his poem "Terence, This Is Stupid Stuff."

9. Our english bulldog is gentler than he looks; on the other hand, our little Pekingese is quite fierce.

10. When congressman Elliott McNeill stepped up to the speaker's stand, we knew we were in for an inspirational pep talk.

11. "Don't tease the baby," said mother. "you are going to make her cry."

12. Although Jeanne is generally good at languages, she cannot seem to master german.

13. Carol is planning to work at least a year before she decides which University to attend.

14. The Jacksonville police department had its hands full yesterday because there was a pile-up accident on the St. Johns river bridge.

15. I went to the Doctor last week for my annual checkup, and I was pleased with the results.

Exercise 75 Italics

In the following sentences underline all words that should be italicized and remove italics that are incorrectly used, replacing them with other marks if necessary. If a sentence is correct as it stands, mark it **C**.

Example: An interesting book called "A Night to Remember" is an account of the sinking of the ship *Titanic* in 1912.

An interesting book called <u>A Night to Remember</u> is an account of the sinking of the ship *Titanic* in 1912.

1. I wonder how many people confuse the meanings of the two words "imply" and "infer."

2. Traveling through Provence last summer, we found a small auberge where our lunch was so delicious that we decided to stay for the evening meal.

3. I am sure that you misunderstood me, Harry; I said that *ain't* is *never* an acceptable expression.

4. Monet's painting of his garden pool with water lilies is almost as famous as van Gogh's "Sunflowers."

5. My uncle was managing editor of the Denver Post for twenty years.

6. Ruth always puts two m's in the word *coming*.

7. Mary Lou, I don't think — I know — that it's time to change the oil in your car!

8. At a tiny candy shop in Rouen, I bought a box of gingembre glacé, a delicious crystallized ginger, for my friend Renée.

9. Those who have been fans for years of the novel "Gone with the Wind" seem to be enjoying its long-awaited sequel, "Scarlett."

10. Yesterday the temperature reached ninety-nine — yes, I said ninety-nine — before 3:00 P.M.

11. *Deck the Halls with Boughs of Holly* has always been a very popular Christmas carol.

12. The long-running television show Cheers will probably be available to its admirers in reruns for a long time to come.

13. Dad loves to collect salad dressing recipes that appear in his favorite magazine, *Bon Appétit*.

14. Of all Burl Ives's recorded songs, my favorites are *The Fox* and *Killigrew's Soiree*.

15. Our friends the Moores will be sailing in July from New York to London aboard the "Golden Odyssey."

16. Several people I know always mispronounce the word cavalry.

17. Probably the most famous painting in the Louvre Museum is da Vinci's "Mona Lisa."

18. Gunther's grandfather, who was born in Germany, always meets me with the greeting *"Guten Tag!"*

19. It is hard to remember that the singular form of data is datum.

20. I don't know whether this figure on his check is a 1 or a 7.

Exercise 76   The Apostrophe

In the following sentences underline all words that should have apostrophes and all
those that have apostrophes incorrectly used; then write the word(s) correctly in the
space at the right. If a sentence is correct, mark it **C.**

Example: Have'nt we been out to the Martin's lake   *Haven't,*
house before?   *Martins'*

1. After two years study in Spain, Guy could speak
   fluent Spanish.   _____

2. Ive been thinking seriously of joining the Air Force;
   don't you think thats a good idea?   _____

3. Denny's and Mario's fishing camp is out on Lake
   Jackson, not far from Macon.   _____

4. Barry, try to leave out some of the ers when you
   make your speech tomorrow.   _____

5. The Joneses cats are Siamese, and except for their
   voices I like them very much.   _____

6. Ted's grandmother attended Wesleyan College,
   where she graduated in the class of 34.   _____

7. We had a fourteen day's delay in starting our trip
   because our tour guide had become ill.   _____

8. Lillian say's that she doesn't like Dickens's novels
   because they are too dreary.   _____

9. Dad complains bitterly because mens' suits have
   increased greatly in price in the last few years.   _____

10. Isn't it interesting, Mrs. Calabash, that you and I
    have similar tastes in food and are especially partial
    to chocolate?   _____

11. Those stucco houses red tile roofs remind me of the
    year we spent in Italy.   _____

12. My dog has hurt it's leg badly on the barbed wire
    fence in the back yard.   _____

13. These boy's clothes are too small for Robert; he'd
    better try the men's department.   _____

14. I could hardly believe the story about Frances acci-
    dent yesterday; she's a very good driver.   _____

15. The officer's who arrived on the scene said that visi-
    bility was poor because of the misting rain.   _____

16. Frances thinks that the slippery streets were also
    part of the problem.   _____

17. Millie's and Joe's new sofa has plaid upholstery,
    and the bright colors are attractive.   _____

18. Last months' bills came in today, so Father's in a
    grouchy mood.   _____

19. We watched television until eleven oclock, and
    then we decided to order pizza before going to bed.   _____

20. Sally, would you mind if I bought a yellow sweater
    just like your's?   _____

Exercise 77 The Hyphen

In the following sentences underline the incorrect compounds and write the correct forms at the right. If a sentence is correct, mark it **C.** Some sentences contain more than one error. If you are doubtful about whether a term should be hyphenated, consult a dictionary for guidance.

Example: <u>Three year old</u> Bobby received a
third large serving of ice cream from   *Three-year-old,*
his <u>ever indulgent</u> mother.   *ever-indulgent*

1. Jennifer had that "don't you dare" look on her face when Marty began the story about our losing the way to Savannah.   _____

2. My history professor is a Chinese porcelain collector who is also fond of jade.   _____

3. Aunt Caroline says that she has recovered her old down comforter a dozen times over the past thirty-five years.   _____

4. We continued our snaillike pace up the hillside, stopping often for water or a moment's rest.   _____

5. Frank received an extra-ordinary letter from his Belgian friend, inviting him to spend the summer with him and his family.   _____

6. Scattered throughout the South are a number of beautiful antebellum mansions, many of which belong to descendants of the original owners.   _____

7. I believe that John's uncle is an old silver authority; perhaps he will appraise your tea service for you.   _____

8. The ex-German chancellor visited the United States recently and stopped off in Atlanta.   _____

9. This hand knit sweater is very warm
   because it is made of a wool and mohair
   yarn.   _____

10. The Jacksons told us that they stayed at a
    really first class hotel in Tampa.   _____

11. George has been well-paid for his summer
    job; he is hoping to have it again next year.   _____

12. My well meant criticism was not well
    received by the group that was playing
    the loud music.   _____

13. My great grandfather, a Montana rancher,
    is eighty seven years old; he rides
    horseback every day.   _____

14. Jake led a hand to mouth existence for five
    years, but then he found a steady job as an
    accountant.   _____

15. Two thirds of our time at the mountain
    cabin was spent in looking for matches for
    the fire-place.   _____

16. Robert Louis Stevenson, the poet novelist,
    is probably best known for his children's
    novel *Treasure Island*.   _____

17. It surprises no-one to learn that I am a
    self-taught typist.   _____

18. The temperature reached the hundred
    degree mark again today; I hope it will
    be cooler for the weekend.   _____

19. Mrs. Marlborough is trying a new thirty
    day diet plan, but after ninety days it still
    isn't working.   _____

20. I think Mrs. Marlborough forgets to count
    her ice-cream sundaes as calories.   _____

Exercise 78 | Review of Mechanics

Underline the errors in the following sentences and then write the correct forms in the spaces at the right. If a sentence is correct, mark it **C.**

Example: I hope it <u>wo'nt</u> rain tomorrow
because I want to go <u>sight-seeing</u>
in Williamsburg.

won't,
sightseeing

1. The Chicago Cub's last home game will be thursday afternoon at Wrigley Field.

_____

2. One of the most popular songs of all time is *White Christmas*, by Irving Berlin.

_____

3. I want to thank-you, Nita, for lending me your raincoat last night during the thunderstorm.

_____

4. Your not planning to leave for Miami at this time of night, are you?

_____

5. We can't get over Marie's eloping with a ne'er do well like Frankie.

_____

6. Tony said, "Your handwriting is illegible; is this word 'beat' or 'best'?"

_____

7. The stew that Harriet served last night contained a soupçon of garlic that added to its flavor.

_____

8. Johnny's feet have grown so much in the past six months that he now wears a mens size eleven shoe.

_____

9. Mr. Franklin asked for a two day leave-of-absence in order to take his daughter to summer camp.

_____

10. Sailing South from Miami, we made our first stop at Key West.

_____

11. Henry Wadsworth Longfellow wrote the long narrative poem "The Courtship Of Miles Standish," which tells of the English people who came over on the *Mayflower*. _____

12. My Father told us children that we could stop at Black Rock Mountain on the way to Highlands. _____

13. The Broadway musical that you are referring to is Lerner's and Loewe's *Guys and Dolls*. _____

14. Do'nt you think its high time to wash the dishes and go to bed? _____

15. Goodness! Josh has eaten fully one half of the chocolate cake. _____

16. Evelyn has developed a real stick in the mud attitude about playing hockey for our team. _____

17. The commercial says that ninety-nine percent of all dentists prefer Glisten toothpaste. _____

18. Mr. Larson has given his Grandson a Shetland pony for his birthday. _____

19. Are you planning to major in history or spanish? _____

20. James Whitcomb Riley's poem starts with these lines: "Little Orphan Annies come to our house to stay / an' wash the cups and saucers up an' brush the crumbs away. . . ." _____

Use of the Dictionary

A convenient and valuable source of linguistic information is a standard dictionary. It is easy to use, and, if used intelligently, very informative. Many people do not realize that a dictionary contains important facts far beyond simple definitions and guides to pronunciation and spelling. One of the best investments that you can make is the purchase of a standard collegiate dictionary. Your frequent use of a good dictionary, besides being a necessary step toward the development of an effective vocabulary, is essential for understanding the material you encounter daily. In any college course, in the newspapers, and in regular communication with others, you will read and hear unfamiliar words. Your desire to learn the meaning, spelling, and pronunciation of a new word should lead you to a dictionary providing this information along with other features such as the derivation of the word and its level of usage. The dictionary may also discuss the word's synonyms and frequently an antonym to illuminate still further its precise shade of meaning.

The best dictionaries have taken years of preparation by hundreds of workers directed by the finest scholars of the time. Unabridged dictionaries are comprehensive in their explanations and descriptions of words, containing thousands more entries than the more commonly used desk dictionary. In the United States perhaps the best-known unabridged dictionary is *Webster's Third New International Dictionary of the English Language*, often called simply *Webster's Third*. It was published by the G. & C. Merriam Company of Springfield, Massachusetts, in 1961; there have been several subsequent printings and supplements. This work, though it is too bulky to be used as a casual desk dictionary (and for most purposes unnecesary), may be found in a college library.

Any one of several extremely reliable collegiate dictionaries is the best choice for you. Severely abridged paperback editions of these dictionaries are a poor substitute, as they do not contain the detailed information that you may find necessary for specialized assignments in your college courses. Most language authorities recommend the latest editions of the following standard college dictionaries: *Webster's Ninth New Collegiate Dictionary*, published by Merriam-Webster Inc., Springfield, Massachusetts; *Webster's New World Dictionary of the American Language*, Simon and Schuster, New York; *The American Heritage Dictionary of the English Language*, The American Heritage Publishing Co., Inc., and Houghton Mifflin Co., Boston; *The Random House Dictionary of the English Language*, Random House, New York; *Funk and Wagnall's Standard Collegiate Dictionary*, Harcourt, Brace and World, Inc., New York.

Select one of these dictionaries and buy it as soon as you get to college; then follow the list of suggestions given below in order to familiarize yourself with the dictionary and the ways in which you can get the maximum use from this very handy and easy-to-use reference work.

1. Read all the introductory material in the front of the dictionary because this explains what information the book has to offer. If some of it seems too scholarly for you to understand, read on, and at least find out what it is mainly concerned with and what you can expect to find in its entries.

2. Study carefully the key to pronunciation, and check it with words that you know so that you will be sure of understanding it. A need for guidance in pronunciation is one of the most common reasons for consulting a dictionary.

3. Refer often to the table of abbreviations, which is most likely to be found inside the front cover of your dictionary. To save space, dictionaries necessarily use many abbreviations, and these are explained in the table. Become familiar with these abbreviations so that no piece of information escapes your notice.

4. Examine the appendixes to learn what information is given in them. Some dictionaries list biographical and geographical information in their appendixes; others list such information in the main entries in the book. Other information often found in the appendixes of a dictionary includes tables of interpretations of various specialized symbols, like those connected with mathematics, chemistry, music, chess, medicine, and pharmacy; a table of weights and measures; a dictionary of English given names, and so on.

One of the most important things a dictionary can tell you is the *level of usage* of a given term. The English language, ever-changing and full of colorful informality, functions on many levels. Young people may use the expression *laid back* to describe a person who has a relaxed, uncomplicated approach to life. Politicians and reporters use the term *bottom line* to mean the end result of something. An educated adult may in conversation refer to *lots of trouble*. And an editor of a magazine may write of the *dichotomy between work and leisure classes* or, in a book review, of an *involuted search for self*. Each of these expressions is in a sense proper in its own context. Judgment of a term as "good English" is usually determined by the level on which it is used. The magazine editor would not in a formal article use the term *laid back;* the youth of today would hardly think or write using terms like *dichotomy.* Your dictionary will tell you whether the use of a word in a particular sense is slang, informal (colloquial), dialectal, archaic, obsolete, or none of these, i.e., Standard English.

Slang is the term used to describe the spontaneous, vivid, and sometimes racy inventions used frequently in the speech and writings of groups like teenagers, gangsters, popular musicians, soldiers, and sports writers — not that these groups necessarily have anything else in common. The life of a slang expression is usually short, but sometimes, if it is striking enough and colorful enough, it may gain universal usage and become at least an informal part of the national vocabulary.

The term *informal* or *colloquial* is applied to words or expressions that are acceptable in the speech of the educated but not in formal writing. It is all right to say, "He's going to have *lots of trouble* explaining his whereabouts on the night of June third," but it is not Standard English to write this statement formally.

Dialect, another usage label, means that a word or expression is common to the speech of a particular group or geographical region. *Archaic* means that the word or term is rarely used today, except in certain contexts like church ritual, but that it may be found fairly frequently in early writings. *Obsolete* means that the term is no longer used but may be found in early writings. In addition, as a part of its usage discussion, a dictionary will inform you if a word or term is commonly considered obscene, vulgar, or profane.

To see how a dictionary presents its information, consider now the following entry from *The Random House Dictionary of the English Language:**

> **bur·den**[1] (bûr′d³n), *n.* **1.** that which is carried; load: *a horse's burden of rider and pack.* **2.** that which is borne with difficulty; obligation or trouble: *the burden of leadership.* **3.** *Naut.* **a.** the weight of a ship's cargo. **b.** the carrying capacity of a ship: *a ship of a hundred-tons burden.* **4.** *Mining.* the earth or rock to be moved by a charge of explosives. **5.** *Accounting.* overhead (def. 6). —*v.t.* **6.** to load heavily. **7.** to load oppressively; trouble. [ME, var. of *burthen.* OE *byrthen;* akin to G *Bürde,* Goth *baurthei;* see BEAR[1]] —**bur′den·er,** *n.* —**bur′den·less,** *adj.* —**Syn. 1.** See **load. 2.** weight, encumbrance, impediment.

Here we are given the correct spelling of the word *burden* and its proper division into syllables. The small numeral (1) after the entry word indicates that this is the first of two or more words with the same spelling but differing radically in meaning and derivation and therefore listed separately. Next, the proper pronunciation is given. It becomes clear immediately that you need to learn the significance of the signs, called diacritical marks, that indicate pronunciation. In this entry the first five numbered definitions are preceded by *n* (for *noun*) and the last two by *v.t.* (for *verb, transitive*). After 3, *Naut.* (*Nautical*) means that the

* Reproduced by permission from *The Random House Dictionary of the English Language.* The Unabridged Edition. Copyright © 1983 by Random House, Inc.

definitions given under 3 are special technical senses of the word as used in shipping. The same interpretation is true of definitions 4 and 5. The information in brackets gives the derivation or origin of the word. It tells that *burden* is a variant form of the older word *burthen*, which is derived from the Old English form *byrthen*, and that the word is linguistically akin to the word *bear* as described in the first *bear* entry elsewhere in the dictionary. Finally we learn that the synonyms of *burden*[1] are discussed under the entry *load*. The second entry, *burden*[2], is arranged on the same principles.

Consider now the following entry from *Webster's New World Dictionary of the American Language:**

> **drunk** (druŋk) *vt., vi.* [ME *dronke* < *dronken*, DRUNKEN] *pp. & archaic pt. of DRINK* —*adj.* 1 overcome by alcoholic liquor to the point of losing control over one's faculties; intoxicated 2 overcome by any powerful emotion [*drunk* with joy] 3 [Colloq.] DRUNKEN (sense 2) Usually used in the predicate —*n.* 1 [Colloq.] a drunken person 2 [Slang] a drinking spree
> **SYN.**—**drunk** is the simple, direct word, usually used in the predicate, for one who is overcome by alcoholic liquor [he is *drunk*]; **drunken**, usually used attributively, is equivalent to **drunk** but sometimes implies habitual, intemperate drinking of liquor [a *drunken* bum]; **intoxicated** and **inebriated** are euphemisms; there are many euphemistic and slang terms in English expressing varying degrees of drunkenness: e. g., **tipsy** (slight), **tight** (moderate, but without great loss of muscular coordination), **blind drunk** (great), **blotto** (to the point of unconsciousness), etc. —*ANT.* **sober**

Here we learn that the adjective *drunk,* with the specific meanings that follow, is the past participle and was formerly a past tense of the verb *to drink.* Two definitions are given: the first of these is the common one; the second is often used figuratively. The discussion of synonyms gives us the fine shades of distinction among a group of words that mean essentially the same thing. In addition, one antonym, or word of opposite meaning, is given. The final part of the entry, defining *drunk* as a noun, explains that when the word is used as a noun, meaning a person in a drunken condition or a period of heavy drinking, the word is slang.

The kind of knowledge that a good dictionary can give you far exceeds what has been discussed here. Most good dictionaries, for instance, pay special attention to biography and geography. One can learn when Beethoven died and the name of the capital of Peru. One can find the height of Mt. Everest and the approximate number of islands in the Philippines. Literature, mythology, and particularly science are well covered in the modern dictionary. Finally, special appendixes sometimes include such miscellaneous information as the meanings of common Christian names, foreign words and phrases, abbreviations, and the symbols used in the preparation of copy for the printer and in proofreading. Some books even contain a dictionary of rhymes. The following exercises illustrate the variety of information one may obtain from a good dictionary.

---

* From *Webster's New World Dictionary.* Copyright © 1988. Used by permission of the publisher, Webster's New World Dictionaries/A Division of Simon & Schuster, New York.

Exercise 79   Word Origins

After each of the following words indicate in the first column at the right the first systematically recorded language from which the word is derived, and in the second column the meaning(s) of the source word(s).

	Language	Root meaning
Example: candid	*Latin*	*bright; white*
1. abet		
2. abhor		
3. assassin		
4. bead		
5. belfry		
6. burlesque		
7. caravan		
8. carnivorous		
9. charismatic		
10. congregation		
11. curfew		
12. disciple		
13. ecstasy		
14. fool		
15. hate		
16. hoard		
17. misanthrope		
18. neighbor		
19. pastor		
20. polygamist		
21. pseudonym		
22. shampoo		
23. sofa		

	Language	Root meaning
24. sophomore	_____	_____
25. tycoon	_____	_____

Exercise 80 British and American Usage

The following words illustrate the differences between British and American usage. Write the equivalents of these British terms:

Example: geyser _____*hot-water heater*_____

1. bonnet _____
2. bowler _____
3. braces _____
4. carriageway _____
5. chemist _____
6. chips _____
7. crisps _____
8. draper _____
9. dustman _____
10. football _____
11. gaol _____
12. holiday _____
13. ironmonger _____
14. jumper _____
15. lift (n.) _____
16. lorry _____
17. paraffin _____
18. pasty (n.) _____
19. petrol _____
20. plimsolls _____
21. pub _____
22. queue (n.) _____
23. rates _____
24. removal _____

25. runners _____

26. spanner _____

27. subway _____

28. sultanas _____

29. sweet (n.) _____

30. tipping (n.) _____

31. torch _____

32. trolley _____

33. underground (n.), tube _____

34. verge _____

35. vest _____

Exercise 81 Plurals

Write the plural form of each of the following nouns:

Example: ego   *egos*

1. alley   _____
2. ally   _____
3. alumna   _____
4. axis   _____
5. bacterium   _____
6. basis   _____
7. bus   _____
8. Christmas   _____
9. child   _____
10. complex   _____
11. criterion   _____
12. datum   _____
13. deer   _____
14. focus   _____
15. half   _____
16. hero   _____
17. intricacy   _____
18. innuendo   _____
19. iris   _____
20. man-of-war   _____
21. medium   _____
22. monkey   _____
23. moose   _____
24. mother-in-law   _____
25. nucleus   _____

26. piano   _____
27. self   _____
28. plateful   _____
29. radio   _____
30. roof   _____
31. syllabus   _____
32. thief   _____
33. tooth   _____
34. thesis   _____
35. vertebra   _____

Exercise 82 Levels of Usage

After each of the following sentences indicate the level of usage of the *italicized* word or expression, using these abbreviations:

     A for archaic,   **I** for informal (colloquial),

     D for dialectal (regional),   **S** for slang.

Note: Although most current standard collegiate dictionaries agree in their classifications of these words and expressions, even these books may differ in their classifications (or show no label at all). For the most reliable information about the level of usage of a word or expression, consult an up-to-date collegiate dictionary.

Dictionary used for this exercise: _____

Example: I don't care for those *boughten* cookies.   _D_

1. This restaurant is frequented by *yuppies* because of its unique atmosphere and gourmet food. _____

2. That last touchdown by Herschel Walker was *awesome*! _____

3. I would hate to baby-sit for Dennis the Menace; he's too *hyper*. _____

4. *Yon* Cassius hath a lean and hungry look. _____

5. Brother fought *agin* brother in the War Between the States. _____

6. I was so tired that I *crashed* as soon as I got home. _____

7. After a seemingly endless exam week, we spent another week just relaxing and *goofing off*. _____

8. I think her curtains are *tacky*. _____

9. I *reckon* I'm ready to go to town. _____

10. It's been a hard day; let's just go home and *chill out* for a while. _____

11. Most people don't like Mary because she is *stuck-up*. _____

12. Put the provisions in the *buttery*. _____

13. *Cool it*, Bill — everything has turned out well. _____

14. My uncle is *fixing* to leave right now. _____

15. I have to do my *stupid* chores before I can go to the movie. _____

16. I decided to *cut* class and sleep late. _____

17. The dark of the night *affrights* me. _____

18. Either Tom is a spendthrift, or he just has a lot of *moola*. _____

19. I don't want to eat that *yucky* black bean and liver casserole ever again. _____

20. *Quoth* the raven, "Nevermore." _____

21. They're celebrating for me and my *gal*. _____

22. Can *you-all* come to the picnic next Sunday? _____

23. He looks like a derelict from *skid row*. _____

24. I think that new lifeguard at the Bishop Park pool is a real *hunk*. _____

25. *Verily*, those who tell the truth are blessed. _____

Exercise 83 General Information

Refer to your dictionary for the information you will need to fill in the blanks below. Remember that some of the information may be found in the appendix.

Example: Father of Romulus, founder of Rome _____ *Mars* _____

1. Birth and death years of Harry S Truman _____
2. Greek name for Roman god Bacchus _____
3. Capital of New Hampshire _____
4. Genus of honeysuckle _____
5. Identity of Thor _____

6. Meaning of *SASE* _____
7. Country to which the Azores belong _____
8. Symbol for the chemical element silver _____

9. Meaning of the Italian *a cappella* _____
10. Fate of the prophecies of Cassandra _____

11. Definition of *agoraphobia* _____
12. Country of origin of the Siamese cat _____
13. Population of San Francisco _____
14. State for which *ME* is the abbreviation _____

15. Identity of Faust _____
16. Location where the sarong is worn _____
17. Meaning of the French word *mousse* _____
18. Location of Rutgers University _____
19. Nonsexist word for *policeman* _____
20. Meaning of *ASAP* _____

Exercise 84 Borrowed Foreign Expressions

The following words occur frequently in our everyday speech and writing. They have been borrowed in their original forms from languages other than English and have in most instances become integral parts of our language. After consulting your dictionary, write the meaning of each expression and the language from which it was borrowed.

Example: canoe   *light, narrow boat propelled by paddling*

(Spanish, from Arawak)

1. ad hoc   _____

_____

2. ad hominem   _____

_____

3. ad infinitum   _____

_____

4. à la mode   _____

_____

5. alter ego   _____

_____

6. alma mater   _____

_____

7. chalet   _____

_____

8. charlotte   _____

_____

9. emeritus   _____

_____

10. et cetera   _____

_____

11. joie de vivre   _____

_____

12. kamikaze   _____

_____

13. karate   _____

_____

14. patio   _____

_____

15. pueblo   _____

_____

16. regatta   _____

_____

17. status quo   _____

_____

18. sauna   _____

_____

19. sauerbraten   _____

_____

20. video   _____

_____

Diction

Diction is one's choice of words in the expression of ideas. Because one speaks and writes on various levels of usage, the same expression may be appropriate to one level but not to another. The diction, for instance, of formal writing seems overprecise in informal conversation, and the acceptable diction of everyday speech seems out of place in serious, formal composition. But on all levels of speech and writing, faulty diction appears — in wordiness, in trite expressions, and in faulty idiom.

■ 22a Wordiness

Wordiness is the use of too many words — more words, that is, than are necessary to express an idea correctly and clearly. Many sentences written by college students may be greatly improved by reducing the number of words. The following kind of sentence is common in student themes:

> WORDY: There is a man in our neighborhood, and he has written three novels.
>
> BETTER: A man in our neighborhood has written three novels.
>
> A neighbor of ours has written three novels.

What is called **excessive predication** is responsible for a common type of wordiness. Usually this fault results from the too frequent use of *and* and *but*. It may usually be remedied by proper subordination:

> WORDY: The test was hard, and the students were resentful, and their instructor was irritated.
>
> BETTER: Because the students resented the hard test, their instructor was irritated.

Another kind of wordiness originates in the desire to impress but ends in pretentious nonsense. It is the language of those persons who refer to bad weather as the "inclemency of the elements," who speak of "blessed events" and "passing away" instead of birth and death. Following are further examples of this kind of wordiness:

Our horse Hap has gone to the big round-up in the sky.

Our horse Hap has died.

Due to the fact that he was enamored of Angela, Thomas comported himself in such a way as to appear ridiculous.

Because he was in love with Angela, Thomas behaved foolishly.

I regret extremely the necessity of your departure.

I am sorry you must go.

Sometimes, of course, expressions like these are used facetiously. But do not make a habit of such usage.

Jargon is also a kind of wordiness, popular among people of specialized occupations. It has now spread to much everyday writing and speaking, probably because it is believed to make its users sound and appear knowledgeable. It is the jargon of government officials, social workers, educators on all levels, and others. Its basic principles seem to be these: Never use one word where two or more will do the work. Never use a concrete expression if it is possible to use an abstract one. Never be plain if you can be fancy. The clear sign of this kind of writing and speaking is the repeated use of such phrases as *frame of reference, in terms of, point in time,* and compounds formed with the suffix *-wise.* The writers of this new jargon never simply look at the budget; they "consider the status budgetwise." They don't study crime among the young; they "examine social conditions in terms of juvenile delinquency." They "critique," they "utilize," they "expedite," and they "finalize." They speak of the "culturally deprived," the "classroom learning situation," "meaningful experiences," "togetherness," and "lifestyle." All these expressions reflect a desire to be a part of the "in-group" (another example of this jargon) by picking up catchwords that seem to show a certain sophistication; what they really show is a failure to use precise language and a lack of judgment.

Redundancy, or unnecessary repetition, is another common type of wordiness, due to carelessness or ignorance of the meanings of certain words. Note the following examples of redundancy:

Repeat that again, please. [Why *again*?]

His solution was equally as good as hers. [Why *equally*?]

The consensus of opinion of the group was that Mrs. Jacobs will make a good mayor. [Use either *consensus of the group* or *the opinion of the group*.]

This location is more preferable to that one. [The word *preferable* means "more desirable"; therefore, the word *more* is unnecessary. The sentence should read *This location is preferable to that one.*]

The union continues to remain at odds with factory management. [*Continues* and *remain* mean essentially the same thing. Say, *The union continues at odds with factory management* or *The union remains at odds with factory management.*]

It was a dog large in size and brown in color. [*It was a large brown dog.*]

Mrs. Frost rarely ever wears her fur coat. [*Mrs. Frost rarely wears her fur coat.*]

◼ 22b Vagueness

A general impression of vague thinking is given by the too frequent use of abstract words instead of concrete words. Note especially the vagueness of such common words as *asset, factor, phase, case, nature, character, line,* and *field.* All these have basic meanings and should be used cautiously in any other sense. The following examples show that the best way to treat these words is to get rid of them:

In cases where drivers receive tickets for speeding, they must pay a fine of fifty dollars. [*In cases where* can be replaced with the single word *If.*]

Industry and intelligence are important assets in business success. [Omit *assets* and the sense remains the same.]

The course is of a difficult nature. [*The course is difficult.*]

Jerry was aware of the fact that he was risking his savings. [*Jerry was aware that he was risking his savings.*]

Whenever you are tempted to use such words, stop and ask yourself just what you are trying to say. Then find the exact words to say it, cutting out all the "deadwood."

◼ 22c Triteness

Trite means worn. Certain phrases have been used so often that they have lost their original freshness. Oratory, sermons, newspaper headlines and captions, and pretentious writing in general are frequently marred by such diction. Expressions of this kind are often called **clichés.** The following list is merely illustrative; you can probably think of numerous ones to add to these:

upset the applecart	proud possessor
an ace up his sleeve	nipped in the bud
dull thud	few and far between
one fell swoop	on pins and needles
up on Cloud Nine	make one's blood boil
grim reaper	eat one's heart out
last but not least	having a ball
face the music	as luck would have it
as straight as a die	quick as a wink
bitter end	gung ho

Avoid also quotation of trite phrases from literature and proverbs. Expressions like the following have already served their purpose:

a lean and hungry look	the best laid plans of mice and men
a sadder but wiser man	where angels fear to tread
a rolling stone	love never faileth
those who live in glass houses	to be or not to be

■ 22d Euphemisms

Euphemisms are expressions used to avoid the outright statement of disagreeable ideas or to give dignity to something essentially lowly or undignified. The Victorians were notoriously euphemistic: they called their legs "limbs," and instead of the accurate and descriptive terms *sweat* and *spit,* they substituted the vague but more delicate words "perspire" and "expectorate." Unfortunately, the Victorians were not the last to use euphemisms. While we cannot admire or condone some of today's obscenely explicit language, there is little justification for the fuzzy-minded delicacy of euphemisms. There is a decided difference between choosing an expression that offers a tactful, rather than hurtful, connotation and choosing an expression that is deliberately misleading. Pregnancy is euphemistically referred to as "expecting"; a garbage collector is a "sanitation engineer"; a janitor is a "superintendent," etc. *Death,* of course, has numerous euphemistic substitutes such as "passing on" or "going to his reward."

Again, it should be emphasized that the laudable wish to spare the feelings of others is not to be confused with the sort of prudery or false sense of gentility that most often produces euphemisms. Unless your use of a euphemism is inspired by the necessity to soften a blow or to avoid offensiveness, use the more factual term. Ordinarily, avoid euphemisms — or change the subject.

■ 22e Idiom

Construction characteristic of a language is called **idiom.** The established usage of a language, the special way in which a thing is said or a phrase is formed, must be observed if writing is to be properly idiomatic. In English the normal sentence pattern has the subject first, then the verb, and then the direct object. In French, if the direct object is a pronoun, it usually (except in the imperative) precedes the verb. In English an adjective that directly modifies a noun usually precedes it. In French the adjective usually follows the noun. In English we say, "It is hot." The French say, "It makes hot." Such differences make learning a foreign language difficult.

Another meaning of the word *idiom* is somewhat contrary to this one. The word is also used for all those expressions that seem to defy logical grammatical practice, expressions that cannot be translated literally into another language.

"Many is the day" and "You had better" are good examples. Fortunately, idioms of this sort cause little trouble to native speakers.

In English, as in most modern European languages, one of the greatest difficulties lies in the idiomatic use of prepositions after certain nouns, adjectives, and verbs. Oddly enough, one agrees *with* a person but *to* a proposal, and several persons may agree *upon* a plan. One may have a desire *for* something but be desirous *of* it. One is angry *at* or *about* an act but *with* a person. These uses of prepositions may seem strange and perverse, but they are part of the idiomatic structure of English and must be learned. Good dictionaries frequently indicate correct usage in questions of this kind. Do not look up the preposition but rather the word with which it is used. The definition of this word will usually indicate the correct preposition to use with it.

■ 22f Connotation

In selecting words that will express their thoughts accurately, careful writers pay attention to the **connotations** of certain expressions. *Connotation* is the associative meaning, or what the word suggests beyond its literal definition.

Through popular usage certain terms convey favorable or unfavorable impressions beyond their literal meanings; they frequently have emotional or evaluative qualities that are not part of their straightforward definitions. Careless use of a word with strong connotations may cause faulty communication of your ideas. On the other hand, skillful use of connotation can greatly enrich your ability to communicate accurately. For example, you would not refer to a public figure whom you admire and respect as a "politician," a term that suggests such qualities as insincerity and conniving for personal gain. The word *childish* is inappropriate when you mean "childlike." The adjective *thin* suggests something scanty or somehow not full enough (especially when describing a person's figure); but *slim* and *slender*, two words close to *thin* in literal meaning, imply grace and good proportion.

Again, your dictionary can provide these shades of meaning that will keep you from writing something far different from your intention and will help you develop a vocabulary you can use accurately.

■ 22g Slang

Slang is, as you know, one of the usage labels given in a dictionary to define extremely informal language, frequently earthy but often vividly expressive. It usually has no true equivalent in Standard English and has the advantage of being forceful and dynamic. Although many slang terms, because of these qualities, eventually become acceptable as colloquial English, many more remain current for only a year or two; then, like all overused expressions, they gradually lose their force. Old slang expressions are constantly being abandoned, while new ones are constantly coming into use. There is no need to list slang expressions here, as they so quickly become dated. Be aware, however, that they are easily recognizable and that you must avoid them in all but the most informal written contexts.

Glossary of Faulty Diction

The following glossary should help you rid your speech and writing of many errors. The term **colloquial** means that an expression is characteristic of everyday speech. **Dialectal** means that an expression is peculiar to a particular place or class.

Note: Remember that colloquialisms, the language we use in our everyday conversation with friends and associates, are perfectly acceptable in informal writing and speech. The purpose of this Glossary of Faulty Diction is to point out that some of the listed expressions should be avoided in formal writing; others can never be considered correct.

About, Around. *About* means *rather close to,* usually referring to time or number (*about a year, about forty*). *Around* is concerned with spatial arrangement (*They sat around the table*) and is colloquial when used to mean *about.*

Above. Avoid the use of *above* as a modifier in such phrases as *the **above** reference, the **above** names.* An exception to this rule is that the word is proper in legal documents.

Accept, Except. *To accept* is *to receive; to except* is *to make an exception of, to omit. Except* (as a preposition) means *with the exception of.*

Accidently. There is no such word. The correct form is *accidentally,* based on the adjective *accidental.*

A.D. This is an abbreviation of *Anno Domini* (in the year of our Lord). Strictly considered, it should be used only with a date: ***A.D.*** *1492.* But it has recently come to mean *of the Christian era,* and expressions like *the fifth century **A.D.*** have become common. Here logic has bowed to usage.

Adapt, Adopt. *To adapt* is *to make suitable; to adjust. To adopt* is *to accept* or *to take as one's own.* (*He adapted to his environment; They adopted a child.*)

Administrate. There is no such word. The verb is *administer;* the noun formed from it is *administration.*

Adverse, Averse. *Adverse* means *unfavorable* (*The meteorologist forecast **adverse** conditions for the yacht race*). *Averse* means *opposed to* (*Mother was **averse** to our plans for ice skating at midnight*).

Affect, Effect. In common usage *affect* is a verb meaning *to influence, to have an effect upon* or *to like to have or use* (*He **affects** a gold-headed cane*) or *to pretend* (*She **affects** helplessness*). *Effect* is both verb and noun. *To effect* is *to produce, to bring about.* The noun *effect* is a *result,* a *consequence.*

Aggravate. Colloquial when used to mean *provoke* or *irritate. Aggravate* means *to make worse* (*The rainy weather **aggravated** his rheumatism*).

Agree to, Agree with, Agree upon or **on.** One agrees *to* a proposal, *with* a person, and *upon* or *on* a settlement (*We **agreed to** his suggestion that we go,*

*The boy did not **agree with** his father, The two factions could not **agree upon** a settlement*).

Ain't. This form is occasionally defended as a contraction of *am not*, but even those who defend it do not use it in writing.

Alibi. Colloquial for *excuse*. In formal usage *alibi* has legal significance only and means a confirmation of one's absence from the scene of a crime at the time the crime was committed.

All ready, Already. *All ready* means simply that all are ready (*The players were* **all ready**). *Already* means *previously* or *before now* (*He has **already** gone*).

All together, Altogether. *All together* means all of a number taken or considered together (*She invited them **all together***). *Altogether* means *entirely, completely* (*He was **altogether** wrong*).

Allusion, Illusion. An *allusion* is a casual or indirect reference to something, usually without naming the thing itself (*The quotation in her speech was an **allusion** to Shakespeare's* Macbeth). An *illusion* is a false or unreal impression of reality (*After his unkind treatment of the puppy Mildred lost her **illusions** about Arthur*).

Alright. This is not an acceptable alternate spelling for the words *all right*.

Alumnus, Alumna. *Alumnus* is masculine and has the plural *alumni*. *Alumna* is feminine and has the plural *alumnae*.

Among, Between. The common practice is to use *between* with two persons or objects (***between** a rock and a hard place*) and *among* with more than two (*The crew quarreled **among** themselves*). Exception: *The plane traveled **between** New York, Chicago, and Miami*. Here *among* would be absurd.

Amount, Number. *Amount* is a total mass or body, considered as one entity (*He spent a large **amount** of money*). *Number* refers to a group of things made up of individual parts that can be separated and counted (*A **number** of errors appeared in his essay*).

Anxious, Eager. *Anxious* means *fearful; worried*. *Eager* means *showing keen desire; ardent*. (*Jane was **eager** [not anxious] to go to summer camp*.)

Anyone, Any one. *Anyone*, the indefinite pronoun, is one word. *Any one*, meaning any single person or any single thing, should be written as two words (***Any one** of your friends will be glad to help you*).

Any place, No place. Dialectal corruptions of *anywhere* and *nowhere*.

Apt, Liable, Likely. *Apt* means *suitable, appropriate, tending to*, or *inclined to* (*an **apt** phrase, a man **apt** to succeed*). *Liable* means *exposed to something undesirable* (***liable** to be injured, **liable** for damages*). *Likely* means *credible, probable, probably* (*He had a **likely** excuse*). It can also overlap to some extent with *apt* in its sense of probability (*It is **likely** — or **apt** — to rain today*).

As far as. This expression is frequently misused when it is not followed by words that would complete a clause (***As far as** her ability she is perfectly able to do the work*). This expression should always function as a subordinating conjunction, introducing both a subject and a verb (***As far as** her ability **is concerned**, she is perfectly able to do the work*).

Asset. In its essential meaning this word is used in law and accounting (*His **assets** exceeded his liabilities*). But it seems to have established itself in the meaning of *something useful or desirable.* When used in this sense, it is frequently redundant.

Attend, Tend. *Attend* means *to be present at.* When meaning *to take care of,* it is followed by *to* (*He **attends to** his own business*). *Tend* without a preposition also means *to take care of* (*He **tends** his own garden*). *Tend to* means *to have a tendency to* (*She **tends to** become nervous when her children are noisy*).

Audience, Spectators. *Audience,* interpreted literally, means *a group of listeners; spectators* are *a group of viewers.* The distinction need not be rigid, but it is better not to say "*The **spectators** applauded loudly at the end of the concert,*" or "*The **audience** booed the rude tennis player.*"

Author, Host, Chair, Position. These nouns and many others like them are frequently misused as verbs (*She has **authored** three best-sellers, The Joneses plan to **host** a party for their friends, The woman who **chairs** the committee is a lawyer, Please **position** the chairs around the table*). In these four sentences there are perfectly adequate verbs that should be used: *written, give, is chairman of,* and *place.*

Awful, Awfully. Either of these is colloquial when used to mean *very.*

Awhile, A while. *Awhile* is used as an adverb (*They stayed **awhile** at their friend's house*). When used after the preposition *for, while* is a noun, the object of the preposition (*I thought for **a while** that you were going to miss the plane*). The adverb is written as one word; the object of the preposition and its article are written as two.

Bad, Badly. *Bad* is an adjective, *badly* an adverb. Say *I feel **bad,*** not *I feel **badly,*** if you mean *I am ill* or *I am sorry.*

Balance. Except in accounting, the use of *balance* for *difference, remainder, the rest* is colloquial.

Being as. Dialectal for *since* or *because.*

Beside, Besides. *Beside* is a preposition meaning *by the side of* (*Along came a spider and sat down **beside** her*). *Besides* is a preposition meaning *except* (*He had nothing **besides** his good name*) and an adverb meaning *in addition, moreover* (*He received a medal and fifty dollars **besides***).

Blame on. Correct idiom calls for the use of *to blame* with *for,* not *on.* (*They **blamed** the driver **for** the accident,* not *They **blamed** the accident **on** the driver.*) *Blame on* is colloquial.

Boyfriend, Girlfriend. These two terms are colloquial, meaning *a favored male or female friend, a sweetheart.*

Bring, Take. *Bring* means to convey to this place here (*Please **bring** me my scissors from the den*). *Take* denotes conveyance away from the place of speaking or the point from which the action is regarded (*Marjorie is going to **take** a heavy coat on the camping trip tomorrow*).

Burst, Bursted, Bust. The principal parts of the verb *burst* are *burst, burst,* and *burst.* The use of *bursted* or *busted* for the past tense is incorrect. *Bust* is either sculpture or a part of the human body. Used for *failure* or as a verb for *burst* or *break,* it is slang.

But. When *but* is used to mean *only,* it should not be used with a negative verb (*I **haven't but** one dollar in my wallet*). The correct form is *I **have but** one* *dollar in my wallet.* Of course, the more natural expression is *I have only one dollar in my wallet.*

But what.   Use *that* or *but that* instead of *but what* (*They had no doubt **that** help would come*).

Calvary, Cavalry.   Mistakes here are chiefly a matter of spelling, but it is important to be aware of the difference: *Calvary* is the name of the hill where Jesus was crucified; *cavalry* refers to troops trained to fight on horseback, or more recently in armored vehicles.

Cannot.   This word is the negative form of *can.* It is written as one word.

Cannot help but.   This is a mixed construction. *Cannot help* and *cannot but* are separate expressions, either of which is correct (*He **cannot but** attempt it,* or *He **cannot help** attempting it*).

Capital, Capitol.   *Capital* is a city; *capitol* is a building. *Capital* is also an adjective, usually meaning *chief, excellent.*

Case.   This is a vague and unnecessary word in many of its common uses today. Avoid *case* and seek the exact word.

Chairperson.   Use the terms *chairman* and *chairwoman* in preference to *chairperson,* which should be used only if it is an official title in an organization or if you are quoting directly someone who has used the term.

Chaise lounge.   The second word in this term is *longue,* not *lounge.* It is a French expression meaning "long chair," and the word *longue* is pronounced the same as the English *long.* Many people simply misread the similar spelling and think that the word is our English word *lounge.*

Childish, Childlike.   *Childish* strongly implies the lack of maturity or of reasonable attitude characteristic of childhood (*She behaved **childishly** in refusing to eat*). *Childlike* has the connotation of innocence, faith, or trust (*He has a **childlike** faith in the power of good*).

Cite, Site.   Cite means *to quote,* or *to summon officially to appear in court* (*Thomas **cited** Einstein as his authority, George was **cited** by the police for drunken driving*). *Site* is the position or area on which anything is, has been, or will be located (*We visited the **site** where our new home will be built*).

Claim.   Do not use simply to mean *say.* In the correct use of *claim* some disputed right is involved (*He **claims** to be the heir of a very wealthy man*).

Clear.   When *clear* is used to mean *all the way* (*The ball rolled **clear** across the road*), it is colloquial.

Complement, Compliment.   In its usual sense *complement* means *something that completes* (*Her navy blue shoes and bag were a **complement** for her gray suit*). A *compliment* is an expression of courtesy or praise (*My **compliments** to the chef*).

Connotate.   There is no such verb as *connotate;* the verb is *connote,* and its noun form is *connotation.*

Consensus of opinion.   The word *consensus* alone means *general agreement.* The phrase *of opinion* is redundant.

Considerable.   This word is an adjective meaning *worthy of consideration, important* (*The idea is at least **considerable***). When used as a noun to denote a great deal or a great many, *considerable* is colloquial or informal.

Contact.   Colloquial and sometimes vague when used for *see, meet, communicate with*, as in *I must **contact** my agent*.

Continual, Continuous.   *Continual* means *repeated often* (*The interruptions were **continual***). *Continuous* means *going on without interruption* (*For two days the pain was **continuous***).

Convince, Persuade.   Do not use *convince* for *persuade* as in *I **convinced** him to wash the dishes*. *Convince* means *to overcome doubt* (*I **convinced** him of the soundness of my plan*). *Persuade* means *to win over by argument or entreaty* (*I **persuaded** him to wash the dishes*).

Couple.   This word, followed by *of*, is informal for *two* or *a few*.

Credible, Creditable.   *Credible* means *believable* (*His evidence was not **credible***). *Creditable* means *deserving esteem or admiration* (*The acting of the male lead was a **creditable** performance*).

Critique.   This word is a noun, not a verb; it means a critical review or comment dealing with an artistic work. The correct verb is *evaluate* or *review*.

Cupfuls, Cupsful.   The plural of cupful is *cupfuls*, not *cupsful*.

Data.   *Data is the plural of datum, something given or known.* It usually refers to a body of facts or figures. It normally takes a plural verb (*These **data** are important*). At times, however, *data* may be considered a collective noun and used with a singular verb.

Definitely.   This is frequently used to mean *very* or *quite*. A trite expression, it should be avoided for this reason as well as for its lack of accuracy.

Desert, Dessert.   The noun *desert(s)* means *a deserved reward or punishment* (*to receive one's just deserts*). Do not confuse this word with *dessert*, which is *the sweet course served at the end of a meal*.

Different than.   Most good writers use *different from*, not *different than*.

Disburse, Disperse.   *Disburse* means *to pay out; spend* (***disbursement** of funds*). *Disperse*, which is sometimes confused with *disburse*, means *to scatter* (*The crowd **dispersed** quickly*).

Disinterested.   Often confused with *uninterested*. *Disinterested* means *unbiased, impartial; uninterested* means *lacking interest in*.

Don't.   A contraction of *do not*. Do not write *he, she,* or *it don't*.

Drapes.   Incorrect when used as a noun to mean *curtains*. *Drape* is the verb; *draperies* is the correct noun form.

Due to.   Do not use *due to* for *because of* as in ***Due to** a lengthy illness, he left college*. *Due to* is correctly used after a noun or linking verb (*His failure, **due to** laziness, was not surprising. The accident was **due to** carelessness*).

Dyeing, Dying.   *Dyeing* refers to the coloring of materials with dye. Do not omit the *e*, which would confuse the word with *dying*, meaning *expiring*.

Each other, One another.   *Each other* is used to denote two people (*Nancy and John like **each other***); *one another* involves more than two people (*All human beings should try to be kind to **one another***).

Emigrant, Immigrant.   A person who moves from one place to another is both an *emigrant* and an *immigrant*, but one emigrates *from* one place and immigrates *to* the other.

Enormity.   This words means *great wickedness; a monstrous or outrageous act*. It should not be used to mean great size or vastness (*The* **enormity** *of his crime was shocking,* not *The* **enormity** *of his generosity is wonderful*).

Enthuse, Enthused.   These words are colloquial and always unacceptable in writing.

Equally as.   Do not use these two words together; omit either *equally* or *as.* Do not write *Water is* **equally as** *necessary as air;* write *Water is* **as** *necessary as air* or *Water and air are* **equally** *necessary.*

Etc.   An abbreviation of Latin *et* (*and*) and *cetera* (*other things*). It should not be preceded by *and,* nor should it be used as a catch-all expression to avoid a clear and exact ending of an idea or a sentence.

Everyday, Every day.   When written as one word (*everyday*), this expression is an adjective (*Mother's* **everyday** *china is ironstone*). When used adverbially to indicate how often something happens, it is written as two words (*Every day at noon I eat an apple and drink a glass of milk*).

Exam.   A colloquial abbreviation for *examination.* Compare *gym, dorm, lab,* and *prof.*

Expect.   This word means *to look forward to* or *foresee.* Do not use it to mean *suspect* or *suppose.*

Fact that.   This is an example of wordiness, usually amounting to redundancy. Most sentences can omit the phrase *the fact that* without changing the sense of what is said (**The fact that** *he wanted a new bicycle was the reason why he stole the money* may be effectively reduced to *He stole the money because he wanted a new bicycle*). Whenever you are tempted to use this expression, try rewording the sentence without it; you will have a more concise and a clearer statement.

Farther, Further.   The two words are often confused. *Farther* means *at or to a more distant point in space or time; further* means *to a greater extent, in addition.* One says *It is* **farther** *to Minneapolis from Chicago than from here,* but *We will talk* **further** *about this tomorrow.*

Faze.   Colloquial for *to disturb* or *to agitate.* Most commonly used in the negative (*Mother's angry looks didn't* **faze** *Jimmy*).

Feel.   *Feel* means to perceive through the physical senses or through the emotions. This word should not be used as a careless equivalent of *think* or *believe,* both of which refer to mental activity.

Fellow.   Colloquial when used to mean a *person.*

Fewer, Less.   Use *fewer* to refer to a number, *less* to refer to amount (*Where there are* **fewer** *persons, there is* **less** *noise*).

Fine.   Colloquial when used as a term of general approval.

Fix.   *Fix* is a verb, meaning *to make firm or stable.* Used as a noun meaning *a bad condition,* it is colloquial.

Flaunt, Flout.   *Flaunt* means *to exhibit ostentatiously, to show off* (*She* **flaunted** *her new mink coat before her friends*). *Flout* means *to show contempt for, to scorn* (*Margaret often* **flouts** *the rules of good sportsmanship*).

Forego, Forgo.   *Forego* means *to precede* or *go before* (*The* **foregoing** *data were gathered two years ago*). *Forgo* means *to give up, relinquish* (*I am afraid I must* **forgo** *the pleasure of meeting your friends today*).

Formally, Formerly.   *Formally* means *in a formal manner* (*He was **formally** initiated into his fraternity last night*). *Formerly* means *at a former time* (*They **formerly** lived in Ohio*).

Gentleman, Lady.   Do not use these words as synonyms for *man* and *woman*.

Got.   This is a correct past participle of the verb *to get* (*He had **got** three traffic tickets in two days*). *Gotten* is an alternative past participle of *to get*.

Graduate.   The verb *graduate* must be followed by *from* (*Father **graduated from** Harvard University in 1968*). Usage of the verb without *from* (*She **graduated** high school with honors*) is nonstandard.

Guess.   Colloquial when used for *suppose* or *believe*.

Guy.   Slang when used for *boy* or *man*.

Hanged, Hung.   *Hanged* is the correct past tense or past participle of *hang* when capital punishment is meant (*The cattle rustlers were **hanged** at daybreak*). *Hung* is the past tense and past participle in every other sense of the term (*We **hung** popcorn and cranberries on the Christmas tree*).

Hardly, Scarcely.   Do not use with a negative. *I can't hardly see it* borders on the illiterate. Write *I **can** hardly see it* or (if you cannot see it at all) *I **can't** see it*.

Healthful, Healthy.   Places are *healthful* if persons may be *healthy* living in them.

Hopefully.   This word means *in a hopeful manner* (*She **hopefully** began getting ready for her blind date*). Do not use this modifier to mean *it is hoped* or *let us hope* (***Hopefully**, the new rail system for Atlanta will be completed within five years*).

Human.   *Human* is an adjective, preferably not used alone as a noun. *Human being* is the correct term.

If, Whether.   In careful writing do not use *if* for *whether*. *Let me know **if** you are coming* does not mean exactly the same thing as *Let me know **whether** you are coming*. The latter leaves no doubt that a reply is expected.

Impact, Conference, Defense.   Many other nouns are frequently misused as verbs (*New taxes will **impact** modest wage earners, The two prime ministers **conferenced** for several days, The Bears **defensed** poorly in the second half of the game, The Joneses will **host** a party for their friends*). In these four sentences perfectly adequate verbs are available and should be used.

Imply, Infer.   *Imply* means *to suggest, to express indirectly*. *Infer* means *to conclude*, as on the basis of suggestion or implication. A writer *implies* to a reader; a reader *infers* from a writer.

Incidently.   There is no such word. The correct form is *incidentally*, based on the adjective *incidental*.

Into, In to.   *Into* is a preposition meaning *toward the inside* and is followed by an object of the preposition. Do not use the one-word form of this expression when the object of the preposition is the object of *to* only and *in* is an adverbial modifier. Say *He went **into** the building* but *The men handed their application forms **in to** the personnel manager*.

Irregardless.   No such word exists. *Regardless* is the correct word.

Its, It's.   The form *its* is possessive (*Every dog has **its** day*). *It's* is a contraction of *it is* (***It's** a pity she's a bore*).

It's me. Formal English requires *It is I*. *It's me* is informal or colloquial, perfectly acceptable in conversation but not proper for written English. Compare the French idiom *C'est moi*.

Kid. Used to mean a child or young person or as a verb meaning *to tease or jest, kid* is slang.

Kind, Sort. These are singular forms and should be modified accordingly (*this kind, that sort*). *Kinds* and *sorts* are plural, and they, of course, have plural modifiers.

Kind of, Sort of. Do not use these to mean *rather* as in *He was **kind of** (or **sort of**) lazy.*

Last, Latest. *Last* implies that there will be no more. *Latest* does not prevent the possibility of another appearance later. The proper sense of both is seen in the sentence *After seeing his **latest** play, we hope that it is his **last.***

Lay, Lie. *Lay* is a transitive verb, always taking an object and meaning *to make something lie; to set or place* (*Please **lay** the cards on the table*). *Lie*, an intransitive verb, means *to be at rest* (*I will **lie** down for a nap*, not *I will **lay** down for a nap*).

Lend, Loan. The use of *loan* as a verb is incorrect. *Loan* is a noun. The distinction between the two words may be seen in the sentence *If you will **lend** me ten dollars until Friday, I will appreciate the **loan.***

Less, Fewer. These are comparatives. *Less* refers to amount as an inseparable mass or body (*My car weighs **less** than Harry's*). *Fewer* refers to number, things that can be counted (*I had **fewer** colds this winter than last*).

Like, As. Confusion in the use of these two words results from using *like* as a conjunction. The preposition *like* should be followed by an object (*He ran **like** an antelope*). The conjunction *as* is followed by a clause (*He did **as** he wished, He talked **as** though he were crazy*). The incorrect use of *as* as a preposition is a kind of reaction against the use of *like* as a conjunction. Consider the sentence: *Many species of oaks, **as** the red oak, the white oak, the water oak, are found in the Southeast.* Here the correct word is *like*, not *as*.

Literally. The word means *faithfully, to the letter, letter for letter, exactly*. Do not use in the sense of *completely*, or *in effect*. A sentence may be copied *literally*; but one never, except under extraordinary circumstances, *literally* devours a book. Frequently, the word *virtually*, meaning *in effect or essence, though not in fact*, is the correct word.

Lot, Lots. Colloquial or informal when used to mean *many* or *much*.

Mad. The essential meaning of *mad* is *insane*. When used to mean *angry*, it is informal.

Masterful, Masterly. *Masterful* carries the suggestion of being forceful or even domineering (*He is a **masterful** dean of the college*). *Masterly* indicates expertness and skill (*John did a **masterly** job of editing the magazine*).

May be, Maybe. *May be* is a verb phrase (*It **may be** that you are right*). *Maybe* used as an adverb means *perhaps* (***Maybe** you are right*).

Mean. Used for *disagreeable* or *cruel* (*He had a **mean** disposition, She is **mean** to me*), the word is informal or colloquial. (Standard English denotation is *inferior* and *humble*.)

Media. *Media* is the plural of *medium, a means, agency,* or *instrumentality.* It is often incorrectly used in the plural as though it were singular, as in *The media is playing an important role in political races this year.*

Midnight, Noon.   Neither of these words needs the word *twelve* before it. They themselves refer to specific times, so *twelve* is redundant.

Most, Almost.   *Most* is colloquial when used to mean *almost; nearly* (**Most** *all my friends are at the beach*). *Almost* is the correct expression (**Almost** *all the work was finished on time*).

Muchly.   There is no such word as *muchly. Much* is both adjective and adverb (**Much** *water has flowed over the dam. Thank you very* **much**).

Mutual.   The use of *mutual* for *common* is usually avoided by careful writers. **Common** *knowledge,* **common** *property,* **common** *dislikes* are things shared by two or more persons. **Mutual** *admiration* means *admiration of each for the other.*

Myself.   Colloquial when used as a substitute for *I* or *me,* as in *He and* **myself** *were there.* It is correctly used intensively (*I* **myself** *will do it*) and reflexively (*I blame only* **myself**).

Nauseated, Nauseous.   These two words are frequently confused. *Nauseated* means *feeling a sickness at the stomach; a sensation of impending vomiting* (*I was* **nauseated** *because of having eaten my lunch too fast*). *Nauseous* means *sickening, disgusting; loathsome* (*The* **nauseous** *odor of the gas was affecting everyone in the building*).

Nice.   *Nice* is a catch-all word that has lost its force because it has no clearcut, specific meaning as a modifier. When writing in praise of something, select an adjective that conveys more specific information than *nice* does.

Noted, Notorious.   *Noted* means *distinguished; renowned; eminent* (*He was* **noted** *for his skill as a surgeon*). *Notorious* refers to something or someone widely but unfavorably known and discussed (*He was* **notorious** *for his unethical business dealings*).

Of.   Unnecessary after such prepositions as *off, inside, outside* (not *He fell* **off of** *the cliff* but *He fell* **off** *the cliff*).

On account of.   Do not use as a conjunction; the phrase should be followed by an object of the preposition *of* (**on account of** *his illness*). *He was absent* **on account of** *he was sick* is incorrect.

Oral, Verbal, Written.   Use *oral* to refer to spoken words (*An* **oral** *examination is sometimes nerve-wracking for a student*); use *verbal* to contrast a communication in words to some other kind of communication (*His scowl told me more than any* **verbal** *message could*); use *written* when referring to anything put on paper.

Orientate.   There is no such word. The verb is *orient,* meaning *to cause to become familiar with or adjusted to facts or a situation* (*He* **oriented** *himself by finding the North Star*). The noun is *orientation.*

Over with.   The *with* is unnecessary in such expressions as *The game was* **over** *with by five o'clock.*

Party.   Colloquial when used to mean *a person.* Properly used in legal documents (**party** *of the first part*).

Passed, Past.   *Passed* is the past tense and the past participle of the verb *to pass*

(*We **passed** each other in the hall this morning; We must have **passed** the house we were looking for*). *Past* is an adjective (*During the **past** few years he has worked in a factory*); a noun (*In the **past** she was a ballerina*); an adverb (*She waved as she drove **past***); or a preposition (*Ours is the first house **past** the drugstore*). The two words are not interchangeable.

Pedal, Peddle.   *Pedal*, as a verb, means *to operate a lever with the foot* on a machine like a bicycle, a piano, or a sewing machine (*Sam **pedaled** vigorously up the steep hill on his bicycle*). The verb *to peddle* means to travel about selling goods (*The old man **peddled** his wares from door to door*).

Peeve.   Either as a verb or noun, *peeve* is informal diction.

Persecute, Prosecute.   *Persecute* means *to harass persistently*, usually in order to injure, for adherence to principle or religious belief (*Oliver Cromwell **persecuted** Englishmen who were loyal to the Crown*). *Prosecute* means *to institute legal proceedings against a person* (*The man has been indicted, and his case will be **prosecuted** in April*).

Personally.   This word is often redundant and is a hackneyed, sometimes irritating expression, as in ***Personally,** I think you are making a big mistake.*

Plan on.   Omit *on*. In standard practice idiom calls for an infinitive or a direct object after *plan*. *They **planned** to go* or *They **planned** a reception* are both correct usage.

Plenty.   This word is a noun, not an adverb. Do not write *He was **plenty** worried.*

Pore, Pour.   *Pore*, meaning *to meditate* or *to study intently and with steady application*, is a verb used with the preposition *over* (*She **pored over** her chemistry assignment for several hours*). It should not be confused with *pour*, meaning *to set a liquid flowing or falling* (*They **poured** the tea into fragile china cups*).

Principal, Principle.   *Principal* is both an adjective and a noun (***principal** parts, **principal** of the school, **principal** and interest*). *Principle* is a noun only (***principles** of philosophy, a man of **principle***).

Pupil, Student.   Schoolchildren in the elementary grades are called *pupils*; in grades nine through twelve *student* or *pupil* is correct; for college the term must always be *student*.

Quote, Quotation.   *Quote* is a verb and should not be used as a noun, as in *The **quote** you gave is from Shakespeare, not the Bible. Quotation* is the noun.

Real.   Do not use for *really. Real* is an adjective; *really* is an adverb (*The **real** gems are **really** beautiful*).

Reason is because.   This is not idiomatic English. The subject-linking verb construction calls for a predicate nominative, but *because* is a subordinating conjunction that introduces an adverbial clause. Write *The **reason** I was late **is that** I had an accident*, not *The **reason** I was late **is because** I had an accident.*

Regrettable, Regretful.   *Regrettable* means that something is to be regretted (*It was a **regrettable** error*). *Regretful* describes a person who is sorry or rueful about something (*I am **regretful** about my error*).

Rein, Reign.   *Rein* is a narrow strap of leather used by a rider to control a horse; it is frequently used figuratively to indicate control (*He took up the **reins** of government*); it should not be confused with *reign*, having to do with royal power (*Queen Victoria's **reign** lasted sixty-four years*).

Respectfully, Respectively.   *Respectfully* means *with respect*, as in *The young used to act* ***respectfully*** *toward their elders. Respectively* is a word seldom needed; it means *in the order designated*, as in *The men and women took their seats on the right and left* ***respectively.***

Reverend.   This word, like *Honorable,* is not a noun, but an honorific adjective. It is not a title like *doctor* or *president.* It is properly used preceding *Mr.* or the given name or initials, as in *the* ***Reverend*** *Mr. Gilbreath, the* ***Reverend*** *Earl Gilbreath, the* ***Reverend*** *J. E. Gilbreath.* To use the word as a title as in ***Reverend,*** *will you lead us in prayer?* or *Is there a* ***Reverend*** *in the house?* is incorrect. ***Reverend*** *Gilbreath* instead of *the* ***Reverend*** *Mr. Gilbreath* is almost as bad.

Right.   In the sense of *very* or *extremely, right* is colloquial or dialectal. Do not write (or say) *I'm* ***right*** *glad to know you.*

Same.   The word is an adjective, not a pronoun. Do not use it as in *We received your order and will give* ***same*** *immediate attention.* Substitute *it* for *same.*

Savings.   This word is frequently misused in the plural when the singular is the correct form. It is particularly puzzling that many people use this plural with a singular article, as in *The 10 percent discount gives you a* ***savings*** *of nine dollars. A saving* is the proper usage here. Another common error occurs with *Daylight* ***Saving*** *Time;* the right form again is *Saving,* not *Savings.*

Shape.   In formal writing do not use *shape* for *condition* as in *He played badly because he was in poor* ***shape.*** In this sense *shape* is informal.

Should of, would of.   Do not use these terms for *should have, would have.*

Situation.   This is another catch-all term, frequently used redundantly, as in *It was a fourth-down* ***situation.*** Fourth down *is* a situation, so the word itself is repetitious. This vague term can usually be omitted or replaced with a more specific word.

So.   Avoid the use of *so* for *very,* as in *Thank you* ***so*** *much. So* used as an adverb means *thus* or *like this.*

Some.   Do not use for *somewhat,* as in *She is* ***some*** *better after her illness.*

Species.   This word is both singular and plural. One may speak of *one species* or *three species.* The word usually refers to a kind of plant or animal.

Sprightly, Spritely.   *Sprightly* means *animated, vivacious, lively.* There is no such word as *spritely,* but many people use this term, probably because it suggests the word *sprite,* an *elf* or *fairy.* Do not write *Her* ***spritely*** *conversation was fascinating.*

Stationary, Stationery.   *Stationary* means *fixed, not moving.* Remember that *stationery,* which is paper for writing letters, is sold by a *stationer.*

Statue, Stature, Statute.   A *statue* is a piece of sculpture. *Stature* is bodily height, often used figuratively to mean *level of achievement, status,* or *importance.* A *statute* is a law or regulation.

Strata.   This is the plural of the Latin *stratum.* One speaks of *a stratum* of rock but of *several strata.*

Super, Fantastic, Awesome, Terrific, Incredible.   When used to describe something exciting or marvelous, these overworked words actually add little to our everyday conversation because they have lost their original force through constant repetition. They should never be a part of written English because they are both slangy and trite.

Suppose, Supposed.   Many people incorrectly use the first form, *suppose*, before an infinitive when the second form, *supposed*, is needed, as in *Am I suppose to meet you at five o'clock?* The past participle *supposed* must go along with the auxiliary verb *am* to form the passive voice. This error almost certainly arises from an inability to hear the final *d* when it precedes the *t* in the *to* of the infinitive. The correct form is *Am I **supposed** to meet you at five o'clock?*

Sure, Surely.   Do not use the adjective *sure* for the adverb *surely*. *I am **sure** that you are right* and *I am **surely** glad to be here* are correct.

Thusly.   *Thus* is an adverb. The *-ly* ending is not needed (*Baste the seam **thus**, not Baste the seam **thusly***).

Trustee, Trusty.   The word *trustee* means *a person elected or appointed to direct funds or policy* for a person or an institution, as in *Mr. Higginbotham is a **trustee** on the bank's board of directors.* A *trusty*, on the other hand, is a prisoner granted special privileges because he is believed trustworthy, as in *Although he was a **trusty**, Harris escaped from prison early today.*

Too.   *Too* means *in addition*, or *excessively*. It is incorrect to use the word to mean *very* or *very much*, as in *I was not **too** impressed by her latest book* or *I'm afraid I don't know him **too** well.*

Try and.   Use *try to*, not *try and*, in such expressions as *Try **to** get here on time* (not *Try **and** get here on time*).

Type.   Colloquial in expressions like *this **type** book*; write *this **type of** book*.

Undoubtably, Undoubtedly.   There is no such word as *undoubtably*. The correct word is *undoubtedly*.

Unique.   If referring to something as the only one of its kind, you may correctly use *unique*. (*The Grand Canyon is a **unique** geological formation*). The word does not mean *rare*, *strange*, or *remarkable*, and there are no degrees of *uniqueness*; to say that something is the **most unique** thing one has ever seen is faulty diction.

Use to, Use to could, Used to could.   Because the final *d* sound of *used* and the initial *t* sound of *to* are run together in pronunciation, writers often omit the *d* in *used to*. Be sure to include the *d* when writing this expression. The *to* and *could* in *used to could* are incorrect when used together because *to* is part of an infinitive, while *could* is the past tense of *can*. You can express your meaning by saying *once could* or *used to be able to* (*Mother **once could** play the piano beautifully* or *Mother **used to be able** to play the piano beautifully*).

Very.   Do not use as a modifier of a past participle, as in **very** broken. English idiom calls for **badly** broken or **very badly** broken.

Vice, Vise.   *Vice* is an evil or immoral practice or habit (*The **vice** in our city has reached an all-time high*). A *vise* is a clamping device of metal or wood, used in carpentry to hold a piece in position (*The cabinetmaker used a **vise** to hold the tabletop in place*).

Wait for, Wait on.   *To wait for* means *to look forward to, to expect* (*For two hours I have **waited for** you*). *To wait on* means *to serve* (*The butler and two maids **waited on** the guests at dinner*).

Wangle, Wrangle.   *Wangle* is a colloquial expression meaning *to bring about by persuasion or adroit manipulation* (*I managed to **wangle** permission from Mother* *to go to the game*). *Wrangle* means *to quarrel noisily and contentiously* (*I am tired of the children's constant wrangling*). Do not confuse the two words.

Want in, Want off, Want out.   These forms are dialectal. Do not use them for *want to come in, want to get off, want to get out.*

Way.   Colloquial when used for *away,* as in **Way** *down upon the Swanee River.*

Ways.   Colloquial when used for *way,* as in *a long **ways** to go.*

Where . . . at, Where . . . to.   The word *where* is an adverb meaning *in or at what place.* The addition of *at* or *to* is redundant.

Where, That.   *Where* is incorrect when used to mean *that* (*I see in the paper **where** the president will visit Europe next week*). Use *that* instead of *where* in the foregoing sentence.

Whose, Who's.   The possessive form is *whose* (***Whose** book is this?*). *Who's* is a contraction of *who is* (***Who's** at the door?*). The use of *whose* as a neuter possessive is confirmed by the history of the word and the practice of good writers. *The house **whose** roof is leaking* is more natural and less clumsy than *the house the roof **of which** is leaking.*

-Wise.   This suffix has become a cliche', attached indiscriminately to many nouns (*healthwise, budgetwise, fashionwise, ecologywise*). Try not to use this catch-all suffix habitually.

Wrest, Wrestle.   *Wrest* means *to twist violently in order to pull away by force* (*Bob **wrested** the pistol from the burglar*). *Wrestle* means *to struggle bodily with an opponent to force him down* (*The two men **wrestled** until Hugh threw Roger to the mat*). The two words are not interchangeable.

Your, You're.   The possessive form is *your* (*Tell me **your** name*). *You're* is a contraction of *you are.*

Exercise 85   Diction

Rewrite the following sentences, reducing wordiness and/or needless repetition. Be careful that your reduction does not lead to a series of short, choppy sentences, sometimes called "primer style." At the same time, be sure not to omit any information essential to the overall sense of the sentence.

Example: Every once in a while Grandfather reverts back to his childhood days when he was a young boy, and he recalls again the time in the past when life was different from the way it is now.

Occasionally Grandfather recalls his childhood, when life was different from life today.

1. Honestly, I do believe that Harry is about to repeat again that fake excuse that he trumped up about having to take his sister to the airport.

2. The nature of Gwen's financial circumstances is such that she is now able to afford to take the trip about which she has been dreaming about for a long time.

3. Those letters I repeatedly keep getting in the mail tell me that I can receive a free gift just by claiming it.

4. After long consideration Jane came to the conclusion that Joe had been playing fast and loose with the truth and that he was not really planning to get ready to try out for the Olympic cross-country team after all.

5. There is a boy who goes to my school, and he has red hair, and he also has freckles, and his nickname is "Red-Roof."

6. The truth is, Geraldine, that in your case as an undergraduate student, you are not studying adequately enough, and you may find yourself in an awkward predicament sometime soon in the near future.

7. My history teacher is a woman who is frequently discovered to be grouchy and testy; past experience tells me that she is also an instructor who habitually gives low grades.

8. Jerry's new car is a very handsome vehicle, turquoise in color and small but comfortable in size and legroom.

9. Several film stars who have been in the movies have written autobiographies of their lives, one of my favorites being the one by Katharine Hepburn, which she has titled *Me*.

10. When all is said and done, each and every one of you is going to have to preplan for the important basic essentials that will be first priorities in the selection of a career.

Exercise 86 Diction

Rewrite the following sentences, reducing wordiness and/or needless repetition. Be careful that your reduction does not lead to a series of short, choppy sentences, sometimes called "primer style." At the same time, be sure not to omit any information essential to the overall meaning of the sentence.

Example: When it comes to the idea of whether chocolate ripple or pistachio ice cream is more preferable, I'll make pistachio my choice every time.

When given a choice between chocolate ripple and pistachio ice cream, I always choose pistachio.

1. Because of the fact that I am Ellen's senior by being three years older, it is my opinion that Father should allow me to use the car today.

2. With a big smile on his face Hal announced that his fellow schoolmates had elected him Mr. Congeniality and that it also seemed to be the consensus of opinion that he would in all probability be the president of the senior class.

3. Suzanne's dress for the spring formal was created by the famous designer Madame Lasagna, and it is very unique.

4. The dress is a beautiful lime green color, and the length reaches all the way to Suzanne's ankles.

5. Penny and Millie's friendship dates back from grammar school days, and they continue to remain close friends who are completely inseparable companions.

6. Equally as congenial are Jack, Penny's brother, and Rob, Millie's brother; and as a matter of fact, both of them are planning to join the Marines together.

7. Running as rapidly as possible, Jeff went on foot to the nearest house to see whether he might possibly use a telephone with which he could call for someone to come and help him repair his flat tire.

8. Melissa commutes back and forth every day to her job, and she says that never before in the past has she been so much of the opinion that a car air conditioner is an absolute necessity.

9. Both of the Granvilles' daughters have different college majors, and from the standpoint of making good grades, they are both doing well.

10. In this world of today, the usual customs of the bygone era of the past, especially in the area of good manners, seem no longer to be taken into consideration.

Exercise 87 Diction

The following sentences contain one or more trite expressions or euphemisms. Underline the trite and euphemistic phrases, and for each one write either **T** or **E** in the space at the right.

Example: Our neighbor Mr. Franklin says that his <u>better half</u>
is a wonderful golfer.   _____T_____

1. Well, I watched with bated breath while our team scored the winning touchdown just in the nick of time.   _____

2. Janet had such a pain in her tummy that she told us in no uncertain terms that she could not help with the dishes.   _____

3. My old dog Queenie, a seventeen-year-old collie, passed away in the wee, small hours last night.   _____

4. When all is said and done, Peter, you will find that Hugh is second to none in sticking to his guns.   _____

5. Mrs. Frobisher, you have been a tower of strength in the final analysis, and we all appreciate your support.   _____

6. Fortunately, Christine decided to leave her job before she was given a pink slip.   _____

7. Nell's great-grandfather is in his sunset years, but he is always as busy as a bee with various interesting projects.   _____

8. I tried and tried to start my car, but as luck would have it, the battery was dead as a doornail.   _____

9. Little Tommy is a holy terror, but he is the apple of his mother's eye, so far be it from me to correct him.   _____

10. I hear that Mrs. Albright is accepting paying guests, and she hopes that this measure will help her cash-flow problem.   _____

11. Accidents will happen, but I believe that Rick was under the influence when he had his wreck.   _____

12. In Caracas, Venezuela, we toured a deprived area, and each and every one of us felt depressed at the sights we saw.   _____

13. In this day and age, jobs are few and far between, so Ellie heaved a sigh of relief when she finally left the ranks of the unemployed.   _____

14. All the boys were green with envy when they saw Tim's good-looking preowned car.   _____

15. For a senior citizen, Mrs. Appleton looks fit as a fiddle, and we are pleased as punch that she is so hale and hearty.   _____

16. All the children on our street are having a ball because the Newtons have a new swimming pool.   _____

17. I have at long last decided to throw caution to the winds and find out whether blonds really have more fun.   _____

18. Al turned red as a beet when June asked him who his date was last Saturday night.   _____

19. The stork paid a visit to the Underwoods yesterday, and they have named the little bundle of joy after his father.   _____

20. According to the police, the accused man had a controlled substance in his possession at the time of his arrest.   _____

Exercise 88   Diction

The following sentences contain unidiomatic uses of prepositions. Underline each preposition that is incorrectly used and write the correct form at the right.

Example: The opposing armies agreed <u>with</u> a two-day truce
to negotiate a satisfactory settlement.   _____*to*_____

1. Having waited on Larry for almost an hour in the hot
   sun, I finally decided to go home and cool off.   _____

2. Sally put her new sweater in a plastic bag and laid it in
   the drawer.   _____

3. Julia and Gloria have been arguing among themselves
   about who should have to sleep in the upper bunk.   _____

4. It seems unfair on Julia to have the upper bunk, because
   she has had it for the past two years.   _____

5. Laurie was convinced that her headache was brought
   about from studying too hard for her finals.   _____

6. Vince says that he is intimidated and in awe of his new
   supervisor.   _____

7. We couldn't believe our eyes when we came in the room
   and there sat Grandfather, watching and listening at our
   new rock video.   _____

8. Where are you living at, Patrick, now that you have
   moved off of our street?   _____

9. Chris said that she had never been so upset as she was
   at Tom when Tom was driving too fast on Interstate 95.   _____

10. Tom insisted that he was not reckless and that he was
    not driving in excess over the posted speed limit.   _____

11. Paul turned his application form into the personnel man-
    ager, hoping that his qualifications measured up with
    the company's standards.   _____

12. The girl on the stage was obviously quite talented with playing the piano, but she was nervous from stage fright.   _____

13. All the members of the chorus agreed between themselves that "Amazing Grace" should be included into the recital.   _____

14. If you drive between forty-five and fifty miles per hour, Dan, you will be complying to the speed limit.   _____

15. I'm afraid that I must differ from you in reference with this matter; perhaps you will reconsider your view.   _____

Exercise 89   Diction

The following exercises (89–92) are based on the Glossary of Faulty Diction in Chapter 22. Underline all errors, colloquialisms (informal expressions), and slang and write the correct or preferred forms at the right.

Example: It turned out that Polly was <u>disinterested</u> in
learning how to cross-stitch.   *uninterested*

1. Norm lay on the chaise lounge, working a cross-word puzzle and not realizing that he was getting too much sun.   _____

2. Jenny says that she is planning to bring her camera when she goes to her class reunion next week.   _____

3. The capital building was decorated with red, white, and blue swags for the forthcoming inauguration of the governor.   _____

4. Jackie felt badly that she was unable to attend Marian's graduation, but she could not hardly get around since spraining her ankle.   _____

5. The amount of people crowding into the auditorium seemed to mean that the concert would be a financial success.   _____

6. Martha is an alumni of three colleges, and she is planning to attend a fourth, starting next fall.   _____

7. The affect of the antibiotic that Dot was taking was most as bad as her illness.   _____

8. I can't believe that Dr. Lamar told Harry that it was alright for him to go swimming when he had an ear infection.   _____

9. We're hoping to convince Joe to go with us on the camping trip up to Ruby Falls, but he says he must forego the outing.   _____

10. The ones who are going on the trip are very
    enthused; I'm planning to bring warm clothes,
    a change of shoes, and my rain gear.   _____

11. The gentleman who stole Dad's watch was caught
    by the police; they said that he is a noted criminal.   _____

12. The reason I was late again for basketball practice is
    because I lost my gym shoes.   _____

13. As a college pupil I remember pouring over my
    chemistry text, trying to make sense of those com-
    plicated formulas.   _____

14. Next month we start Daylight Savings Time, and
    Jack and myself will be able to play tennis longer in
    the evenings.   _____

15. The principle of Ty's school says that less boys than
    girls make the honor roll.   _____

Exercise 90 Diction

Underline all errors, colloquialisms, and slang expressions in the following sentences and write the correct or preferred forms at the right.

Example: Mrs. Smithson <u>claims</u> that her son Jason is a
child prodigy.   *asserts, says*

1. It was the consensus of opinion at the annual barbecue that Jim Donaldson makes the best Brunswick
stew in Clarke County.   _____

2. After we orientated ourselves, we realized that the
road that goes south is the one we should have
taken.   _____

3. Please wait for me, Seth; I haven't but a few more
pages to read in this chapter.   _____

4. That guy received his just desserts when the judge
sentenced him to five years in prison for burglary. _____

5. I walk my dog Cleo everyday, and she sure enjoys
the exercise.   _____

6. The discredited official reluctantly gave up the
reigns of government when he was threatened with
public disgrace.   _____

7. I saw in the paper where June and Mack will be
married in September and that Reverend Smythe
will officiate at the wedding.   _____

8. Hank was feeling nauseous after going all day without food due to missing lunch.   _____

9. It was an awesome football game, with the Minne-
sota Vikings battling every step of the way for their
fantastic victory.   _____

10. Tina managed to wrangle two tickets to the game,
so she and myself had seats on the fifty-yard line. _____

11. Tracy, you should of known better than to try and run five miles when you're out of condition. _____

12. If I were you, I personally wouldn't plan on passing that English course without really studying. _____

13. Some critics contend that the media often tries to influence voters in political campaigns. _____

14. Irregardless of what Professor Radcliffe says, I feel that Hugh has done a masterful job in his translation of that French novel. _____

15. Several people have offered to loan me their cars for Saturday night; I don't know if I should accept or decline. _____

Exercise 91 Diction

Underline all errors, colloquialisms, and trite expressions; then write the correct or preferred forms at the right.

Example: Those new <u>drapes</u> of Laura's are an unattrac-
tive shade of green.   *draperies*

1. Due to the fact that Alice and Hank were late, we
   missed the first act of the play, and I was really
   aggravated.   _____

2. Johnny inferred that Tech was not defensing well,
   and his implications made Randy mad as hops.   _____

3. I've never had these kind of cookies before; did you
   get them at the Black Forest Bakery?   _____

4. The gray Persian cat was in it's favorite spot on the
   kitchen window sill, laying in wait for the cardinal
   that comes there to feed every morning.   _____

5. Ron has flaunted lots of the college's regulations,
   and I doubt but what he will return next semester. _____

6. Judy accidently knocked over her glass of milk, and
   she was muchly embarrassed at her clumsiness.   _____

7. Anyone of those skirts would compliment your
   blue jacket and shoes, Dorothy.   _____

8. Teddy seemed to have a creditable alibi for his
   stupid behavior, but then Teddy is a well-known
   con artist.   _____

9. The deservedly famous restaurant has been in business continually for thirty years; it is well known
   for its delicious deserts.   _____

10. Although my father was formally a teacher, he now
    spends most of his time authoring textbooks.   _____

11. Thank goodness, the dentist told me that I have
    less cavities than I had this time last year.   _____

12. Julie's new stationary, a garish hot pink, is what I
    would call the pits.   _____

13. I was suppose to receive a savings of twenty-five
    percent on that purchase, but the store manager
    said that my coupon was out of date.   _____

14. Mr. Johnson, the party I am to interface with in a
    conference today, is a very unique individual.   _____

15. I am sure that a man of principal would honor his
    commitment to loan you the money you need, even
    though it is quite a considerable amount.   _____

Exercise 92 Diction

Underline all errors, colloquialisms, and trite expressions. Then write the correct or preferred forms at the right.

Example: When she went to the audition, she believed that she would win the starring role in the movie; unfortunately, her dream was merely an <u>allusion</u>.   *illusion*

1. We could hardly believe the amount of tickets we sold for our big Christmas bazaar.   _____

2. The huge crowd disbursed rapidly when the lightning and thunder became violent.   _____

3. Tom decided to go for broke and put all his money into a business venture to which his family is very adverse.   _____

4. I cannot help but wish that I could learn to play the piano as well as my mother use to.   _____

5. I argued with Gary until I was blue in the face about his spending habits and etc., but he had all ready decided that I was a spoilsport.   _____

6. The audience at the tennis match was so loud and unruly that the officials threatened to stop the game unless the crowd behaved properly.   _____

7. Our hosts had prepared a delightful supper of grits, country ham, black-eyed peas, hot biscuits, and last but not least, a fantastic bread pudding.   _____

8. The lady who cleans the house for us is sort of clumsy, and she has undoubtably broken at least a dozen pieces of our best china.   _____

9. My recipe for pound cake is different than yours, Marcus; it calls for four cupsful of flour instead of five.   _____

10. That back road to Macon that you recommended is actually twelve miles further than the regular highway.   _____

11. My father's old calvary unit is planning to meet for a reunion in San Antonio next month.   _____

12. Frontier justice took over when the posse cornered the cattle thief and hung him from a sycamore tree.   _____

13. I'm hoping against hope that Bill will call to let us know if he is going to the class picnic.   _____

14. Justin said that he is not too happy about the professor whose going to teach physics next year.   _____

15. I understand that Joe wrestled his mother's valuable diamond bracelet away from the burglar, an escaped trustee from the prison in Reidsville.   _____

Building a Vocabulary

As you know from your own experience, one of your greatest needs for successful composition is to improve your vocabulary. One of the best ways to build a vocabulary, of course, is always to look up in a dictionary the meanings of unfamiliar words that you hear or read. This chapter on vocabulary will provide you with a minimal body of information concerning word formation and the derivations of various words comprising the English language. For a more intensified study of all aspects of this fascinating subject, including ways to strengthen your own vocabulary, consult and use frequently a book devoted exclusively to this purpose.

Learning the derivation of a word will fix in your mind the meaning and spelling of that word. Because the largest part of our English vocabulary comes from three main sources — the Old English, the Greek, and the Latin languages — a knowledge of commonly used prefixes, roots, and suffixes from these languages will prove useful.

A *prefix* is a short element — a syllable or syllables — that comes before the main part of the word, which is the *root*. A *suffix* is added to the end of the word. Thus the word *hypodermic* has *hypo-*, meaning "under," as its *prefix; derm*, meaning "skin," as its *root;* and *-ic*, meaning "having to do with," as its *suffix*. You see that the *prefix* and the *suffix* of a word modify the meaning of the *root*. The word *hypodermic,* then, when used as an adjective, means "having to do with something under the skin."

There are actually more words of classical origin, that is, Greek and Latin, than of Old English in our language; however, we use Old English words much more frequently in every sentence that we write or speak. For instance, the Old English prefixes *un-* (not) and *for-* (from) are found in many of our words, such as *unfair* and *forbid*. The Old English root-word *hlaf* (loaf) gives us the word *lord*, a lord being a loafkeeper or warden (*hlaf-weard*). The root-word *god* (God) gives us *goodbye*, a contraction of *God be with ye*. Old English suffixes such as *-ish* (having the qualities of) and *-ly* (like) are seen in many words, such as *foolish* and *courtly*.

If you combine the Greek root *tele*, meaning "at a distance," with *graph* (writing), *phone* (sound), *scope* (seeing), *pathy* (feeling), you have *telegraph* (writing at a distance), *telephone* (sound at a distance), *telescope* (seeing at a distance), *telepathy* (feeling at a distance).

The Latin root *duc* is seen in such words as *adduce, aqueduct, conduce, conduct, induce, produce, reduce, seduce, conductor, ducal*, and *ductile*. If you know that *duc* means "to lead," and if you know the meanings of the prefixes and suffixes combined with it, you can make out the meanings of most of these words.

Each prefix, root, and suffix that you learn may lead to a knowledge of many new words or give a clearer understanding of many you already know. Therefore, a list of some of the most common prefixes, roots, and suffixes is given below. Look up others in your dictionary, or, as suggested earlier, get a good vocabulary textbook and use it often.

■ 23a Prefixes

Prefixes Showing Number or Amount

BI– (*bis–*) two	(*bi*)annual, (*bis*)sextile
CENT– (*centi–*) hundred	(*cent*)enarian, (*centi*)pede
DEC– (*deca–*) ten	(*dec*)ade, (*Deca*)logue
HEMI– half	(*hemi*)sphere, (*hemi*)stich
MILLI– (*mille–*) thousand	(*milli*)on, (*mille*)nnium
MULTI– many, much	(*multi*)form, (*multi*)graph
MON– (*mono–*) one	(*mono*)gyny, (*mono*)tone
OCTA– (*octo–*) eight	(*octa*)ve, (*octo*)pus
PAN– all	(*pan*)acea, (*pan*)demonium, (*pan*)orama
PENTA– five	(*penta*)gon, (*Penta*)teuch
POLY– much, many	(*poly*)glot, (*poly*)chrome
PROT– (*proto–*) first	(*prot*)agonist, (*proto*)type
SEMI– half	(*semi*)circle, (*semi*)final
TRI– three	(*tri*)angle, (*tri*)ad
UNI– one	(*uni*)fy, (*uni*)cameral

Prefixes Showing Relationship in Place and Time

AB– (*a–, abs–*) from, away from	(*a*)vert, (*ab*)sent, (*abs*)tract
AD– (*ac–, af–, al–, ag–, an–, ap–, ar–, as–, at–*) to, at	(*ad*)mit, (*ac*)cede, (*af*)fect, (*al*)lude, (*ag*)gregate, (*an*)nounce, (*ap*)pear, (*ar*)rive, (*as*)sume, (*at*)tain
AMB– (*ambi–*) around, both	(*ambi*)dextrous, (*ambi*)guous
ANTE– (*ant–*) before	(*ante*)cedent, (*ante*)date
ANTI– (*ant–*) against	(*anti*)thesis, (*ant*)agonist

CATA– away, against, down   (*cata*)clysm, (*cata*)strophe
CIRCUM– around, about   (*circum*)scribe, (*circum*)stance
CON– (*com–, col–, cor–*) with, together, at the same time   (*con*)tract, (*com*)pete, (*col*)league, (*cor*)relate
CONTRA– (*counter–*) opposite, against   (*contra*)dict, (*counter*)mand
DE– from, away from, down   (*de*)pend, (*de*)form, (*de*)tract
DIA– through, across   (*dia*)gram, (*dia*)meter
DIS– (*di, dif–*) off, away from   (*dis*)tract, (*di*)verge, (*dif*)fuse
EN– (*em–, in–*) in, into   (*en*)counter, (*em*)brace, (*in*)duct
EPI– on, over, among, outside   (*epi*)dermis, (*epi*)demic
EX– (*e–, ec–, ef–*) out of, from   (*ex*)pel, (*e*)lect, (*ec*)centric, (*ef*)face
EXTRA– (*extro–*) outside, beyond   (*extra*)mural, (*extro*)vert
HYPO– under   (*hypo*)dermic, (*hypo*)crite
INTER– among, between, within   (*inter*)fere, (*inter*)rupt
INTRO– (*intra–*) within   (*intro*)spection, (*intra*)mural
OB– (*oc–, of–, op–*) against, to, before, toward   (*ob*)ject, (*oc*)casion, (*of*)fer, (*op*)press

PER– through, by   (*per*)ceiver, (*per*)ennial
PERI– around, about   (*peri*)meter, (*peri*)odical
POST– after   (*post*)script, (*post*)erity
PRE– before   (*pre*)cedent, (*pre*)decessor
PRO– before in time or position   (*pro*)logue, (*pro*)bate
RETRO– back, backward   (*retro*)gress, (*retro*)spect
SE– aside, apart   (*se*)clude, (*se*)duce
SUB– (*suc–, suf–, sug–, sum–, sup–, sus–*) under, below   (*sub*)scribe, (*suc*)cumb, (*suf*)fer, (*sug*)gest, (*sum*)mon, (*sup*)pose, (*sus*)pect
SUPER– (*sur–*) above, over   (*super*)sede, (*super*)b, (*sur*)pass
TRANS– (*tra–, traf–, tres–*) across   (*trans*)port, (*tra*)vesty, (*traf*)fic, (*tres*)pass
ULTRA– beyond   (*ultra*)marine, (*ultra*)modern

Prefixes Showing Negation

A– (*an–*) without   (*an*)onymous, (*a*)theist
IN– (*ig–, im–, il–, ir–*) not   (*in*)accurate, (*ig*)nore, (*im*)pair, (*il*)legal, (*ir*)responsible

NON– not   (*non*)essential, (*non*)entity
UN– not   (*un*)tidy, (*un*)happy

■ 23b Greek Roots

ARCH   chief, rule   (*arch*)bishop, an(*archy*), mon(*archy*)
AUTO   self   (*auto*)graph, (*auto*)mobile, (*auto*)matic
BIO   life   (*bio*)logy, (*bio*)graphy, (*bio*)chemistry
CAU(S)T   burn   (*caust*)ic, holo(*caust*), (*caut*)erize
CHRON(O)   time   (*chron*)icle, (*chron*)ic, (*chrono*)logy
COSM(O)   order, arrangement   (*cosm*)os, (*cosm*)ic, (*cosmo*)graphy
CRIT   judge, discern   (*crit*)ic, (*crit*)erion
DEM(O)   people   (*demo*)crat, (*demo*)cracy, (*dem*)agogue

DERM	skin	epi(*dermis*), (*derm*)a, pachy(*derm*), (*derm*)ophobe
DYN(A)(M)	power	(*dynam*)ic, (*dynam*)o, (*dyn*)asty
GRAPH	write	auto(*graph*), (*graph*)ic, geo(*graphy*)
HIPPO	horse	(*hippo*)potamus, (*hippo*)drome
HYDR(O)	water	(*hydr*)ant, (*hydr*)a, (*hydro*)gen
LOG(Y), LOGUE	saying, science	(*log*)ic, bio(*logy*), eu(*logy*), dia(*logue*)
MET(E)R	measure	thermo(*meter*), speedo(*meter*), (*metr*)ic
MICRO	small	(*micro*)be, (*micro*)scope, (*micro*)cosm
MOR(O)	fool	(*moro*)n, sopho(*more*)
NYM	name	ano(*nym*)ous, pseudo(*nym*)
PATH	experience, suffer	a(*path*)y, sym(*path*)y, (*path*)os
PED	child	(*ped*)agogue, (*ped*)ant, (*ped*)iatrician
PHIL	love	(*phil*)anthropy, (*phil*)osophy, (*phil*)ander
PHON(O)	sound	(*phono*)graph, (*phon*)etic, (*phono*)gram
PSYCH(O)	mind, soul	(*psycho*)logy, (*psych*)ic, (*Psych*)e
SOPH	wisdom	philo(*sopher*), (*soph*)ist, (*soph*)istication
THEO	god	(*theo*)logy, (*theo*)sophy, (*theo*)cratic
THERM	heat	(*therm*)ostat, (*therm*)ometer, (*therm*)os

■ 23c Latin Roots

AM	love	(*am*)ity, (*am*)orist, (*am*)orous
ANIM	breath, soul, spirit	(*anim*)al, (*anim*)ate, un(*anim*)ous
AQU(A)	water	(*aqu*)educt, (*aqua*)tic, (*aqua*)rium
AUD	hear	(*aud*)itor, (*aud*)ience, (*aud*)itorium
CAPIT	head	(*capit*)al, (*capit*)ate, (*capit*)alize
CAP(T), CEP(T), CIP(T)	take	(*cap*)tive, pre(*cept*), pre(*cip*)itate
CED, CESS	go, yield	ante(*ced*)ent, con(*cede*), ex(*cess*)ive
CENT	hundred	(*cent*)ury, (*cent*)urion, per(*cent*)age
CER(N), CRI(M,T), CRE(M,T)	separate, judge, choose	dis(*cern*), (*crim*)inal, dis(*crete*)
CRED	believe, trust	(*cred*)it, in(*cred*)ible, (*cred*)ulity
CLAR	clear, bright	(*clar*)ity, (*clar*)ify, de(*clar*)ation
CORD	heart	dis(*cord*), con(*cord*), (*cord*)ial
CORP(OR)	body, substance	(*corpor*)al, (*corp*)se, (*corp*)ulent
DOM(IN)	tame, subdue	(*domin*)ant, (*domin*)ate, (*domin*)ion
DON	give	(*don*)or, (*don*)ate
DORM	sleep	(*dorm*)ant, (*dorm*)itory, (*dorm*)ient
DUC	lead	con(*duc*)t, (*duc*)tile, aque(*duc*)t
FER	bear	in(*fer*)ence, (*fer*)tile, re(*fer*)
FORT	strong	(*fort*)ress, (*fort*)e, (*fort*)itude
FRAG, FRING, FRACT	break	(*frag*)ile, in(*fring*)e, (*fract*)ure
GEN	beget, origin	en(*gen*)der, con(*gen*)ital, (*gen*)eration
JAC(T), JEC(T)	cast	e(*jac*)ulate, pro(*ject*), e(*ject*)

LATE	carry	col(*late*), vacil(*late*), re(*late*)
MI(SS,T)	send	dis(*miss*), (*miss*)ionary, re(*mit*)
NOMIN, NOMEN	name	(*nomin*)ate, (*nomen*)clature
NOV	new	(*nov*)el, (*nov*)ice, in(*nov*)ation
PED	foot	(*ped*)al, centi(*pede*), (*ped*)estrian
PLEN, PLET	full	(*plen*)ty, (*plen*)itude, re(*plete*)
PORT	bear	(*port*)er, de(*port*), im(*port*)ance
POTENT	able, powerful	(*potent*), (*potent*)ial, (*potent*)ate
SECT	cut	dis(*sect*), in(*sect*), (*sect*)ion

■ 23d Old English (Anglo-Saxon) Roots

BOC	book	(*bo*)okish, (*bo*)okkeeper, (*bo*)oklet
CELD	cold	*cold*, (*co*)ol, (*ch*)ill, (*je*)ll
DEOP	deep	(*dep*)th, *dip*
EALD	old	(*eld*)er, (*ald*)erman
ETAN	to eat	(*et*)ch, (*ed*)ible
GAST	spirit	*ghost*, breath
GRIM	fierce, savage	*grim*
HIERAN	to hear	(*hear*)say, (*har*)ken
HLAF	bread	bread, *loaf*
MANN	man	*man*, *men*, (*manne*)quin
MORGEN	morn	(*mor*)ning, dawn
NIHT	night	(*ni*)g(*ht*), (*noc*)turnal
SCEAP	sheep	(*sh*)ee(*p*), (*shep*)herd, (*sh*)ee(*p*)ish
SCIP	ship	(*s*)h(*ip*), (*skip*)per
SETTAN	to set	(*se*)at, (*set*)tle, (*ses*)sion
WRITAN	to write	(*writ*), (*writ*)ten, (*wr*)o(*te*)

■ 23e Suffixes

Noun Suffixes

1. *Suffixes Denoting an Agent*

–ANT (*–ent*) one who, that which	ten(*ant*), ag(*ent*)
–AR (*–er*) one who	schol(*ar*), farm(*er*)
–ARD (*–art*) one who (often deprecative)	cow(*ard*), bragg(*art*)
–EER one who	privat(*eer*), auction(*eer*)
–ESS a woman who	waitr(*ess*), seamstr(*ess*)
–IER (*–yer*) one who	cash(*ier*), law(*yer*)
–IST one who	novel(*ist*), Commun(*ist*)
–OR one who, that which	act(*or*), tract(*or*)
–STER one who, that which	young(*ster*), road(*ster*)

2. *Suffix Denoting the Receiver of an Action*

| –EE one who is the object of some action | appoint(*ee*), divorc(*ée*) |

3. *Suffixes Denoting Smallness or Diminutiveness*

–CULE (*–cle*)	mole(*cule*), ventri(*cle*)
–ETTE	din(*ette*), cigar(*ette*)
–LET	ring(*let*), brace(*let*)
–LING	duck(*ling*), prince(*ling*)

4. *Suffixes Denoting Place*

–ARY indicating location or repository	diction(*ary*), api(*ary*)
–ERY place or establishment	bak(*ery*), nunn(*ery*)
–ORY (*–arium, –orium*) place for, concerned with	dormit(*ory*), audit(*orium*)

5. *Suffixes Denoting Act, State, Quality, or Condition*

–ACY denoting quality, state	accur(*acy*), delic(*acy*)
–AL pertaining to action	refus(*al*), deni(*al*)
–ANCE (*–ancy*) denoting action or state	brilli(*ance*), buoy(*ancy*)
–ATION denoting result	migr(*ation*), el(*ation*)
–DOM denoting a general condition	wis(*dom*), bore(*dom*)
–ENCE (*–ency*) state, quality of	abstin(*ence*), consist(*ency*)
–ERY denoting quality, action	fool(*ery*), prud(*ery*)
–HOOD state, quality	knight(*hood*), false(*hood*)
–ICE condition or quality	serv(*ice*), just(*ice*)
–ION (*–sion*) state or condition	un(*ion*), ten(*sion*)
–ISM denoting action, state, or condition	bapt(*ism*), plagiar(*ism*)
–ITY (*–ety*) action, state, or condition	joll(*ity*), gai(*ety*)
–MENT action or state resulting from	punish(*ment*), frag(*ment*)
–NESS quality, state of	good(*ness*), prepared(*ness*)
–OR denoting action, state, or quality	hon(*or*), lab(*or*)
–TH pertaining to condition, state, or action	warm(*th*), steal(*th*)
–URE denoting action, result, or instrument	legislat(*ure*), pleas(*ure*)

Adjective Suffixes

–ABLE (*–ible, –ile*) capable of being	lov(*able*), ed(*ible*), contract(*ile*)
–AC relating to, like	elegi(*ac*), cardi(*ac*)
–ACIOUS inclined to	pugn(*acious*), aud(*acious*)
–AL pertaining to	radic(*al*), cordi(*al*)
–AN pertaining to	sylv(*an*), urb(*an*)
–ANT (*–ent*) inclined to	pleas(*ant*), converg(*ent*)
–AR pertaining to	sol(*ar*), regul(*ar*)
–ARY pertaining to	contr(*ary*), revolution(*ary*)
–ATIVE inclined to	demonstr(*ative*), talk(*ative*)
–FUL full of	joy(*ful*), pain(*ful*)
–IC (*–ical*) pertaining to	volcan(*ic*), angel(*ical*)
–ISH like, relating to, being	devil(*ish*), boy(*ish*)

–IVE inclined to, having the nature of   elus(*ive*), nat(*ive*)
–LESS without, unable to be   piti(*less*), resist(*less*)
–OSE full of   bellic(*ose*), mor(*ose*)
–OUS full of   pi(*ous*), fam(*ous*)
–ULENT (*–olent*) full of   fraud(*ulent*), vi(*olent*)

Verb Suffixes

The following verb suffixes usually mean "to make" (to become, to increase, etc.).

–ATE   toler(*ate*), vener(*ate*)
–EN   madd(*en*), wid(*en*)
–FY   magni(*fy*), beauti(*fy*)
–IZE (*–ise*)   colon(*ize*), exerc(*ise*)

Exercise 93 **Word Analysis: Prefixes**

Break the following English words into their parts and give the literal meaning of each part as derived from the source. Consult the list of prefixes and roots given on the previous pages. Use your dictionary if you find a part not given in these lists. Be sure you know the meaning of each word and can use it in a sentence.

Word	Prefix (and literal meaning)	Root (and literal meaning)	Meaning of Whole Word
panacea	*pan-, all*	*akos, remedy*	*a remedy for all ills; cure-all*
1. abduct			
2. adopt			
3. anteroom			
4. antiseptic			
5. bicycle			
6. circumference			
7. compose			

Word	Prefix (and literal meaning)	Root (and literal meaning)	Meaning of Whole Word
8. deluge	_____	_____	_____
	_____	_____	_____
9. dialect	_____	_____	_____
	_____	_____	_____
10. epidemic	_____	_____	_____
	_____	_____	_____
11. exclude	_____	_____	_____
	_____	_____	_____
12. hypertension	_____	_____	_____
	_____	_____	_____
13. hypothermia	_____	_____	_____
	_____	_____	_____
14. interfere	_____	_____	_____
	_____	_____	_____
15. introvert	_____	_____	_____
	_____	_____	_____
16. monarch	_____	_____	_____
	_____	_____	_____
17. multiply	_____	_____	_____
	_____	_____	_____
18. observe	_____	_____	_____
	_____	_____	_____

Word	Prefix (and literal meaning)	Root (and literal meaning)	Meaning of Whole Word
19. postscript	_____	_____	_____
	_____	_____	_____
20. precede	_____	_____	_____
	_____	_____	_____
21. progress	_____	_____	_____
	_____	_____	_____
22. semiannual	_____	_____	_____
	_____	_____	_____
23. subterranean	_____	_____	_____
	_____	_____	_____
24. superficial	_____	_____	_____
	_____	_____	_____
25. unknown	_____	_____	_____
	_____	_____	_____

Exercise 94   Word Analysis: Suffixes

Break the following English words into their parts and give the literal meaning of each part as derived from its source. Consult the list of suffixes and roots given on previous pages. Use your dictionary if you find a part not given in the lists. Be sure you know the meaning of each word and can use it in a sentence.

Word	Root (and literal meaning)	Suffix (and literal meaning)	Meaning of Whole Word
active	*agere, to act; do*	*-ive, inclined to; having the nature of*	*acting; working; functioning*
1. alienate			
2. anklet			
3. arsonist			
4. buoyancy			
5. capable			
6. clarify			
7. defendant			

359

Word	Root (and literal meaning)	Suffix (and literal meaning)	Meaning of Whole Word
8. dependence	_____	_____	_____
	_____	_____	_____
9. employee	_____	_____	_____
	_____	_____	_____
10. erasure	_____	_____	_____
	_____	_____	_____
11. feminism	_____	_____	_____
	_____	_____	_____
12. girlish	_____	_____	_____
	_____	_____	_____
13. hopeless	_____	_____	_____
	_____	_____	_____
14. kingdom	_____	_____	_____
	_____	_____	_____
15. library	_____	_____	_____
	_____	_____	_____
16. mental	_____	_____	_____
	_____	_____	_____
17. monument	_____	_____	_____
	_____	_____	_____
18. moronic	_____	_____	_____
	_____	_____	_____

Word	Root (and literal meaning)	Suffix (and literal meaning)	Meaning of Whole Word
19. motherhood	_____	_____	_____
	_____	_____	_____
20. opulent	_____	_____	_____
	_____	_____	_____
21. sanity	_____	_____	_____
	_____	_____	_____
22. scandalous	_____	_____	_____
	_____	_____	_____
23. spacious	_____	_____	_____
	_____	_____	_____
24. talkative	_____	_____	_____
	_____	_____	_____
25. terrorize	_____	_____	_____
	_____	_____	_____

Exercise 95   Word Analysis: Roots

For each root listed below write the meaning and at least three words containing the root. Do not use the same word with two roots. If the root given is not among the roots listed on previous pages, look it up in your dictionary, which is also the best source for finding the words you need. Remember that some words containing these roots will have prefixes.

Root	Meaning	Words Containing Root
path	*experience; suffer*	*pathetic, pathology, psychopathic*
1. anim(a)		
2. aqu(a)		
3. aud		
4. auto		
5. bio		
6. capit		
7. clar		
8. corp(or)		
9. cred		
10. crit		
11. derm		
12. dom(in)		
13. fort		
14. fract, frag, fring		
15. graph		
16. hydro		
17. jac(t), jec(t)		
18. log(y), logue		
19. met(e)r		

Root	Meaning	Words Containing Root
20. nomen, nomin	_____	_____
21. nov	_____	_____
22. plen, plet	_____	_____
23. port	_____	_____
24. sceap	_____	_____
25. writan	_____	_____

Exercise 96   Vocabulary: Prefixes and Suffixes

A. Underline the prefix in each of the following words, give its meaning, and use the word in a sentence in order to show the meaning of the prefix.

Word	Meaning of Prefix	Sentence
<u>bi</u>lingual	*two*	*Mr. Boudreau, our French teacher, is bilingual; he speaks both English and French.*
1. antebellum		
2. centipede		
3. exhale		
4. intercollegiate		
5. misdeed		
6. preamble		
7. reunion		
8. submit		
9. tricolor		
10. uplift		

B. In the following list of words underline each suffix, give its meaning, and use the word in a sentence.

Word	Meaning of Suffix	Sentence
stardom	general condition	I am sure that Judy will achieve stardom in the movies.
1. coward		
2. gravitate		
3. lengthen		
4. loveliest		
5. malice		
6. mentor		
7. merriment		
8. morose		
9. ringlet		
10. upward		

Exercise 97 Vocabulary: Greek and Latin Roots

A. Use the derivatives of *aster, astron,* meaning "star," necessary to complete the following statements. (In this and the following exercises remember that these roots may be found in words containing prefixes. The list of prefixes in Chapter 23 may suggest certain words to you, as in the word *diagram,* with the prefix *dia-,* meaning "across," and *gram,* the root, meaning "writing.")

1. The _____, a white, blue, purple, or pink flower with rayed petals, usually blooms in late summer or early autumn.

2. A star-shaped figure (*) used in printing to indicate an omission or reference to a note located elsewhere is called an _____.

3. One who studies the positions and aspects of heavenly bodies in the belief that these influence the lives of human beings is an _____.

4. The National Astronautics and Space Administration is responsible for sending _____ into space as pilots of spacecraft.

5. Many _____ spend their lives in the scientific study of the universe beyond the earth.

B. Use the derivatives of *graphein,* meaning "to write," necessary to complete the following statements.

1. The famous author will be in the bookshop on Saturday to _____ copies of his latest novel.

2. A drawing that shows a relationship, by comparison or contrast, between two sets of numbers is called a _____.

3. When an object or an event is described vividly, it is said to be represented in _____ detail.

4. When writers of fiction use their own lives as thinly veiled bases for their stories, the works are often labeled _____.

5. The soft, black crystallized carbon used to make lead pencils is known as _____.

C. Use the derivatives of *gratus,* meaning "good will," necessary to complete the following statements.

1. The quality that is pleasing for its beauty of form, movement, or proportion is generally called _____.

2. A person who is _____ is one who is characterized by kindness and warm courtesy.

3. "I am very _____ to you for your help in finding my lost necklace," said Mrs. Hartman.

4. On Thanksgiving Day it is traditional to show _____ for the blessings we have received.

5. When one is pleased and satisfied by achieving a desire of some kind, that person is said to be _____.

D. Use the derivatives of *stare, stat,* meaning "to stand," necessary to complete the following statements.

1. One's _____ of mind is the mental or emotional condition with regard to a set of circumstances.

2. A relative position in a ranked group or in a social system is known as _____.

3. The word _____ is a way of referring to the height of a human being or an animal in an upright position.

4. The legislature has enacted a _____ requiring all automobile owners

   to carry accident insurance.

5. I hope that you will _____ nearby during the next few hours, so that

   I can call you if necessary.

Spelling

Spelling is an important aspect of written communication. Instructors seldom have the opportunity, however, to spend adequate classroom time on the subject. The responsibility for the mastery of spelling, therefore, rests almost solely on the individual student.

Here are a few practical suggestions on how to approach the problem of spelling:

1. Always use the dictionary when you are in doubt about the spelling of a word.

2. If there is a rule applicable to the type of words that you misspell, learn that rule.

3. Employ any "tricks" that might assist you in remembering the spelling of particular words giving you trouble. If, for example, you confuse the meaning and hence the spelling of *statue* and *stature*, remember that the longer word refers to bodily "longness." Certain troublesome words can be spelled correctly if you will remember their prefixes (as in *dis/appoint*) or their suffixes (as in *cool/ly*). Also, it might help you to remember that there are only three *-ceed* words: *exceed*, *proceed*, and *succeed*.

4. Keep a list of the words that you misspell. In writing down these words, observe their syllabication and any peculiarities of construction. Try to "see" — that is, to have a mental picture of — these words.

5. Practice the correct pronunciation of troublesome words. Misspelling is often the result of mispronunciation.

Of the many rules governing spelling, four are particularly useful since they are widely applicable. Study these four rules carefully.

◼ 24a Final e

Drop the final **e** before a suffix beginning with a vowel (*ing, -ous*, etc.) but retain the final **e** before a suffix beginning with a consonant (*-ment, -ly*, etc.):

Final **e** dropped: come + ing = coming
                           fame + ous = famous
                           love + able = lovable
                           guide + ance = guidance

Final **e** retained: move + ment = movement
                           fate + ful = fateful
                           sole + ly = solely

Exceptions: Acknowledge, acknowledgment; abridge, abridgment; judge, judgment; dye, dyeing; singe, singeing; hoe, hoeing; mile, mileage; due, duly; awe, awful; whole, wholly. The final **e** is retained after **c** or **g** when the suffix begins with **a** or **o**: peace, peaceable; courage, courageous.

◼ 24b Final Consonant

Double a final consonant before a suffix beginning with a vowel (1) in words of one syllable containing a single vowel, or (2) in words of more than one syllable whose accent falls on the last syllable:

stop + ed = stopped

occur + ence = occurrence

Do not double a final consonant before a suffix beginning with a vowel (1) in words of one syllable but two vowels, or (2) in words of more than one syllable whose last syllable is unaccented:

shout + ing = shouting

benefit + ed = benefited

◼ 24c *ei* and *ie*

When **ei** and **ie** have the long **ee** sound (as in *keep*), use **i** before **e** except after **c**; **i** follows all consonants except **c**, and **e** follows **c**.

ie	*ei* (after *c*)
chief	ceiling
field	receive
niece	deceive
siege	conceit

Exceptions *(grouped to form a sentence):*   Neither financier seized either species of weird leisure.

■ 24d Final *y*

In words ending in **y** preceded by a consonant, change the **y** to **i** before any suffix except one beginning with **i**.

Suffix beginning with a letter other than **i**:

fly + es = flies
ally + es = allies
easy + ly = easily
mercy + ful = merciful
study + ous = studious

Suffix beginning with **i**:

fly + ing = flying
study + ing = studying

■ 24e Homonyms

Homonyms are words that sound alike but have different meanings and spellings. Students need to be especially aware of homonym errors because computerized spelling checkers will not recognize them as spelling errors. The following list gives some common homonyms:

accept/except

affect/effect

everyday/every day

flair/flare

lead/led

principal/principle

their/there

to/too

whose/who's

your/you're

Other sound-confusion errors involve words that end in **-ed** when the **-ed** sound is not clearly enunciated in speech. Be sure to include the **d** in writing such phrases as "suppose*d* to," "use*d* to," and "prejudice*d* against."

■ 24f Spelling List

The following list is made up of approximately 500 frequently misspelled words. Since these are commonly used words, you should learn to spell all of them after you have mastered the words on your individual list.

absence
academic
accelerate
accept
accessible
accidentally
accommodate
accumulate
accustomed
acknowledge
acknowledgment
acquaintance
acquire
across
address
adolescent
advantage
aggravate
allege
all right
a lot
altogether
always
amateur
among
amount
analysis
angel
anonymous
anxiety
apology
apparatus
apparent
appearance
appreciate
appropriate
arctic
argument
arithmetic
around
arrangement
ascend
aspirin
assassin
association
athletics
attendance
attractive
audience
author

automatically
autumn
auxiliary
awkward
bankruptcy
barbarous
becoming
beginning
believe
beneficial
benefited
brilliant
Britain
broccoli
buoyant
bureau
business
cafeteria
caffeine
calendar
camouflage
candidate
capable
captain
carburetor
carriage
category
cavalry
ceiling
cemetery
certain
changeable
characteristic
chauffeur
choose
chosen
clothes
colloquial
colonel
column
coming
commission
committee
comparative
compel
compelled
competent
competition
complement
completely

compliment
compulsory
confident
congratulate
connoisseur
conqueror
conscience
conscientious
conscious
contemptible
continuous
controversy
convenient
coolly
council
counsel
courteous
criticism
curiosity
curriculum
dealt
deceit
decide
defendant
definite
dependent
descend
descent
describe
description
desert
desirable
despair
desperate
dessert
dictionary
dietitian (dietician)
difference
dilapidated
dining
diphtheria
disappear
disappoint
disastrous
discipline
discussion
disease
dissatisfied
dissipate
distribute

divine
division
dormitories
drudgery
dual
duchess
duel
dyeing
dying
ecstasy
efficiency
eighth
eligible
eliminate
embarrassed
eminent
emphasize
enthusiastic
environment
equipped
equivalent
erroneous
especially
exaggerate
excellent
except
exercise
exhaust
exhilaration
existence
exorbitant
expel
expelled
experience
explanation
extraordinary
familiar
fascinate
February
finally
financial
financier
flier
foregoing
forehead
foreign
foreword
forfeit
forgo
formally

formerly
forth
forty
fourth
fraternity
friend
fulfill
fundamental
furniture
futile
gauge
generally
genius
government
grammar
granddaughter
grandeur
grievance
guarantee
guerrilla
handkerchief
harass
having
height
high school
hindrance
hitchhike
hoping
humorous
hygiene
hypocrisy
illusion
imaginary
imitation
immediately
incidentally
independence
indispensable
inevitable
infinite
influential
ingenious
innocence
instance
instant
integrity
intellectual
intelligence
intentionally
interested

irrelevant
irresistible
its
it's
judgment
kindergarten
knowledge
laboratory
led
legitimate
leisure
library
likable
literature
livelihood
loneliness
loose
lose
lovable
magazine
maintain
maintenance
maneuver
manual
manufacture
marriage
mathematics
meant
medicine
mediocre
miniature
mirror
mischievous
misspell
momentous
monotonous
morale
mortgage
murmur
muscle
mysterious
naive
naturally
necessary
nevertheless
nickel
niece
ninety
ninth
noticeable

notoriety
nowadays
nucleus
obedience
obstacle
occasion
occasionally
occurrence
o'clock
off
omission
omitted
operate
opinion
opportunity
optimism
organization
original
outrageous
overrun
paid
pamphlet
parallel
paralysis
paralyzed
parliament
particularly
partner
passed
past
pastime
peaceful
perform
permanent
permissible
perseverance
persistent
personal
personnel
perspiration
persuade
physically
physician
picnicking
piece
pleasant
pneumonia
politician
politics
politicking

possession
possible
practically
precede
precedence
preference
preferred
prejudice
preparation
prevalent
principal
principle
privilege
probably
procedure
proceed
professor
prominent
pronunciation
propaganda
psychology
publicly
purchase
pursue
quantity
quarter
questionnaire
quiet
quite
quiz
quizzes
realize
really
receive
recognize
recommend
referred
region
reign
rein
relevant
religious
remembrance
repetition
representative
resistance
respectfully
respectively
restaurant
rhetoric

rheumatism
rhythm
ridiculous
roommate
sacrifice
sacrilegious
salable
salary
sandwich
schedule
science
scissors
secretary
seize
sense
sentence
separate
sergeant
severely
sheriff
shining
shoulder
shriek
siege
significant
silhouette
similar
sincerely
skiing
sophomore
source
speak
specimen
speech
stationary
stationery
statue
stature
statute
strength
strenuous
stretch
studying
superintendent
supersede
surprise
susceptible
syllable
symmetry
temperament

temperature
tendency
their
thorough
too
tournament
tragedy
transferred
tremendous
truly
Tuesday
twelfth
tying
tyranny
unanimous
undoubtedly

universally
unnecessary
until
unusual
usable
using
usually
vaccine
vacuum
valuable
variety
vegetable
vengeance
vigilance
vigorous
village

villain
waive
wave
weather
Wednesday
weird
whether
wholly
who's
whose
wield
women
writing
written
yacht
yield

Exercise 98 Spelling

A. Combine the specified suffix with each of the following words, and write the correct form in the blank space.

Example: *drop* + *ed*   *dropped*

1. advise + able   _____
2. ally + s   _____
3. argue + ment   _____
4. become + ing   _____
5. busy + ly   _____
6. care + ful   _____
7. definite + ly   _____
8. dine + ing   _____
9. disaster + ous   _____
10. drastic + ly   _____
11. final + ly   _____
12. funny + er   _____
13. happy + ness   _____
14. harass + ment   _____
15. hero + s   _____
16. hope + less   _____
17. hope + ing   _____
18. hop + ing   _____
19. occasional + ly   _____
20. omit + ed   _____
21. peace + able   _____
22. physical + ly   _____
23. prestige + ous   _____
24. public + ly   _____
25. scare + ed   _____

26. scar + ed   _____

27. study + ing   _____

28. tragic + ly   _____

29. true + ly   _____

30. write + ing   _____

B. Supply _ei_ or _ie_ in each of the following words. Then write the correct form in the space provided.

Example: n_ie_ce   _____niece_____

1. ach__ve   _____   11. h__r   _____

2. br__f   _____   12. l__sure   _____

3. caff__ne   _____   13. rec__ve   _____

4. c__ling   _____   14. r__n   _____

5. ch__f   _____   15. rel__ve   _____

6. conc__t   _____   16. s__ze   _____

7. __ther   _____   17. s__ve   _____

8. fr__ght   _____   18. th__r   _____

9. fr__nd   _____   19. v__n   _____

10. gr__ve   _____   20. w__rd   _____

Exercise 99 Spelling

If there is a misspelled word in any of the groups of five words given below, underline it and write it correctly in the space at the right. If all five words are correctly spelled, write **C** in the blank.

Example: *sincerely, truely, likable, probably, schedule*   *truly* _____

1. tying, seperate, necessary, occasion, author   _____
2. immediately, conscious, dissappoint, niece, speak   _____
3. grammar, probably, speech, alright, always   _____
4. atheletics, severely, finally, benefited, imitation   _____
5. original, capable, alot, hygiene, fulfill   _____
6. noticeable, asprin, candidate, muscle, severely   _____
7. secretary, usually, nickel, lonliness, professor   _____
8. environment, fraternity, literature, usable, existance   _____
9. occurrence, parallel, psychology, statue, precede   _____
10. occasion, publically, hypocrisy, coolly, until   _____
11. transferred, definate, across, pleasant, attendance   _____
12. quiz, highschool, government, amateur, cemetery   _____
13. sophomore, competent, yacht, vengeance, studying   _____
14. relevant, dissappear, roommate, dissatisfied, mirror   _____
15. excellent, salary, led, contemptable, inevitable   _____
16. peacefull, experience, possession, ridiculous, salary   _____
17. discipline, exercize, knowledge, omission, realize   _____
18. business, column, conscience, embarrassed, immitation   _____
19. congratulate, intelligence, shoulder, priviledge, procedure   _____
20. automaticly, operate, restaurant, universally, vigorous   _____

Exercise 100 Spelling

Underline any word that is misspelled in the following sentences. Then write it correctly in the space at the right. If a sentence contains no misspelled word, write **C** in the blank. (There is more than one misspelled word in some of the sentences.)

Example: A few days after he had broken his mother's antique vase, Tom's <u>conscious</u> began bothering him.   *conscience*

1. When Lamar asked Gloria to the homecoming dance, she excepted ecstatically.   _____

2. The affects of the war in Yugoslavia are devastating.   _____

3. My professor gave a brillient lecture on the causes of World War II.   _____

4. The principle of Johnstown High School allowed the students to vote on a dress code for sophomores, juniors, and seniors.   _____

5. Everyday I wake up at 7:00 A.M., do my stretching exercises, and run four miles.   _____

6. Some students are prejudice against sorority and fraternity members.   _____

7. On many occasions I have felt embarrased because of my clumsiness.   _____

8. One can remember how to change the clocks for Daylight Saving Time with the saying, "Spring foreward, fall back."   _____

9. When Timmy was lost in the national park, his dog, Lassie, lead the rescue party to him.   _____

10. When Dr. Brown recieved the letter from the publishing company, he opened it immediately.   _____

11. We were quite happy to sit down and enjoy the peace and quiet of the woods.   _____

12. The team was sorry to loose the game, but they re-
    solved that they would definitely do better next
    week.   _____

13. Greenpeace is an organization that promotes
    enviromental concerns.   _____

14. I use to work at a grocery store as a cashier, but
    now I work as a lifeguard.   _____

15. This questionaire asks personal questions about
    one's religous preferences.   _____

16. LaToya was disatisfied with most of the literature
    she discovered at the library.   _____

17. The secretary carefully labeled the files and put
    them into seperate drawers.   _____

18. Tony was susceptable to colds and flu, so his
    mother was surprised when he went through a
    whole winter without getting sick.   _____

19. Dr. Gerber is a history professor and the author of
    a book about William the Conqueror.   _____

21. The *New York Times Book Review* gives enlightening
    descriptions of books on a vareity of subjects.   _____

22. According to many psycologists, adolescence is a
    time for young people to find out who they are and
    what they want to become.   _____

23. Many store owners in the South tell their custom-
    ers, "We appreciate your buisness."   _____

24. The guidance counseler in our highschool gave the
    students some pamphlets on how to choose a
    career.   _____

25. I cannot possibly give my opinion on marrage
    until I have personally experienced that kind of
    relationship.   _____

Paragraph Tests   Paragraph Test 1

Each of the following paragraphs contains twenty errors in grammar, punctuation, mechanics, diction, or spelling. Mark each error that you find with a checkmark (✓) as close to the error as possible or bracket any groups of words that need correction. Then, with these marks as guides, rewrite the paragraph, eliminating all errors. If you find and correct all errors, your score for the paragraph will be 100. Any error that you fail to correct counts off five points. If, in rewriting a paragraph, you eliminate existing errors but make others, each of these will count off five points.

When we were touring the south pacific several years ago, New Zealand was one of my favorite stopovers, however, there was moments when we had cause for concern. In Christchurch, a lovely town that strongly resembles small cities of the English countryside we learned through news accounts that two elderly women who had died of botulism after having eaten some "home-bottled mussels". Their fellow citizen's were naturally distressed at this unusual tradgedy. Our next stop was the city of Auckland, where we found that members of a local civic club had invited we tourists in groups of four or five to have dinner and spend an evening with a local family. Our hosts were Myrtle and George Eastman who were charming and hospitable. They informed us that we would have a typical New Zealand dinner, starting with home-bottled mussels gathered from the beach at their vacation home. I glanced nervously at my fellow traveling companions, and not one of them looked as though they were very happy. The two men bravely accepted some mussels from the platter, but one of the women murmured something about an allergy to fish. I only ate one or two and was relieved to find that I did not immediately start to writhe with stomach pain and getting sicker by the minute. The rest of the evening passed pleasantly; we had roast leg of lamb, potatoes, vegetable salad, and the famous national dessert, Pavlova a meringue like concoction filled with fresh fruits; cherries, oranges, pineapple, and of course kiwi fruit. The Eastman's gave us lemons from the tree in their yard as big as grapefruits. It was an unforgetable experience, and in spite of our fears we luckily suffered no ill effects from eating the notorious home-bottled mussels.

Paragraph Test 2

The summer after my freshmen year in college, I worked in a glove factory in Gloversville New York. My job was to paint the edges of newly sewn black leather gloves with black dye so that no white from the underside of the leather remained, a process called "blackedging." I liked the people I worked with very much. However there was disadvantages to this job, my fingers and clothes were always getting stained, and working from eight to five, little time was available for me to get outside and enjoy the beautifull weather of upstate New York. The summer after my sophmore year I found a job as a clerk in a souvenir store in the resort town of Lake George. There I had no worry about ruining my clothes, moreover, because I worked from 2:30 to 11:30 P.M., I was able to go to the town beach in the morning to swim and lay out in the sun. My last summer job, which I held after graduation from college was as a waitress in a real fancy resterant in Lake George. The work was difficult. Carrying heavy trays and constantly rushing to serve all the customers, my back and feet often hurt at the end of my shift. With tips; however, I made more money than any previous summer, and because you didn't begin work until 4:00 P.M., I had a lot of time to enjoy the outdoors. Today I work as an english teacher, but I will always remember my summer jobs and the different experiences it gave me.

Paragraph Test 3

Several years ago I spent a Winter in what is now called Slovakia; that Central European country once a part of Czechoslovakia. Here I had the opportunity to have recorded for me some of the folktales, that a group of students remembered from its childhood. As interesting as the tales were in theirselves, they were even more interesting because they echoed themes that you hear in folktales told and retold in our own country. In reading the students' papers there were characters that reminded me of many I had met before a old ruler with three sons, each of whom wanted their own kingdom; a great giant who had long ago visited the massive castle still looming above the capitol city; a virtuous maiden and a courageous knight who died for love in nearby Devin's castle; the Danube's enchanted fish king with his bright, shining scales, and the wicked woman whom the villagers discovered had committed unspeakable crimes in her search for eternal youth. Why do these characters and their circumstances seem familiar to us. Folklorists offer at least 2 reasons. First, as men, women and children have traveled across the world; they have taken there stories with them along with their other prized possessions. Second, the same archetypal themes lay in the unconscious of human beings everywhere, surfacing again and again in all their art forms — including the very old one that we call the folktale.

Paragraph Test 4

In highschool Lyle Alzado was an awesome football player, however, in college he was afraid, that he was not big enough too be successful. Thus in 1969 he started taking anabolic steroids, both oraly and by injection. His size did subsequently increase, and over the next fifteen years he played professional football for three teams; the Denver Broncos, the Cleveland Browns and the Los Angeles Raiders. However, Alzado paid a terrible price for this success his brain was effected. He began to have terrible mood swings. He described himself as a maniac, violent on the field and off it. He would get into fights, yell all the time, and slept only three or four hours a night. In 1985 at the age of thirty-six, Alzado retired from the Raiders, but he continued to take steroids, then, for an attempted comeback in 1990, he began to take human growth hormones. Alzado's career, however, was over. His comeback failed, and not long afterward he began to suffer from loss of coordination, fainting spells, and double vision. Tests finally showed that he had brain cancer. When a reporter asked one of his doctors Robert Huizenga, if Alzados cancer could of been caused by the drugs he had taken the doctor replied, "I think there's no question." The doctor went on to point out that according to estimates, a million people in the United States uses steroids. "I think," he concluded, "We have a real time bomb on our hands." Weak, hairless, some sixty pounds lighter, and clearly dying, Alzado offered this advice in a 1991 issue of Sports Illustrated, "If you're on steroids or human growth hormone, stop. I should have."

Paragraph Test 5

I agree that us Americans have love affairs with our cars. But even the most ardent love affairs have their dismal moments, at one time or another devoted companions entertain thoughts of closing the door, and walking away. As for me, I have been associated with many cars in my life some were objects of my affection, a few strained all my charitable instincts. There was a long two-tone station wagon who's fuel gauge ceased to function shortly after the vehicle had been driven off the used car lot. One night it ran out of gas as three of us — my two older brothers and me — were on our way to a wedding. I remember too the car that sort of late in its life was christened "the green dragon". It drank quart after quart of oil and spasmodically spewed steam from beneath its' hood. Then there was the most unforgettable of cars — a chunky black sedan through whose floorboards you could see the pavement whizzing passed. I could only manage to back it up the slightest incline, and when I needed to get the spare tire, the trunk door more than opened, indeed, it came completely off. Nevertheless I am pleased that my partners in these affairs ca'nt respond to my remarks, for they would be liable to recall times when I was the offending party; denting fenders, miring down on muddy roads, spinning wheels in the sand, and — greatest of all automotive sins — to forget to change the oil.

Paragraph Test 6

Whenever I visit in Savannah, Georgia I get in touch with old friends who live there, and usually drop by there apartment. Their beautiful four-story building, designed by a famous southern architect is in the restored area of the city. The only trouble is that it's elevator is now over sixty-five years old and temperamental at best. On a recent visit I stepped into the small, rickety elevator, which already had four passengers. I hesitated before getting in but decided to go ahead. On the next floor we stopped, and there stood three people; a large women and two very large, young men. The woman lunged forward, beckoning to the men to join her. I immediately pointed out that they would overload the six-person capacity of the car. The woman loudly and rudely told me to keep quiet, again urging her companions to enter. They crammed themselves in, and we made a jerky takeoff then we stopped abruptly between floors. I felt as though I couldn't hardly breathe in that crowded space glaring accusingly at the woman who had caused the trouble. She didn't flinch, however, and did not acknowledge her guilt. We were stuck there for over thirty minutes, with the building superintendent calling encouraging messages that he would have us out shortly. The workers finally got us to the next floor, and as the door opened I haughtily suggested that those three people take the stairs when they were ready to leave. I was breathing hard and really shook up, having thought that the old car may suddenly drop to the basement. On my way out of the building I took the stairs, and to my surprise had the misfortune to see those three again — also on the stairs! At last the big arrogant woman gave me a sheepish look and said, "Sorry", before hurrying down ahead of me. I think it cost her alot to utter that one word apology.

Paragraph Test 7

During my high school years my best friend was Susan Miller a girl whom had lived down the street from me all her life. We knew each other well, and had many interests in common. One way in which we were different; however, was in our shopping habits. When I shopped I always knew what I wanted, got it quickly, and left. For Susan, shopping was a game. She spent all day at it; examining, comparing, and finally, if conditions was right, buying. All to often I have spent hours waiting for her to make up her mind. In fact, my longest "shopathon" was on a Christmas Eve when Susan and myself went to pick up a few last-minute gifts. She wanted a gift for her Father, and I had to get something for my youngest sister Sara. We started at 9:00 A.M., and by 10:15 I had bought Sara her gift a toy Dalmatian. Then I just trudged around the mall after Susan. By one o'clock she still had not made a purchase, and the mall was becoming human gridlock. Finally feeling some compassion Susan bought herself and I each a slice of pizza. We had to eat standing up the tables were all filled. Then, walking and walking through endless stores, the shopping continued. She examined shirts, scarves, ties, knickknacks. Her responses to every possibility was negative, her father had it, he wouldn't like it, this was too expensive, that was too cheap. Nothing seemed right for Susans father. Finally, fifteen minutes before the mall was scheduled to close, she came out of a store in triumph. "I got it!" she said. I looked up from where I was sitting on a bench, rubbing my swollen feet. "What?" I asked weakly. She held up a peice of paper. "A gift certificate!" she exclaimed. "With this my father can get whatever he wants."

Paragraph Test 8

Some of todays social commentators argue that television is destroying america's children. These critics describe grade-school children coming home from school and spend the next five to seven hours crouched like zombies in front of a brightly colored screen, watching program after program. The children do not even stop to eat, they have there meals in front of the television set. In fact, according to these critics, modern children are so dominated by television that they have almost no social interaction with parents or friends. I think such descriptions are exaggerated; they do not apply to the children I know, and they certainly do not apply to me and my family. Six to eight years ago as a youngster, television only played a small roll in my life. When my brother and I got home from school we would not go directly to the television set, we would go straight out the back door to play. With the other children in the neighborhood we would organize games of kickball, hide-and-seek, and sometimes we played softball. When dad got home from work, he would call my brother and I in for dinner. My parents, my brother and I would then eat together as a family, which gave us an opportunity to catch up on each others news. After dinner my brother and I would do our homework (we didn't have much in grade school), then sometimes we would, I admit, watch television. However, if we found nothing to interest us we either would read or play board games. About nine o'clock the bedtime ritual began: we would bathe, brush our teeth, and say our prayers with either our mother or our father. I have happy memories of those early childhood years — memories, that are not at all dominated by bright, flickering images on a television screen.

Sentence-Combining Exercise 1

A. Combine the following pairs of sentences, changing one of the two to a participial phrase. Punctuate each newly formed sentence correctly.

Example: I found an ink stain on my new white blouse. I tried without success to remove the stain.

Having found an ink stain on my new white blouse, I tried without success to remove it.

1. Tom hoped to make a good grade on his history essay. He was disappointed when he received a C+.

2. Julie wanted to be on time for her date with Terry. She started dressing at three o'clock.

3. The Martins are busily studying house plans at the moment. They will start building their new home in April.

4. Dwight was annoyed by the loud, discordant noises in his dormitory. He finally decided to study in the library.

5. The big dog was sitting in the doorway. Louise was afraid to enter the house.

6. Jake was engrossed in the new science-fiction novel. He forgot to go to football practice.

7. Dad tried to teach Helen to ice-skate. He became frustrated when she kept falling down.

8. Tina and I made a list of the guests to invite to our party. We found that the final list added up to too many people.

9. Our area is suffering from a terrible drought. There has been no rain here for more than six weeks.

10. That young man is a college student. He wants a summer job in order to earn next quarter's tuition.

B. Combine the following pairs of sentences, changing one of the two to a gerund phrase. Punctuate each newly formed sentence correctly.

Example: Rod has cultivated his apple trees properly. His efforts have paid off with a bumper crop.

Cultivating his apple trees properly has paid off for Rod with a bumper crop.

1. Glenda tried out for the college glee club. It was an ordeal.

2. Dave thought that he could skip class with no problem. He didn't know that Dr. Moseley would give a pop quiz that day.

3. Jane and her mother agreed to shop at Lenox Square. Afterward they concluded that they had made the right decision.

4. Perhaps we can persuade Ms. Phelps to participate in our Christmas bazaar. Her help would ensure its success.

5. Joe sent for a mail-order book titled *How to Be Your Own Mechanic*. He made a mistake in judgment.

6. I swim ten laps in our pool every day. This exercise is helping me lose weight.

7. Sam, I think that you have the opportunity to make the basketball team. You must practice faithfully every day.

8. Meg gets up early every morning and swims fifty laps at the pool. This exercise keeps her fit.

9. Jim knows that he has a high average in chemistry. This knowledge has encouraged him to apply for a loan for graduate study.

10. I have been lying in this hammock all day. I will certainly not be able to finish my book report on *Intruder in the Dust.*

Sentence-Combining Exercise 2

A. Combine the following pairs of sentences, changing one of the two to an appositive phrase. Punctuate each newly formed sentence correctly.

Example: Peonies are my favorite spring flower. They grow well in our climate.

Peonies, my favorite spring flower, grow well in our climate.

1. Pete Larkins is a classmate of mine. He has asked me to room with him next year.

2. Mrs. Ashford-Forsyth is the president of her garden club. She bores all the members with her lengthy, gushy reports.

3. I am surprised that Jackie looks so sloppy today. She is usually a well-groomed person.

4. I have a first cousin called Marian. She and I have the same birthday.

5. My very first car was a Ford Mustang. It was bright red, with a black leather top.

6. Peter's mother is a descendant of General "Stonewall" Jackson. She and her family have lived in Virginia for many years.

7. Tom Glavine was the recent winner of the Cy Young Award. He has been a pitcher for the Atlanta Braves for several years.

8. Helen Keller was born both blind and deaf. She learned to read, write, and speak and became an author and lecturer.

9. Our next-door neighbor is a real grouch. He often yells at the neighborhood children.

10. Mariana is my closest friend. She gave me a book of poetry for my birthday.

B. Combine the following pairs of sentences, changing one of the two to an absolute phrase. Punctuate each newly formed sentence correctly.

Example: The rain had been falling heavily. Lars regretted that he had not brought his poncho.

The rain having been falling heavily, Lars regretted that he had not brought his poncho.

1. Bill's Spanish professor announced a test for Friday. Bill knew that he would have to change his weekend plans.

2. The air conditioner had not run for hours. The temperature in our room rose to ninety-eight degrees.

3. The Secretary of State called a news conference for 4:00 P.M. Members of the media hurried to find strategic seats in the large room.

4. The baby has finally cried himself to sleep. Mother is trying to get a few minutes' rest before he awakes.

5. Katherine's beautiful cheese soufflé was ruined. She wondered what she could substitute as a dinner entreé.

6. Lewis passed the football fifteen yards to Dodd in the end zone. The crowd screamed with delight at the touchdown.

7. Millie wrote an enthusiastic letter to Franklin about her new job. Franklin was pleased to learn that she was happy.

8. The dean arranged a schedule of morning classes for me. I then started looking for an afternoon job.

9. This summer has been very hot and dry. I am afraid that the usual lovely autumn colors will not appear in the mountains.

10. Jack has finished reading *War and Peace*. His next reading assignment is Shakespeare's *King Lear*.

Sentence-Combining Exercise 3

A. Combine the following pairs of sentences, making one of them an adverbial clause. Be careful to avoid upside-down subordination in your formulation of the new sentence. Punctuate each new sentence correctly.

Example: I cannot lift this heavy bag from the trunk of the car. Otherwise, I would be glad to help you, Aunt Martha.

If I could lift this heavy bag from the trunk of the car, I would be glad to help you, Aunt Martha.

1. I learned to ride a bicycle on my sixth birthday. It was a happy day for me.

2. David has not yet completely mastered the use of a computer. He learns something new every day.

3. It is hard for Jill to speak in public. She becomes very nervous and unsure of herself.

4. We need a list of camping provisions. We should make the list before going to the supermarket.

5. Larry made his plane reservations two weeks ahead. He wanted to be sure to arrive in Denver in time for his brother's wedding.

6. Marilyn plans to work next summer in San Francisco. She has always heard that it is a wonderful city.

7. Charlotte, North Carolina, is growing rapidly. Its population has greatly increased in the past ten years.

B. Combine the following pairs of sentences, making one of the two a noun clause. Punctuate each newly formed sentence correctly.

Example: John and his sister are leaving today. I learned about their departure this morning.

I learned this morning that John and his sister are leaving today.

1. Karen was in doubt about her plans for the future. She could not decide between college and a job.

2. The contents of the refrigerator were not at all promising. Harry decided to go out for some fast food.

3. To be a doctor of veterinary medicine is her greatest wish. We all hope for her success.

4. You were forty minutes late for our aerobics class today. The instructor would like to know the reason.

5. Louisa has decided to tell James about her engagement to Rob. She wants him to be the first to know her plans.

6. Gloria has learned the news of Fred's big honor. He is to be valedictorian of his graduating class.

7. My word processor is still a mystery to me. I do not understand the basic principles behind its function.

C. Combine the following pairs of sentences, making one of the two an adjective clause. Punctuate each newly formed sentence correctly.

Example: That woman with red hair is my neighbor. I introduced her to you at the party Saturday.

That red-haired woman, whom I introduced to you at the party Saturday, is my neighbor.

1. I asked Uncle Ralph for his Brunswick stew recipe. He served us the stew at his barbecue last summer.

2. These figures were compiled by the graduate school. They show the number of students receiving graduate degrees for the past five years.

3. Laurie says that she will always remember her sixteenth birthday. She got her driver's license that day.

4. Mrs. Hopkins spent her entire vacation visiting patients in a local nursing home. She is a wonderfully kind person.

5. My old car is a 1970 model. It still provides me with reliable transportation.

6. The young man out in our carport is looking for the pruning shears. He takes care of our lawn and garden.

Sentence-Combining Exercise 4

Combine the following pairs of sentences to form one effective simple or complex sentence. Use phrases or dependent clauses of any type as a way to give variety and coherence to your sentences through subordination. Punctuate each newly formed sentence correctly.

Example: Ted used all his knowledge and skill to start the motorboat. He could not make the engine turn over.

Although Ted used all his knowledge and skill to start the motorboat, he could not make the engine turn over.

1. Mr. Whittier had spent the entire weekend hiking with a troop of Boy Scouts. He was ready for civilization and a hot shower.

2. I hope you can manage to meet us by ten o'clock. Then we can ride to the airport with Martin.

3. I was watching an old movie on television. I fell asleep on the sofa.

4. Wallace wants a job in an architectural firm. First, however, he must get his degree.

5. Juan's mother threw out his treasured collection of comic books. He could hardly believe the bad news.

6. Barbara registered early. She wanted to get the courses necessary for graduation.

7. Prices of new houses are now very high. Most buyers have to save money for several years to make a down payment.

8. Rosita was very happy. She was going out for pizza with her new boyfriend.

9. I was surprised at Tommy's low grade on the final. He is usually an A student.

10. The hockey team has made a request for new uniforms. This request seems reasonable to the Athletic Board.

11. We have just heard the good news about the Levines' son. He has won a Rhodes scholarship.

12. The dramas of Sophocles are greatly admired by literary scholars. This fact is certainly well known.

13. I will be frank with you. I do not like your new haircut.

14. The physics class had already begun. Dr. Miller scowled fiercely at Earl for being late.

15. My drive on the freeway in rush-hour traffic frustrated me. It was an unpleasant experience.

16. Mike plants shrubs in an unusual way. I do not understand the reasoning behind his method.

17. Henry tried manfully to control his temper. He left the meeting without a word.

18. Retirement for a professor at our college comes at age seventy. Dr. Jane Smithson will meet that requirement next year.

19. Carmen is feeling dejected. She did not pass the entrance test for law school.

20. I respect Ms. Howard's opinion. She is an advocate for environmental protection.

Sentence-Combining Exercise 5

Combine the following pairs of sentences to form one effective simple or complex sentence. Use phrases or dependent clauses of any type as a way to give variety and coherence to your sentences through subordination. Punctuate each newly formed sentence correctly.

Example: At first Margaret could not decide between pink and blue wallpaper for her bedroom. She finally selected the blue.

Though undecided at first between pink and blue wallpaper for her bedroom, Margaret finally selected the blue.

1. Jim was heading for the bus stop on his way to work. Then he saw the bus disappearing down the road toward town.

2. The girl screamed. She stared fearfully at the snake coiled to strike.

3. Our dog Prince is a nine-year-old collie. He was a gift to our family from Uncle Charlie.

4. The police questioned the suspect for five hours. She refused to change her assertion of innocence.

5. Chaucer is the father of English poetry. He is held by many to be the equal of Homer.

6. Robert and Laura plan to spend their honeymoon in Europe. They will spend a month in either Switzerland or Italy.

7. We returned from a long, cold day of skiing. Cups of hot tea and a roaring fire revived us quickly.

8. The city of Paris on Bastille Day is a thrilling place. We stood in a crowd on the Champs Élysées and listened to the music of "La Marseillaise."

9. Mark Twain was famous for his sardonic humor. He is said to have remarked that reports of his death were highly exaggerated.

10. Leningrad, Russia, is now called St. Petersburg. The name was changed in 1991, reverting to the city's original name.

11. The Smiths have a camellia bush with delicate pink flowers. Its name is Pink Perfection.

12. The tall-case clock in our front foyer is made of mahogany. My great-grandfather brought it here from Scotland in 1849.

13. Hank wanted to borrow a book from Ginny. He walked to her house in pouring rain.

14. Yesterday Billy almost had an accident. He swerved in the road to avoid hitting a small dog.

15. We believe that autumn is finally on its way. The dogwood, maple, and sourwood leaves are showing beautiful colors.

16. I was confused and nervous on my freeway drive through an unfamiliar city. I took the wrong exit and was soon hopelessly lost.

17. Mark has a new red convertible. This car has made him very popular with all his college classmates.

18. We filled our hummingbird feeder with a sugar-and-water solution. The feeder now attracts dozens of the little birds.

19. Sue warned Tommy repeatedly that he would run out of gas through failure to watch the meter. Saturday Tommy ran out of gas.

20. The television meteorologist has just announced that a tornado warning is in effect. We will take the precautions that he suggests.

Sentence-Combining Exercise 6

Combine the following pairs of sentences, making one of the two a participial phrase, a gerund phrase, an infinitive phrase, an absolute phrase, or an appositive phrase. Punctuate each sentence correctly.

Example: Suzanne has enjoyed cooking for many years. She now has a sizable collection of cookbooks.

Having enjoyed cooking for many years, Suzanne now has a sizable collection of cookbooks.

1. Mario made the most of his time. He systematically listed the things that needed to be accomplished each day.

2. We had grown tired of listening to Mimi's tapes. We finally decided to go by the Music Shop to look for some new ones.

3. Neither of us was ready to take the test for a ham radio license. We asked Father to drill us on Morse code.

4. The doctor had traveled to the villages along the river for many years. He now looked forward to having still another generation of patients.

5. I had never lived anywhere but at home. I was a bit uneasy about renting an apartment in St. Paul with Elinor and her sister.

6. Kim wanted to swim well in the spring meet. She knew that she must make practice a daily priority.

7. Their son is a highly respected landscape architect in the Southwest. Photographs of some of his work are on display in the downtown library.

8. My friends restored the Hampton house in less than a year. They worked most weekends and holidays.

9. The Scholarship Awards Committee interviewed Dorothy about her desire to major in archaeology. Then the members voiced their reactions to her replies.

10. The music reminded Irwin of the summer just past. He thought of all the good times he had had at Birch Lodge.

11. The letter arrived yesterday. Fran now knows that her interview for the job at the insurance company is scheduled for a week from Friday.

12. He really did not understand how to access the database that he needed. He went in search of the student on duty in the computer lab.

13. Christina is an agronomist with the U.S. Department of Agriculture. She recently appeared on television as a participant in a roundtable discussion.

14. Tom started to mow the lawn. Then he thought better of the idea and decided to get up a golf game with Stan.

15. Today Dad drove into a service station off the parkway. He was amused to see parked there a lavender motorcycle with yellow wheels.

16. Joe Edwards is president of the local union. At last night's meeting he announced plans to open contract negotiations with the plant management.

17. Barbara had never met her cousin or his fiancée. She was having difficulty deciding on a wedding gift.

18. Delia discovered that she still had $216.58 in her bank account. She went shopping for a dress to wear that night.

19. Friday had finally arrived. The office manager had only to deposit the week's receipts and head for the ballpark.

20. The dancers anticipated each other's movements. They attracted the attention of the audience and the judges alike.

Sentence-Combining Exercise 7

Combine the following pairs of sentences, making one of the two an adverbial clause, an adjective clause, a noun clause, or an elliptical clause. Punctuate each sentence correctly.

Example: Mr. Corsini has not seen a car in the garage or a light on in the living room. He thinks that his neighbors have already left for Hawaii.

Because Mr. Corsini has not seen a car in the garage or a light on in the living room, he thinks that his neighbors have already left for Hawaii.

1. The noise along the hall interfered with her powers of concentration. Jodie grabbed up her books and headed for the library to finish her geology paper.

2. Mary Beth has gone to Canada to visit friends. She met them last year when she was studying French in Montreal.

3. The theater was small. Nevertheless, it was the ideal place to present the experimental play.

4. My letter must reach Miami by Thursday. Robert and Al are leaving for Key West on Friday.

5. The idea is absolutely inspired. We should ask Rigney to house-sit for us next week.

6. Holly assures me that she has packed only the bare necessities. Nevertheless, her suitcase is almost too full to close.

7. Mrs. Nettles is always more than willing to show us pictures of her cat. She brought it home from the Humane Society's shelter.

8. My sister and I are always interested in going to the farmers' market. There we can buy fruits and vegetables from all over the world.

9. Vivian had thought that she would order just a cup of coffee. Then she saw a boy at the next table eating a tempting concoction of chocolate and nuts.

10. She erased a resolution regarding sweets from her memory. She searched the menu for the name of her neighbor's dessert.

11. The search committee was elated. An innovative young coach from a small college in the Midwest had accepted its offer.

12. Shirley bought a linen blazer on sale at Liza's. She told me about it this morning at breakfast.

13. The members of the senior class have had a long discussion about the homecoming dance. They have been arguing about when they should schedule it.

14. Early this morning the telephone rang insistently. Doug knew that his mother would be on the other end of the line.

15. The tourist became lost in the maze of narrow streets. He used the cathedral spire as a landmark to lead him back to his hotel.

16. Travis's father and mother agreed. Travis should work a year before applying to graduate school.

17. Even the children look forward to the flower show. It takes place every May in the exhibition hall overlooking the river.

18. Uncle Neil won't give up his old blue sweater. It has a hole in the elbow of one sleeve and two missing buttons.

19. It is a complete surprise to all of us. Larry and Beth plan to be married in August.

20. Your brother Kelly is one of those generous human beings. He is willing to share bed and board with a host of friends.

Sentence-Combining Exercise 8

In the following exercise combine the ideas in each of the groups of sentences into one effective simple or complex sentence.

Example: Bill was an eighteen-year-old college student at the University of Georgia.
He worked part-time at a video store.
The money he earned helped pay his college expenses.

Bill, an eighteen-year-old college student at the University of Georgia, worked part-time at a video store to help pay his college expenses.

1. Michelle has a sports car.
   It was given to her by her parents.
   It has two airbags and antilock brakes.

2. Animal-rights advocates are increasing in numbers.
   They believe that animals are not means to human ends.
   They believe that animals are beings with interests of their own.

3. Pine beetles have invaded the pine tree.
   The pine tree is eighty feet high.
   It shades our whole back yard.

4. The pine tree was cut down.
   Its branches were carted off for firewood.
   Our back yard seemed very empty.

5. *Eyes on the Prize* is a series of six films.
   The films cover the civil rights movement in the United States from 1954 to 1965.
   More civil rights legislation was passed in America during these years than ever before.

6. Euthanasia is another term for mercy killing.
   Many people believe that euthanasia should be legalized.
   In the United States euthanasia is generally considered murder.

7. Allan Bloom wrote *The Closing of the American Mind*.
   The book argues that American universities have abandoned traditional liberal arts courses.
   According to Bloom, universities are now often teaching "relevant," trendy courses.

8. My brother's desk was cluttered.
   Books, papers, and pens were scattered on its surface.
   Half-eaten pizza crusts, empty soda cans, and crumpled potato-chip bags could also be seen.

9. The Writing Center offers tutorial help in writing.
   This help is offered to any student registered for classes at the University.
   The Writing Center is located in Room 25 of Memorial Library.

10. Walking is a low-risk exercise.
Almost everyone can walk.
Thus walking is often called the ideal low-stress exercise.

11. *Parade* is a magazine supplement to many Sunday newspapers in the United
States.
In 1993 *Parade* conducted interviews on law and order with 2,512 men and
women.
The men and women were between the ages of eighteen and seventy-five.
The men and women were representative of the population as a whole.

12. Eighty-two percent of the people surveyed said they had a positive attitude
toward the police.
Only 23 percent believed that juries usually convict the guilty and free the
innocent.
These figures are from *Parade*.

13. The Holocaust Museum is located just behind the Washington Monument.
It is our country's tribute to those killed by Hitler's regime.
Six million Jews were killed by Hitler's regime.

14. I went on a trip.
I was gone for five days.
When I returned, my houseplants were drooping.
They needed water.

15. Juan worked as a city lifeguard last summer.
    He was assigned to the Rock Springs Pool.
    He enjoyed the job.

16. Benny Goodman was the son of impoverished Jewish immigrants.
    They lived in Chicago.
    Goodman took his first music lessons in a neighborhood synagogue.

17. Goodman was a renowned clarinetist during the 1930's and 1940's.
    He helped establish jazz as an art.
    He became known as the "King of Swing."

18. My only sister lives in Upper Saddle River, New Jersey.
    Her name is Dorothy.
    She is one of my best friends.

19. Edward tore the anterior cruciate ligament in his right knee.
    He had surgery.
    The surgery reconstructed his knee.

20. Alice Walker was born in Georgia in 1944.
    She is the author of the novel *The Color Purple*.
    The Color Purple was published in 1982.
    Walker won the Pulitzer Prize for that novel.

Sentence-Combining Exercise 9

In the following exercise combine the ideas in each of the groups of sentences into one effective simple or complex sentence.

Example: We bought a microwave oven.
It heated up leftovers very effectively.
We never again threw away any leftover food.

The microwave oven we bought heated up leftovers so effectively that we never again threw away any leftover food.

1. The kitten was black.
It belonged to my son.
It disappeared from our yard one day.
I put up signs around the neighborhood.
The signs asked whether anyone had seen the kitten.

2. The next day a young girl rang our doorbell.
She wore a Catholic school uniform.
The uniform was a plaid jumper and a white blouse.

3. She told us about a stray black kitten.
It had been hiding in the bushes in her back yard.
The kitten cried at night.

4. My son and I went to the girl's house.
We saw a black kitten peeping out from under a bush.
The kitten was ours.

5. The kitten must have learned from its experience.
   It never wandered from our yard again.
   It lived for sixteen years.

6. Jacques-Louis David painted a picture called *The Dead Marat*.
   It shows a man who has been murdered in his bathtub.
   The man was Jean Paul Marat.
   Marat was an important political figure in the French Revolution.

7. We ate at a Mexican restaurant last night.
   We ate tacos and burritos.
   Then we had an American fudge sundae for dessert.

8. Peter Taylor is the author of short stories, plays, and novels.
   He has won prizes for his work.
   He grew up in Nashville and Memphis, Tennessee.

9. One of Taylor's novels is *A Summons to Memphis*.
   It won the Pulitzer Prize.
   The novel is based in part on some of Taylor's boyhood experiences in
      Nashville and Memphis.

10. There are ways for students to get good grades on exams.
    They should review the material carefully.
    They should also get a good night's sleep the night before.

11. Maya Angelou is an African-American writer and performer.
    Maya Angelou read a poem at President Clinton's inauguration.
    She had written the poem especially for the occasion.

12. In 1993, five hundred candidates auditioned to become the new stadium
    announcer for the San Francisco Giants.
    Sherry Davis was chosen for the position.
    Sherry Davis was a legal secretary.

13. Davis was a long-time baseball fan.
    She had had training in television voice-overs.
    She was the first woman to be a full-time professional baseball announcer.

14. I like writing on a word processor.
    I can correct my errors easily.
    I don't have to read my own handwriting.

15. The day was dark and cloudy.
    Mary wore a raincoat.
    It had a hood.
    It was waterproof.

16. Aunt Mary pulled a leather strap out of her purse.
    She snapped it onto a ring on the side of her suitcase.
    Her suitcase was large and heavy.
    Then she briskly pulled the suitcase along behind her on its wheels.
    It was like walking a dog on a leash.

17. My mother retired from her job.
    She had worked as a high school teacher.
    Then she had time to crochet many brightly colored afghans.
    She gave them to my sister and me.

18. Janet fell asleep in the sun.
    A straw hat was over her face.
    Thus the tan on her face matched the mesh of her hat.

19. Willa Cather wrote *O Pioneers!* and *My Antonia*.
    She attended the University of Nebraska from 1891 to 1895.
    During her last two college years she helped pay her expenses.
    She worked those years as a newspaper columnist.

20. Mary often forgets her dental appointments.
    She also often forgets her term-paper deadlines.
    However, she never forgets her Saturday-night dates.

Review Tests **Test on Chapters 1–7**

A. In each of the following sentences underline the subject once and the verb twice; then circle the complement (or complements). In the first column at the right tell whether the verb is transitive active (**TA**), transitive passive (**TP**), or intransitive (**I**). In the second column tell whether the complement is a direct object (**DO**), an indirect object (**IO**), a predicate nominative (**PN**), a predicate adjective (**PA**), or an objective complement (**OC**). Note that not all sentences have complements.

1. Jamie reads the newspaper the first thing every morning. _____ _____

2. Everyone was given an opportunity to see the exhibit. _____ _____

3. He felt really good after that test. _____ _____

4. The party was planned for you and me. _____ _____

5. One of my worst experiences was my first blind date. _____ _____

6. Paul did not attend many football games. _____ _____

7. Last night's freeze killed all of the flowers. _____ _____

8. The coach appointed him team mascot. _____ _____

9. The cheerleaders will decorate the gym for the dance. _____ _____

10. The decorator painted the dining room yellow. _____ _____

11. Her father frequently brings her a surprise. _____ _____

12. There is someone in your office. _____ _____

B. What part of speech is each of the following underlined words?

1. first in the first sentence above _____

2. Everyone in the second sentence above _____

3. after in the third sentence above _____

4. me in the fourth sentence above _____

5. date in the fifth sentence above _____

6. many in the sixth sentence above _____

7. all in the seventh sentence above _____

8. <u>team</u> in the eighth sentence above _____

9. <u>for</u> in the ninth sentence above _____

10. <u>yellow</u> in the tenth sentence above _____

11. <u>frequently</u> in the eleventh sentence above _____

12. <u>office</u> in the twelfth sentence above _____

C. In each of the sentences below identify the *italicized* expression by writing one of the following numbers in the space at the right:

1 if it is a *prepositional phrase*,   **6** if it is an *absolute phrase*,
2 if it is a *participial phrase*,   **7** if it is a *noun clause*,
3 if it is a *gerund phrase*,   **8** if it is an *adjective clause*,
4 if it is an *infinitive phrase*,   **9** if it is an *adverbial clause*.
5 if it is an *appositive phrase*,

1. We arrived *at Fort Largo* Wednesday afternoon. _____

2. Amy Tan, *who is Kim's favorite author,* has written a new novel. _____

3. For many Americans, *watching television* is their only entertainment. _____

4. Fortunately, he knows exactly *what he wants.* _____

5. *After we eat dinner,* will you tell us a ghost story? _____

6. The President spent several hours *consulting with his advisers.* _____

7. *To play Scrabble well* requires attention to the game. _____

8. *The clock having struck midnight,* Cinderella had to leave the ball. _____

9. Her two grandsons, *Paul and William,* are both living in New York City. _____

10. Rumors are *that Dr. Hanna will be the college's next president.* _____

D. Underline the dependent clause (or clauses) in each of the following sentences. In the first column at the right tell whether the clause is a noun clause (**N**), an adjective clause (**Adj**), or an adverbial clause (**Adv**). In the second column tell how the noun clause is used (that is, whether it is a subject, direct object, etc.), or what the adjective or adverbial clause modifies.

1. I recently learned that for graduation I do not need to take History 205. _____   _____

2. We will reach the campground before dark unless we have difficulty finding the cut-off.   _____   _____

3. The cut-off, which is not marked, is easily missed.   _____   _____

4. Dr. Crawford is someone whose sense of humor never fails him.   _____   _____

5. What he wants to do the rest of his life Carlos has not decided.   _____   _____

6. Because we were early, we were asked to help set up the film projector.   _____   _____

7. What I found difficult to understand was his obsessive interest in insects.   _____   _____

8. Before he leaves his apartment, he sets his computer to receive voice mail.   _____   _____

9. The subjects that I like best are English, history, and theology.   _____   _____

10. What is the name of the professor whom everyone recommends for Western Civilization?   _____   _____

E. In the following sentences insert all necessary commas and semicolons. Rewrite sentence fragments in such a way as to make complete sentences. If a sentence is correct, mark it **C.**

1. When he walked into the room everyone turned and stared.

2. The department store had a one-day sale everything was half price.

3. Homer's *Iliad* an epic poem which describes the adventures of Achilles.

4. Kay bought a large dog a Rhodesian Ridgeback for her son.

5. Her wedding is tomorrow and she is hoping that it will not rain.

6. Our favorite restaurant having had a grease fire several weeks ago, now scheduled to reopen in July.

7. Before starting on a long trip Ken has his car checked for mechanical safety.

8. After the play is over we will all meet at the Buckhead Diner for dinner then some of us will go dancing.

9. The reason that he gave for missing the homecoming game was somewhat far-fetched.

10. He rushed into the house dropped his coat on a chair threw his books on the desk and opened the refrigerator to look for something to eat.

Test on Chapters 8–18

Correct all errors in the following sentences. Many sentences will have to be rewritten. In some cases a misplaced element may be circled and its correct position indicated by a caret ($\wedge$). Other errors may be crossed out and corrections written above the sentence. If a sentence is correct, write **C.**

1. He always has and always will believe that he left his camera at the sidewalk café near the Fitzgerald Book Shop.

2. While driving back to school, the thought occurred to me that I should have packed my hiking boots.

3. The wedding present for Nat and Gail is setting on the desk in the living room.

4. Parking at the main post office is difficult, which is particularly annoying in the late afternoon.

5. Critics think that of the three principal characters the father has the better understanding of the girl's problem.

6. As the passengers filed past, an attendant asked each of them to present their boarding pass.

7. The panel member who the question was addressed to has a great deal of experience in community service.

8. The criteria for the position of managing editor was discussed at last night's staff meeting.

9. The reason that Barbara doesn't know how to manage her financial affairs is because she has never been entrusted with the responsibility.

10. The witness remembers only seeing two men leave the bank.

11. Caught in a downpour this morning, everything from my hair clips to my shoestrings got soaking wet.

12. There is a food court in the mall, and it is on the first level, and I think we should meet there at noon.

13. If I was Helen, I would get a madras shirt to wear with that new white skirt.

14. He is a man with a great deal of common sense and who also appreciates it in others.

15. The cat that was startled suddenly darted up the sycamore tree.

16. Marvin, I approve of your buying this truck: its motor really runs smooth.

17. Even though I have had bridge lessons, I still don't understand all of the fine points of the game.

18. Vanilla yogurt with a nut topping make a great pick-me-up on a hot afternoon.

19. Which country has the greatest trade surplus of any other country that we have studied?

20. Father is still reading Winston Churchill's account of the Norman Conquest on the porch.

21. After looking through the files for a third time, Don's letter from the insurance company turned up in a very unlikely folder.

22. Stuffing the envelopes on Thursday, the campaign workers sealed and stamped them on Friday.

23. I'm sure that Dad feels well; he looks splendidly.

24. Generally speaking, taking a sweater or jacket to the game is not a bad idea.

25. The memo states that everybody should pick up their new telephone directory at the front office.

26. Because he putted more consistent than anyone else, I wasn't surprised when he won the tournament.

27. Even though he grew up in a family of politicians, he doesn't seem to be interested in it.

28. Organizing the Halloween party won't be difficult if we divide the work among us — you, Agnes, and I.

29. To get to the river, it is necessary that we walk from here.

30. It is I who have forgotten to pick up the groceries and you who is getting the blame.

31. I wish that I was as far along with my sociology paper as Michael seems to be with his.

32. The congregation rose to its feet as the bride entered the church on the arm of her father.

33. Beverly, we really appreciated you bringing us the casserole the day that we moved.

34. If Pat will look at the map, she will see that it is more than five hundred miles from here to Tucson.

35. The local media recognized its need to report all the facts about the developer's intentions.

36. I didn't know who was supposed to receive the letter of recommendation, so I addressed it simply "To Who It May Concern."

37. In writing a paper for Ms. Thistleberry, the opening paragraph must contain an explicit thesis statement.

38. Our neighbors can't sell their house because they are asking more for it.

39. The letter to the *Herald* was written by my friend Joel and was addressed by him to the editor of the editorial page.

40. "Mystery!" is one of those television programs that offers suspense on the one hand and escape on the other.

41. Tina, you either need some rose velvet pillows for this couch or some tapestry ones with a background in that color.

42. Hugh has a great sense of humor, so one shouldn't take him too serious.

43. The foreign trade statistics submitted to the congressional subcommittee speak for themselves.

44. Gerald is the person whom I suppose will spearhead the fund drive for the Heart Association.

45. According to historical records, the cornerstone for the White House was lain on October 13, 1792.

46. By getting up early and staying up late was the way that Harvey had his portfolio ready to present to the head of the art department.

47. The juvenile court is interested and supportive of the community's desire to offer fresh opportunities to young offenders.

48. In the fall our small mountain town has a harvest festival, and we often block off the streets, and then we set up booths, and we sell our local wares.

49. Even people who seldom remember dates recall that 1066 was the date of the Battle of Hastings.

50. Anthony acknowledged that during spring quarter how difficult carrying an overload was going to be.

Test on Chapters 19–24

A. In the following sentences insert all necessary punctuation marks and correct all errors of punctuation and mechanics.

1. Frankly Tom your plan to paint the house yourself, is a terrible idea.

2. When we saw the beautiful gingko tree last fall we were struck, by it's brilliant yellow foliage.

3. My oldest brother Martin is a gifted pianist and he also plays the clarinet.

4. The cat said Laura is waiting for her milk but we don't have any.

5. "Has anyone seen my car keys"? George asked frantically. "I am late for class already".

6. Though it is a very old musical I understand that its touring company last year played to record audiences.

7. Dont be afraid to disagree with Mrs. Jacobson; her bark is actually — well, it's worse than her bite, to coin a phrase.

8. In our new pamphlet you will find full-color photographs page 5 of several new varieties of camellias.

9. Here is the list of supplies, you will need for your art class a sketch pad, a palette, an easel, oil paints, and pastel chalk.

10. Above the clouds had turned a dark threatening black, I wanted to get home before the storm broke.

11. "This news of his brother's selection for the olympic swimming team is most gratifying," said Harold McPherson.

12. I hear youve been wanting to see me about something important can you wait, until tomorrow afternoon?

13. Let's take the time to swing by Carey's and Jackie's house to see their new car; we can still be home by seven oclock.

14. The four year old child, the Greene's youngest boy, is a little imp.

15. Miriam is reading Faulkner's "The Sound And The Fury" for the first time, and she is going to write an essay about the book for her english class at Emory university.

B. After each of the following groups of words indicate the level of usage of the *italicized* word(s), using the following abbreviations: **A** for archaic, **D** for dialectal, **I** for informal (colloquial), and **S** for slang. Use your dictionary for this test.

1. It looks as though I will have to *tote* these groceries all the way home. _____

2. That movie last night really *turned* me *on*. _____

3. Jim was all *tuckered out* after driving five hundred miles. _____

4. My Uncle Simon says he never tires of eating *goobers.* _____

5. Shakespeare's Sonnet 73 begins with the following lines: "That time of year thou *mayst* in me behold / When yellow leaves or none, or few, do hang / Upon those boughs which shake against the cold, . . ." _____

6. Frank said he was *leery* of that *con man* right from the start.   _____

7. Genevieve is an interesting person, but she *gripes* too much.   _____

8. Some *hoods* broke out the windshield on my car last night, and I am really *aggravated*.   _____

9. Last night for supper Mother cooked a *mess* of catfish.   _____

10. Milton reports that his date last night was a real *doll*.   _____

C. The following section is based on the Glossary of Faulty Diction. Underline all errors or colloquialisms and write the preferred forms above each sentence.

1. Loretta bursted into tears when Ruth treated her rudely, and I felt very badly about the incident.

2. Our whole class is enthused at the news that a notorious journalist will be visiting our campus next month.

3. Regretfully, Terry and I will not be able to come to your party; I know it will undoubtably be an awesome affair.

4. I don't know who's idea it was to go swimming today, but I sure do think the water is plenty cold.

5. Gary and myself will be in Salt Lake City in January for a skiing vacation.

6. Uncle Foster and Aunt Josephine were muchly impressed with the delicious dessert that Bonnie made; incidently, Bonnie is only ten years old.

7. I see in the paper where the mayor is going to dedicate a stature in front of city hall today.

8. That was Reverend Sims whom we saw at the reception; I feel that he is a real nice person.

9. The reason I like Doris is because she has a good disposition; she never gets peeved with anyone.

10. Gladys woke up feeling nauseous this morning; if she had eaten less candy bars last night, she would be all right.

11. Will was laying on his bed, trying to decide if he would go out to the lake with Sam and Mark.

12. Being as you plan on getting your degree next June, I cannot help but think that you should be working on your thesis everyday.

13. After she had orientated herself in the darkness, Helen was aware of the fact that she was further from home than she had thought.

14. Mrs. Worthington inferred in her remarks that Mrs. Smythe was sort of irresponsible.

15. Jerry was watching his favorite television show when he should of been pouring over his Latin book.

D. Give the meaning of each of the following prefixes or roots; then write two words containing each prefix or root.

1. *inter-*   _____

   (1) _____   (2) _____

2. *pre-*   _____

   (1) _____   (2) _____

3. *cred*   _____

   (1) _____   (2) _____

4. *hydr(o)*   _____

   (1) _____   (2) _____

5. *contra-*   _____

   (1) _____   (2) _____

6. *multi-* _____

   (1) _____   (2) _____

7. *derm* _____

   (1) _____   (2) _____

8. *theo* _____

   (1) _____   (2) _____

9. *circum-* _____

   (1) _____   (2) _____

10. *super-* _____

   (1) _____   (2) _____

E. If there is a misspelled word in any line of five words given below, write it correctly in the space at the right. If all five words are spelled correctly, write **C** in the space.

1. extrordinary, restaurant, possible, occasion, sandwich _____

2. likable, morgage, partner, foreign, height _____

3. harass, fullfil, hygiene, fascinate, accustomed _____

4. arctic, broccoli, caffeine, benefitted, becoming _____

5. calendar, rhythm, salary, marriage, camoflage _____

6. superintendant, awkward, nickel, exhaust, partner _____

7. yacht, villain, sophomore, seize, ninty _____

8. sherriff, writing, twelfth, shining, scissors _____

9. village, until, transferred, definite, pamphlet _____

10. murmur, minature, necessary, psychology, descent _____

11. noticeable, sacreligious, pursue, divine, despair _____

12. dissipate, niece, mirrow, possess, repetition _____

13. precede, indispensable, mediocre, flier, dutchess _____

14. gauge, eminent, grandaughter, curiosity, desperate

   _____

15. recommend, mathematics, predjudice, weird, surprise

   _____

Name _____   Score _____

Achievement Test

A. In the following sentences identify the part of speech of each *italicized* word by writing one of the following numbers in the space at the right:

1 if it is a noun, **5** if it is an adverb,
2 if it is a pronoun, **6** if it is a preposition,
3 if it is a verb, **7** if it is a conjunction,
4 if it is an adjective, **8** if it is an interjection.

1. *One* of my best friends spent a year in Bratislava, Czechoslovakia. _____

2. Winters in the Adirondacks are *extremely* cold. _____

3. In the legends and myths of the Plains Indians the coyote *is respected* for its cunning. _____

4. Sheep's milk is richer than *either* goat's *or* cow's milk. _____

5. Joan brought me *that* from New Zealand. _____

6. The *Mojave Desert* is strange and beautiful. _____

7. *Throughout* the field there are paths for hikers. _____

8. Now for the first time I understand *calculus*. _____

9. On the elevator *were* two of my high school friends. _____

10. Mr. Frank Farmer will be the *guest* speaker at the luncheon. _____

11. *Wow!* Am I really going to the circus with Jimmy and his grandfather? _____

12. Benji *is picking* blackberries down by the creek. _____

13. For several weeks each year Sandra visits her grandparents *in* Idaho. _____

14. An afghan is a soft *blanket* that is crocheted or knitted. _____

15. *Talk* radio is listened to by more people than any other type of radio programming. _____

16. Harley has lived in Brazil, *and* he has only recently moved here. _____

17. Rosemary, *who* graduates in June, will spend the summer in Europe. _____

18. I *seldom* understand what my attorney friends are saying to each other. _____

19. She opened the letter and then gave *it* to me. _____

20. Flying squirrels and flying snakes *do exist.* _____

21. The teaching method used in *most* law schools is case study. _____

22. *Annually* hundreds of humpback whales migrate from Alaska to Hawaii. _____

23. We will divide the entrée *between* us and spend less money. _____

24. Dolly Parton has made over fifty *record* albums. _____

B. Each of the following sentences either contains an error of grammar or is correct. Indicate the error or the correctness by writing one of the following numbers in the space at the right:

> **1** if the case of the pronoun is incorrect,
> **2** if the subject and the verb do not agree,
> **3** if a pronoun and its antecedent do not agree,
> **4** if an adjective or adverb is used incorrectly,
> **5** if the sentence is correct.

25. The newspaper account of the meetings is completely incorrect. _____

26. Mt. Everest is higher than any mountain peak in the world. _____

27. After work Van is bringing my sister and I something sweet from the bakery. _____

28. Many vegetables — such as tomatoes, eggplant, and turnip greens — can be grown indoors. _____

29. Oil spills ruins our sea life, shorelines, and beaches. _____

30. Everyone is ready for their final tryout. _____

31. Both Leon and Marilyn is sailing to Europe on the *Queen Elizabeth II.* _____

32. Several of we football players will be taking the same math course. _____

33. Neither of the classrooms were large enough for Political Science 101. _____

34. Rumor has it that the next chairman of the board is to be him. _____

35. Brown & Brown had an ad in last night's paper announcing their sale on Wednesday. _____

36. Russell Baker's book was one of those that is appreciated by young and old alike. _____

37. The large woman sitting next to me at the lunch counter talked steady all the way through my chicken sandwich. _____

38. Once he had studied the data, he knew that it would support his argument. _____

39. Everyone but Bret and Theo want to eat tonight at El Sombrero. _____

40. If anyone is interested in going to the tournament, they can buy a ticket from a member of the squad. _____

41. Next week every book, magazine, and newspaper are to be moved to the new library building. _____

42. Ask whomever is at the clinic's reception desk how to get to Dr. Murphy's office. _____

43. Tell Rachel that both chips and another salad is needed for the potluck supper. _____

44. The alumni met in Webster Hall this morning and elected their new officers. _____

45. Because Leah had felt badly all morning, she decided to leave the office at noon. _____

46. I am sure that any one of those children are capable of programming the VCR. _____

47. His physics professor was surprised at him knowing nothing about quarks. _____

48. We heard that a poet and novelist have been invited to address the spring writers' conference. _____

49. While waiting in the airport, the team occupied itself talking, reading, and sleeping. _____

50. It's some farther from here to Scranton than it is from Baltimore to Scranton. _____

C. Each of the following sentences either contains an error in sentence structure or is correct. Indicate the error or correctness by writing one of the following numbers in the space at the right:

   1 if the sentence contains a *dangling modifier,*
   2 if the sentence contains a *misplaced modifier,*
   3 if the sentence contains a *faulty reference of a pronoun,*
   4 if the sentence contains *faulty parallelism,*
   5 if the sentence is correct.

51. Always asking questions, there was no way to satisfy the two-year-old's curiosity. _____

52. The athletic program in this school is as good, if not better than, any other that we know of. _____

53. The detective had only rung the bell once when an expression-less butler opened the door. _____

54. The man appointed chief executive officer at the mine recently moved with his family into the house on the corner. _____

55. Murray's last dive was nearly perfect, which meant that the gold medal was his. _____

56. After turning on the television, the news about the British Open caught Dad's attention. _____

57. I believe that I like the taste of Golden Delicious apples better than Red Delicious. _____

58. When starting the treadmill, do not stand on the belt. _____

59. Yesterday we began discussing the causes of the Great Depression in economics class. _____

60. If anybody wants to give one of these games for Christmas, they need to shop early. _____

61. The producer of this television program is a person of great creativity and who also understands what the public wants. _____

62. Written hurriedly, I could hardly read Laurie's card from Ontario. _____

63. Peg is a talented commercial artist and hopes to make a career of it. _____

64. We read about Hemingway's interest in bullfighting last year in Professor Twigley's class. _____

65. I think that it is as hot and dry this summer as it has been any summer this decade. _____

66. Since finding himself, his mother is expecting great things of Oscar. _____

67. It costs more to execute criminals than putting them in prison for fifty years. _____

68. Beach music is played every evening, which keeps spring fever in all of us. _____

69. A football helmet cannot protect a player from all injuries; when used incorrectly, a head blow may cause paralysis. _____

70. Trying to appear sophisticated, my first question concerned the novelist's most recent work. _____

71. When Margaret received good grades her first semester at college, it pleased her parents. _____

72. The ants spoiled the picnic for the children, swarming all over the fried chicken and potato salad. _____

73. I chose to work at Macy's rather than at a fast-food restaurant last summer because Macy's had better pay, shorter working hours, and prestigious. _____

74. If soaked with enough brandy, you will enjoy this bread pudding. _____

75. The trip was stimulating, educational, and exhausting. _____

D. Each of the following sentences contains an error in punctuation or mechanics or is correct. Indicate the error or the correctness by writing one of the following numbers in the space at the right:

> **1** if a comma has been omitted,
> **2** if a semicolon has been omitted,
> **3** if an apostrophe has been omitted,
> **4** if quotation marks have been omitted,
> **5** if the sentence is correct.

76. The Great Awakening a widespread religious revival took place in America in 1740. _____

77. Influenced by the dramatic sermons of the Reverend George Whitefield thousands of American colonists felt that they had been "born again." _____

78. The citys recycling bins are located in the parking lot at the end of Clayton Street. _____

79. The sky was black, thunder crashed, and wind began tearing at the leaves on the trees. _____

80. The hymn I liked best at the wedding was Ode to Joy. _____

81. The bride, who looked radiant, was wearing her mothers bridal gown and carrying a bouquet of red and white roses. _____

82. There were five bridesmaids four of them I recognized as classmates of the bride. _____

83. Its hard to believe that summer is almost over. _____

84. My favorite foods are spaghetti ice cream and chocolate chip cookies. _____

85. Some historians criticize Benjamin Franklin for not being more idealistic, however, I admire him for being realistic. _____

86. If it were not for the diversity of customers my job as a grocery store cashier would be boring. _____

87. Our second-grade teacher often said, An inquiring mind is an expanding mind. _____

88. The papers that were written at the beginning of the semester were stolen. _____

89. Last nights party was fun for the guests, but not for the neighbors. _____

90. Millie rushed back to her room and finished her English homework, then she took a long nap. _____

91. Most students really like discussing Shirley Jackson's short story The Lottery. _____

92. In the morning I am never hungry, at night I am ravenous. _____

93. Janice will you stop at the grocery store and pick up a loaf of bread for our sandwiches? _____

94. In the Midwest there were floods in the South there was drought. _____

95. Preregistration for fall semester begins on May 21, 1993 and ends on June 7. _____

96. Financial-aid checks will be available in the Business Services Building, 424 East Broad Street, Athens, Georgia from 8:00 A.M. to 5:00 P.M. _____

97. Lucy asked Charley Brown to show her where to put the commas in her paper, or, as she said, where to sprinkle in the little curvy marks. _____

98. Members of the English department will miss their colleague Elaine who is leaving to take a new job. _____

99. Many tourists go to Memphis to see Graceland, Elvis Presleys home. _____

100. The drought was disastrous for the South, trees everywhere were dying. _____

Glossary of Grammatical Terms

Absolute phrase. A construction grammatically independent of the rest of the sentence. It is formed by use of a noun followed by a participle. It is not a subject and does not modify any word in the sentence.

> *The rain having ended,* we decided to walk home.

Abstract noun. A noun that names a quality, condition, action, or idea; it cannot be perceived by one of the five physical senses.

> kindness   truth   courtesy   dishonesty

Active voice. The form of a verb indicating that the subject of the sentence performs the action of the verb.

> The dog *ate* its supper.
>
> Mary *is going* to town.

Adjective. A word that modifies, describes, limits, or adds to the meaning of a noun, pronoun, or any other substantive.

> *Your late* arrival caused trouble.
>
> Ellen is *beautiful.*

Adjective clause. A dependent clause that modifies a noun, pronoun, or any other substantive.

> The girl *whom you met* is a flight attendant.
>
> The place *where I was born* is a thousand miles from here.

Adverb. A word that modifies or adds to the meaning of a verb, adjective, or other adverb. It may also modify or qualify a phrase or clause, adding to the meaning of the whole idea expressed in the sentence.

> I finished the test *quickly.*
>
> Trent is *truly* worthy of this award.
>
> *Luckily,* we got to class on time.

Adverbial clause. A dependent clause that functions exactly as if it were an adverb. It modifies verbs, adjectives, adverbs, or the whole idea expressed in the sentence's independent clause.

> *When I was a child,* I lived in Missouri.
>
> *After you have eaten lunch,* I will help you wash dishes.
>
> *Because you are tired,* I will drive home.
>
> Don't leave here *until you have finished your work.*

Ambiguous modifier. A modifier carelessly placed between two sentence elements so that it may be taken to modify either element.

> The boy who had been walking *slowly* came into our driveway.

Ambiguous pronoun reference.   Improper use of a pronoun that may grammatically refer to more than one word as its antecedent in a sentence.

> John told Fred that *he* should lose weight.

Antecedent.   The substantive to which a pronoun refers and with which it must agree in person, number, and gender.

> *Peter* told Sue that *he* would be late for dinner.

Apostrophe.   A mark of grammatical mechanics used to show possession, indicate omitted letters in contractions, or show plurals of letters or numerals.

> Ted's glove
>
> It's raining.
>
> Mind your *p*'s and *q*'s.

Appositive.   A word or phrase that explains, identifies, or renames the word it follows and refers to.

> William Faulkner, author of "The Bear," was a native Mississippian.

Archaic words.   Words that are out of date and no longer in general use.

> "*Oft* in the *stilly* night."

Articles.   Three words, classified as adjectives, that appear before nouns or certain other substantives. *A* and *an* are indefinite articles; *the* is a definite article.

Auxiliary verbs.   Verbs that help to form the various tenses of main verbs. The use of auxiliary verbs creates verb phrases and enables the writer to express time and time relationships much more precisely than by using simple present and past tenses. *Was, have,* and *will* are the auxiliary verbs in these examples:

> She *was going* with me.
>
> I *have finished* my work.
>
> Tom *will go* to New York.

Brackets.   Marks of grammatical mechanics used to enclose any interpolation or insertion added to material being quoted.

> "Four score and seven years ago [Lincoln began] our forefathers brought forth on this continent. . . ."

Broad pronoun reference.   Incorrect use of a pronoun to refer broadly to the whole idea of the preceding clause.

> She was late, *which* made me angry.

Capitalization.   The use of capital letters for the first word of a sentence, a line of traditional poetry, or a direct quotation. Capitals are also used for the first letter of proper nouns, days of the week, months, holidays, and historical periods.

Case.   The inflection of a noun or pronoun to show its relationship to another word or sentence element. Nouns change form only to show the possessive case. Pronouns have three forms to show case: nominative, objective, and possessive.

Clause.   A group of words containing a subject and a verb. The two types of clause are independent and dependent. Dependent clauses cannot stand alone as completed thoughts; independent clauses express complete thoughts.

Cliché.   An overused expression that has lost its original freshness.

dull thud	one fell swoop
bitter end	through thick and thin
having a ball	last but not least

Collective nouns.   Those nouns that name groups of persons, places, or things functioning as units.

jury   team   class   club   herd

Colloquialism.   Words or expressions (also referred to as informal diction) that are acceptable in the speech of the educated person but not in formal writing.

We have *lots* of apples on our trees this year.

Colon.   The mark of punctuation that introduces a formal list or an explanation or amplification of a statement. Also used after the formal salutation in a letter, between hour and minute numerals of time, between chapter and verse of Bible references, and between titles and subtitles of books.

Comma.   Punctuation mark used to indicate the smallest interruptions in thought or grammatical construction.

Comma splice.   Incorrect use of a comma as punctuation between two independent clauses not joined by a coordinating conjunction. A stronger separation must be shown through use of a semicolon or a period.

I saw the plane landing, it was a 747 jet.

I saw the plane landing; it was a 747 jet.

Common noun.   A noun that names a class of persons, places, things, or ideas.

woman	honesty
book	friendship
house	

Comparative degree.   The inflection of an adjective or adverb that compares two things, persons, or actions.

Peggy's camera is *better* than yours.

Marcia felt the disappointment *more keenly* than Harry did.

Comparison.   Indication of the extent to which one noun or verb has a particular quality in common with another noun or verb through use of the comparative degree of an adjective or adverb.

Complement.   A word, phrase, or clause that completes the action of the verb and the sense of the sentence. It may be a direct object, an indirect object, a predicate adjective, a predicate noun, an objective complement, or a retained object.

Complex sentence.   A sentence that contains one independent clause and one or more dependent clauses.

> I know what you are going to say.

Compound sentence.   A sentence that contains at least two independent clauses and no dependent clause.

> I will ride with you, and Patsy will stay at home.

Compound-complex sentence.   A sentence that contains at least two independent clauses and one or more dependent clauses.

> I was sorry that I could not attend the meeting, but my throat was sore.

Concrete noun.   A noun that names a person, place, or thing that can be perceived by one of the five physical senses.

> desk   chocolate   aroma   shout   rain

Conjugation.   The showing of all forms of a verb in all its tenses.

Conjunction.   A word used to join words or groups of words. Coordinating conjunctions (like *and* and *but*) join sentence elements of equal rank. Subordinating conjunctions introduce subordinate, or dependent, elements, joining them to the main part of the sentence.

Conjunctive adverb.   An adverb (sometimes called a transitional adverb) used to connect two independent clauses while modifying the sense of the sentence and showing the relationship between the two clauses.

> I had neglected to buy coffee yesterday; *consequently*, my breakfast today lacked a vital ingredient.

Connotation.   The associative meaning of a word or expression; connotation goes beyond the literal dictionary definition.

Coordinate elements.   Elements of equal rank within a sentence. They may be single words, phrases, or clauses, but they must have similar values as sentence parts.

Coordinating conjunction.   A conjunction that joins two sentence elements of equal rank. The coordinating conjunctions are *and, but, or, nor, for, yet* in the sense of *but*, and *so* in the sense of *therefore*. The correlative conjunctions *either . . . or* and *neither . . . nor* are also coordinating conjunctions.

Correlative conjunctions.   Coordinating conjunctions used in pairs, as shown in the entry on coordinating conjunctions.

> *either . . . or*   *neither . . . nor*
> *both . . . and*   *not only . . . but also*

Dangling modifier.   A phrase or elliptical clause that does not modify any particular word in the sentence.

> *To be a good cook,* the kitchen must be conveniently arranged.

Dash.   A mark of punctuation that indicates an abrupt shift or break in the thought of a sentence or sets off an informal or emphatic parenthesis. It is also used to set off an appositive or parenthetical element that is internally punctuated.

> I'm trying to be sympathetic, but — oh, Mack, you aren't even listening.

> The three of us — Jim, Susan, and Dot — are trying out for parts in the play.

Demonstrative adjective.   An adjective that modifies a substantive by pointing it out.

> *this* picture   *these* glasses
> *that* woman   *those* apples

Demonstrative pronoun.   A pronoun that points out persons, things, qualities, or ideas.

> *Those* are my friends.

> *These* are the problems.

> *That* is the question.

> My answer is *this.*

Dependent clause.   A group of words that contains a subject and a verb but that cannot stand alone as a complete thought. It begins with a subordinating word. Dependent clauses function as grammatical units within a sentence: that is, as nouns, adjectives, and adverbs.

Dialectal words.   Words whose usage is common to the speech of a particular group or geographical region.

> *branch* for creek

> *polecat* for skunk

> *poke* for sack or bag

Diction.   One's style of writing or speaking in terms of word choice.

Direct object.   A noun or other substantive that completes the verb and receives the action expressed in the verb.

> The child ate the *candy.*

> Carol hates *arithmetic.*

> Frank thought the *fine* excessive.

Elliptical clause or expression.   A grammatically incomplete expression whose meaning is nevertheless clear; frequently a dependent clause from which subject and/or verb is omitted.

> *When a child,* I had a great many freckles.

Essential appositive.   An appositive that positively identifies that which it renames, most frequently by use of a proper noun. Essential appositives are not set off by commas.

> The actress *Katharine Hepburn* has had a long and distinguished career.

Essential clause (modifier).   An adjective or adverbial clause that is necessary in a sentence because it identifies or points out a particular person or thing. An essential clause is not set off by commas.

> A child *who grows up in the country* learns a great deal about nature.

Euphemism.   An expression used to avoid the outright statement of a disagreeable, delicate, or painful idea, or to give dignity to something essentially lowly or undignified.

> The Jacobs family had a *blessed event* at their house last week.

> Mr. Thompson's present *financial embarrassment* is said to be the result of *uneven cash flow*.

> Sally received a *pink slip* in her pay envelope last week.

Excessive predication.   The use of too many independent clauses, strung together with coordinating conjunctions. Proper subordination of less important ideas is the remedy for excessive predication.

> I went to a movie, and I ate two boxes of popcorn, and I later had a stomachache.

Expletive.   An idiomatic introductory word, used to begin a sentence when the subject is deferred to a later position.

> *There* are too many cooks in this kitchen.

> *It* has been raining since Monday.

Gerund.   A verbal used as a noun. In its present tense it always ends in *-ing*. It may function as a sentence element in any way that a noun can.

> *Riding* a bicycle in the street can be risky.

Homonyms.   Two or more words that sound alike but have different meanings and spellings. Following are examples of some common homonyms:

> *accept / except*
>
> *affect / effect*
>
> *principal / principle*
>
> *their / there*
>
> *who's / whose.*

Hyphen.   A mechanical mark that is used in compound numbers and other compound words formed from phrases. It is also used at the end of a line to indicate the division of a word continued on the next line.

> *thirty-four*   *ex-governor*
>
> *sister-in-law*   *sixteen-year-old* boy

Idiom.   The characteristic construction used to form sentences in a particular language; the pattern and sequence of words normal to that language.

Illogical comparison.   Comparison, usually through careless writing, of two things that do not have a point of similarity. In "My car is newer than Mark," *car* and *Mark* have no point in common to be compared. A logical comparison would state:

> My car is newer than Mark's.

Indefinite pronouns.   Pronouns that do not point out a specific person, place, or thing, but only a general class. Many indefinite pronouns are concerned with indefinite quantity:

> some   any   each   everyone   several

Independent clause.   A group of words containing a subject and verb and expressing a complete thought. It may stand alone as a simple sentence, or it may be combined with other independent clauses or with dependent clauses to form a compound or complex sentence.

Indirect object.   A word or words denoting the person or thing indirectly affected by the action of a transitive verb. It is the person or thing to which something is given or for which something is done. Words such as *give, offer, grant, lend* represent the idea of something done for the indirect object. The idea of taking something away can also have an indirect object, with the use of words such as *deny* and *refuse*.

Infinitive.   A verbal consisting of the simple form of a verb preceded by *to,* and used as a noun, adjective, or adverb.

> I want *to win*.
> I have work *to do*.
> You must leave now *to get* there on time.

Inflection.   A change in the form of a word to indicate a change in its meaning or use. Nouns show inflection only in plural and possessive forms. Some pronouns are inflected to show case, number, and gender. Verbs are inflected to show person, number, tense, voice, and mood. Most adjectives are inflected to show comparative and superlative degrees.

Informal diction.   Words or expressions that are acceptable in the speech of the educated but not in formal writing. Also called colloquial diction.

Intensive pronouns.   Pronouns combined with *-self* or *-selves* and used in conjunction with nouns and simple pronouns for emphasis.

> I *myself* will write the letter.
> Frank did the work *himself*.

Interjection.   An exclamatory word thrown into a sentence or sometimes used alone. It is grammatically independent of the rest of the sentence.

> *Oh,* why are you doing that?
> *Goodness!* I am hot!

Interrogative adverb.   An indefinite adverb that asks a question, namely *how*, *when*, *where*, or *why*.

> *How* are you going to pay for that car?
>
> *When* will you leave for the airport?
>
> *Where* does Dorothy live?
>
> *Why* did you call me at midnight?

Interrogative pronoun.   A pronoun that is part of a sentence asking a question.

> *What* is that noise?
>
> *Which* of the cakes do you prefer?

Intransitive verb.   A verb whose action is not directed toward a receiver.

> Mike *walked* around the block.
>
> The river *is overflowing*.
>
> You *are* foolish.

Irregular verb.   A verb that forms its past tense not by the addition of *-d* or *-ed* but by a change in the vowel of the root verb.

sing	sang	begin	began	choose	chose
ride	rode	give	gave	do	did

Italics.   A device of mechanics that uses a printing style sloping to the right in the manner of handwriting. Italics are used to emphasize a word or expression or to designate book, play, opera, symphony, magazine, newspaper, painting, sculpture, movie, and ship titles. In typing or handwriting, italics are shown by underlining.

Jargon.   Vague, pretentious language so general in meaning that many words may be omitted without loss of the sense of a statement.

Levels of usage.   Divisions of usage within the categories of Standard and Substandard English. The following are usage labels usually applied by most dictionaries and grammarians: formal, informal, dialectal, slang, archaic, and obsolete.

Linking verb.   An intransitive verb that makes a statement not by expressing action but by indicating a state of being or a condition. It follows the subject and must be followed by a predicate noun or predicate adjective to complete the sense of the sentence. The verb *to be* in all its forms is the most common linking verb; however, any other verb that expresses a state of being and is followed by a noun identifying the subject or an adjective describing it is a linking verb. Some examples are *appear, become, look, seem, smell, sound, taste,* and *feel*.

Misplaced modifier.   A word or phrase that by its position in the sentence does not seem to modify the word it is intended to modify. A modifier should be as close as is logically possible to the word it modifies.

The crystal chandelier brilliantly lit the huge banquet table that hung from the ceiling.

Correction:

The crystal chandelier that hung from the ceiling brilliantly lit the huge banquet table.

Mixed construction.   A shift in the original construction of a sentence, causing the sentence to be confused in its meaning and incorrect in its grammatical structure.

Honesty is *when someone is truthful in word and deed.*

Modifier.   A word, phrase, or other sentence element that describes, qualifies, or limits another element in the same sentence.

Mood.   The form a verb may take to indicate whether it is used to make a statement, give a command, to express a condition contrary to fact. Moods of a verb are *indicative, imperative,* and *subjunctive.*

Nominative case.   The case of a noun or pronoun that is the subject or the predicate noun of a sentence. Nouns in the nominative case are not inflected; personal pronouns have inflections for each of the three cases.

Nonessential appositive.   An appositive that is not necessary in the identification of the word with which it is in apposition. It merely provides additional information as a method of renaming. Note that a nonessential appositive is set off by commas.

P. D. James, *a mystery novelist,* is an Englishwoman.

Nonessential modifier.   A modifier that is not necessary to the meaning of the sentence but simply provides additional description rather than identification. Nonessential modifiers are set off by commas.

My father, *who is a lawyer,* often has to travel in connection with his practice.

Noun.   The part of speech that names a person, place, thing, or idea.

Noun clause.   A dependent clause that functions within the sentence as a noun.

Tell me *what you want for breakfast.*

Number.   Inflection of verbs, nouns, and pronouns indicating whether they are *singular* or *plural.*

| *tree* | *trees* | he *loves* | they *love* |
| *woman* | *women* | *I* | *we* |

Object.   A sentence element that receives directly or indirectly the action of a verb, gerund, participle, or infinitive; or shows relationship as object of the preposition to some other element in the sentence.

Object of a preposition.   The substantive that follows a preposition and shows a relationship between the object of the preposition and some other element in the sentence.

Objective case.   The case of a noun or pronoun that receives the action of a verb, either directly or indirectly, or that refers to that receiver. The object of the preposition is also in the objective case.

Objective complement.   A noun, pronoun, or adjective that completes the action of the verb and refers to the direct object.

> Henry VIII made Catherine of Aragon his *queen.*
>
> Todd considers Marilyn quite *intelligent.*

Parallelism.   The use of equal, or parallel, grammatical constructions within a sentence. Coordinate elements of equal rank should be expressed in parallel language.

> The girl was tall, slender, and beautiful. (*Three adjectives are used.*)
>
> She is a woman who is conscientious and who is a splendid worker. (*Two adjective clauses are used.*)

Parentheses.   A device of punctuation that encloses parenthetical information like a brief explanation of a foregoing term or a figure repeated to ensure accuracy.

> Lincoln said (in the Gettysburg Address), "Four score and seven years ago. . . ."
>
> I am enclosing eight dollars ($8) to cover the cost of my order.

Parenthetical expressions.   Expressions that are not a part of the central statement of a sentence but are used as comments upon the statement. Parenthetical expressions are usually, but not always, enclosed by commas.

> He is, *as the saying goes,* a real football buff.
>
> What *do you suppose* can be done?

Participle.   A verb form that functions as an adjective while retaining some of the characteristics of a verb. It is called a *verbal.*

> *shining* light   *worn* coat   *known* danger.

Parts of speech.   The various elements that go to make up a sentence. There are eight parts of speech: noun, pronoun, adjective, verb, adverb, preposition, conjunction, and interjection.

Passive voice.   The inflection of a transitive verb showing that the subject of the sentence is the receiver of the verb's action.

> He *was taken* to jail.

Person.   The inflection of verbs and personal pronouns indicating the speaker (first person), the person spoken to (second person), or the person or thing spoken about (third person).

Personal pronouns.   Pronouns used in one of the three persons (*I; you; he, she, it*) and their plural forms as well.

Phrase. A group of words generally without a subject and predicate, used as a single part of speech.

> *Living alone* has some advantages. (*gerund phrase, used as subject*)
>
> Marcia, *waving wildly*, tried to catch our attention. (*participial phrase, used to modify* Marcia)
>
> I want *to go to Paris*. (*infinitive phrase, used as direct object*)
>
> His cousin, *a computer specialist*, lives in Nevada. (*appositive phrase, in apposition with* cousin)
>
> We climbed *up the mountain*. (*prepositional phrase, used adverbially*)

Positive degree (of adjectives and adverbs). The regular form of an adjective or an adverb.

Possessive case. The inflection of a noun or pronoun, showing possession.

> *Janet's* last name is Rogers.
>
> *My* friend has moved away.
>
> The cat has lost *its* tongue.
>
> *Mine* is the only true story of the incident.

Predicate. The part of the sentence that makes a statement about the subject. It always includes the sentence verb.

Predicate adjective. The adjective in the predicate that describes or modifies the subject. It follows a linking verb.

> Charlotte is *friendly*.
>
> This soup smells *good*.
>
> Mr. Thomas appears *ill*.

Predicate noun or nominative. The noun in the predicate that renames or identifies the subject. It follows a linking verb.

> That woman is a *lawyer*.
>
> Jim was *master* of ceremonies.

Prefix. A short element (a syllable or syllables) that comes before the main part of the word (the root), adding to or modifying its meaning.

> *sub*marine   *centi*pede   *contra*dict

Preposition. A part of speech that shows a relationship between its object (a substantive) and some other word or sentence element.

> She is a friend *of* the family.

Primer style. The monotonous style of writing that reflects no relative importance of ideas and no emphasis. Primer style is found in writing that does not vary sentence structure through subordination or other rhetorical devices, but uses only simple sentences without variation.

Principal parts (of a verb).   The principal parts of a verb are *first-person singular, present tense; first-person singular, past tense;* and *past participle.* Knowledge of these three principal parts enables one to conjugate any verb.

Pronominal adjective.   An adjective that is the possessive form of a pronoun:

> *your* hat, *their* intentions, *our* home, *my* watch

or a pronoun used to modify a substantive:

> *this* house, *that* glove, *these* grapes, *those* books, *some* people, *any* students, *either* dress

Pronoun.   A word used in place of a noun; it sometimes refers to a noun or other substantive already mentioned.

Pronoun-antecedent agreement.   The agreement that must exist between a pronoun and its antecedent in person and number.

> Each girl was told to bring *her* lunch with *her* for the outing.

Proper noun.   A noun that names a particular person, place, or thing. It always begins with a capital letter.

> Angela   Senator Smith   Christmas   Atlanta   Idaho

Quotation marks.   Punctuation marks used to enclose direct quotations, titles of short works, smaller units of books, television programs, and words from special vocabularies.

Redundancy.   Unnecessary repetition.

> *Repeat* that *again.*
> She *returned back* to her home.
> The coat that I bought is *blue in color.*

Reflexive pronouns.   Pronouns ending in *-self* or *-selves* and indicating that the subject acts upon itself.

> Jack bruised *himself* on the leg at the playground.
> Millie treated *herself* to a hot fudge sundae.

Relative pronoun.   A pronoun used to introduce a dependent adjective clause.

> The information *that* I gave you is correct.
> My uncle, *whom you met last year,* is coming for a visit.

Retained object.   A noun or other substantive remaining as the object when a verb that has both direct and indirect objects is put into the passive voice.

> President Rogers has been given a *vote* of confidence by the student body. (*Vote* is the retained object.)

Root.   The central or main part of a word. A prefix may begin the word, and a suffix may end it, each one modifying the meaning of the root.

> peri*meter,* post*script, wis*dom, *false*hood

Run-together sentences.   Sentences without punctuation between independent clauses not joined by a coordinating conjunction.

> Mark ran quickly to the door he opened it and saw the burglar.

Semicolon.   Punctuation mark used to separate independent clauses not joined by a coordinating conjunction, coordinate elements internally punctuated with commas, and independent clauses joined by a coordinating conjunction but heavily punctuated internally.

Sentence.   A group of words combined into a pattern that expresses a complete thought.

Sentence fragment.   A part of a sentence written and punctuated as though it were a whole sentence (a complete thought), although some necessary element has been omitted.

> The baby crying.
>
> Because I was tired.
>
> When we arrived at the hotel.

Simple sentence.   A single independent clause that has one subject and one predicate. It may have more than one noun or pronoun as its subject and more than one verb in its predicate.

> The dog ran across the street.
>
> The dog ran across the street and barked at the cat.
>
> The dog and the cat fought and made noise.

Squinting modifier.   Another name for ambiguous modifier, which is a modifier carelessly placed between two sentence elements so that it may be taken to modify either element.

> The boys who were eating *noisily* complained that there was no dessert.

Subject.   The person, place, or thing being spoken or written about in a sentence.

Subject-verb agreement.   The agreement in person and number that each verb in a sentence must have with its subject. The verb is inflected as to person and number according to those of the clause's subject.

Subjunctive mood.   The mood used in a verb to express a wish or to state a condition contrary to fact. It is also used to express certain formal suggestions or proposals.

> I wish that I *were* going with you.
>
> If I *were* president, no one would go hungry.
>
> I move that the nominations *be* closed.

Subordinate clause.   See **Dependent clause.**

Subordination.   In writing or speaking, the reflection that one sentence element is less important or worthy of emphasis than another. Dependent clauses, phrases, and single words may be used instead of full-fledged independent clauses to convey subordinate ideas.

> Jenny Martin is my cousin, and she is a senior in high school, and she has just been awarded a scholarship to Tulane. (*no subordination*)

> My cousin Jenny Martin, who is a senior in high school, has just been awarded a scholarship to Tulane. (*subordination through use of appositive phrase and dependent adjective clause*)

> My cousin Jenny Martin, a senior in high school, has just been awarded a scholarship to Tulane. (*subordination through use of two appositive phrases*)

Subordinating conjunctions.   Conjunctions that introduce dependent clauses, subordinating them in rank to the idea expressed in the independent clause.

Substantive.   A noun, pronoun, or any other word or group of words that is used as a noun.

Suffix.   A word part that is added to the end of a word and modifies the meaning of the root.

> accura*cy*   law*yer*   young*ster*   commun*ion*   altru*ism*

Superlative degree.   The inflection of an adjective or an adverb indicating the highest degree of quality, quantity, or manner. It is formed by adding *-est* as a suffix to the simple form of the adjective, or, with adverbs or adjectives of several syllables, by preceding the word with *most.*

> kindest   most agreeable   most thoughtfully
> poorest   least honorable   most nearly

Tense.   The form that a verb takes in order to express the time of an action or a state of being.

Tense sequence.   The logic that governs time relationships shown by the verbs in a sentence. If the action in one verb or verbal form occurs before or after the action in the main verb, these differences must be indicated by differences in the tenses.

Terminal marks.   The marks of punctuation that signal the end of a sentence. They are the *period,* the *question mark,* and the *exclamation mark.*

Transitional adverb.   The adverb, sometimes called conjunctive adverb, that introduces the second of two independent clauses, showing the relationship between the two clauses and frequently modifying the entire sense of the sentence. Sometimes the second adverb comes within the second clause.

Transitive verb.   A verb whose action is directed toward a receiver, which may be the object of the verb or (with a transitive verb in the passive voice) its subject.

Bob Horner hit the ball.

A home run was hit by Bob Horner.

Triteness. The use of stale, hackneyed expressions that have lost their original freshness. See also **Cliché.**

Upside-down subordination. The subordination of an important idea to a less important one through careless writing.

Although the accident occurred, Tom had tried to prevent it.

Vagueness. The too-frequent use of abstract words instead of concrete ones.

The fact that the plan was of a risky nature was known by everyone.
Correction:
Everyone knew that the plan was risky.

Verb. A word used to state or to ask something, expressing action or a state of being. Every sentence must contain a verb.

Verbal. A verb form made from a verb but performing the function of a noun, an adjective, or an adverb. The three verbal forms are the *gerund,* the *participle,* and the *infinitive.*

Verbal phrase. A group of words that contains a verbal and all its modifiers and complements.

Your running too fast has left you out of breath.

Voice. The form of a verb that indicates whether the subject of the sentence performs the action or is the receiver of the action of the verb. If the subject performs the action, the verb is in the *active voice;* if the subject receives the action, the verb is in the *passive voice.*

The chorus sang "America" at the end of the program. (*Chorus* is the subject; *sang* is the verb in the active voice.)

"America" *was sung* by the chorus at the end of the program ("America" is the subject; *was sung* is the verb in the passive voice.)

Weak pronoun reference. Faulty reference by a pronoun to a word that has been merely implied by the context.

Mother made delicious grape jelly yesterday; I gathered *them* for her.

Wordiness. Use of more words than are necessary to express an idea clearly and accurately. Excessive predication, redundancy, and certain abstractions are all forms of wordiness, also known as verbosity.

Index